Avebury Cosmos

The Neolithic World of Avebury henge, Silbury Hill, West Kennet long barrow, the Sanctuary & the Longstones Cove

Avebury Cosmos

The Neolithic World of Avebury henge, Silbury Hill, West Kennet long barrow, the Sanctuary & the Longstones Cove

Nicholas R. Mann

BOOKS

Winchester, UK
Washington, USA

First published by O-Books, 2011
O-Books is an imprint of John Hunt Publishing Ltd., Laurel House, Station Approach, Alresford, Hants, SO24 9JH, UK
office1@o-books.net
www.o-books.com

For distributor details and how to order please visit the 'Ordering' section on our website.

ISBN: 978 1 84694 680 6

A CIP catalogue record for this book is available from the British Library.

Design: Stuart Davies

Printed in the UK by CPI Antony Rowe
Printed in the USA by Offset Paperback Mfrs, Inc

CONTENTS

View south from the northern bank of Avebury henge, mid-third millennium BCE. The Southern Cross rose over Waden Hill in the small hours of each winter morning, bringing with it the Milky Way.

Introduction

It is no exaggeration to say that astronomy has existed as an exact science for more than five millennia... it is a barren society that has no myth-making surrounding the heavens.

Professor John North

Five thousand years ago, an extraordinary sight was visible in the night sky over the British Isles. Every winter night, over the course of several hours, the Neolithic people of Britain saw the galaxy form a complete circle around the horizon. At the same time, the brilliant stars of Crux, the Southern Cross, as well as alpha and beta Centauri, were visible deep in the southern sky. These first-magnitude giants were embedded like radiant jewels within the complete ring of the Milky Way. This awe-inspiring sight was due to a slow, 26,000-year rotation of the axis of the Earth, known as the precession of the equinoxes. Those of us who live at this latitude today can no longer see these southern stars; only our distant ancestors were privileged to see the expanse of the galaxy extending around the horizon.

In this book I describe how the unique night skies of their time inspired and influenced the people who built Avebury henge, Windmill Hill, Silbury Hill, the Longstones Cove, the Sanctuary, West Kennet long barrow and other Neolithic monuments near the source of the River Kennet, in Wiltshire, Britain. I show that these awe-inspiring monuments were closely oriented to the sky, and that their makers were familiar with not only the cycles of the Sun and Moon but also those of the stars.

Extensive evidence assembled in the relatively new research field of archaeoastronomy has now confirmed beyond any doubt that when European prehistoric peoples began to build their first great monuments they possessed considerable knowledge of the heavens. This knowledge had presumably been developed over tens of thousands of years, in the previous hunter-gatherer Mesolithic and Palaeolithic eras, as part of a rich, oral, mythic and spiritual tradition. Like all tribal peoples these people experienced the world as full of a purposeful and animating force, an *anima mundi* or world spirit. This power was present on the Earth in all life forms, as well as in the sky: as thunder, lightning, fire, Sun, Moon and stars. The Neolithic Britons would have venerated these powers in their stories and traditions, as well as in their skilfully constructed structures of earth, wood, and finally, stone.

Indeed, its builders conceived Avebury on such a scale that it seems their goal was to incorporate the spirit of *everything* into the fabric of their monument. The Neolithic people wanted Avebury to be a mirror of the cosmos, a place that honoured, told and retold *all* its stories, on Earth and in the heavens. They pursued this objective with extraordinary hard work, dragging megaliths and carrying chalk over many centuries, until they had laid out a monumental centre that still moves us today. This place was a powerful expression of their identity, and of their relationship with the surrounding forces of nature and the cosmos. The sites at Avebury were in use for almost two thousand years. Although they changed their character over this time, they provided a focus for activities that united a widely spread people, establishing codes, laws, conduct and the calendar among the many practicalities of their lives.

With the passage of time, however, the monument-builders would have realised that the familiar backdrop of the sky—the seemingly constant or 'fixed' stars—were moving against their permanent stones and great earthworks. Eventually, even the Milky Way appeared to be falling away from the complete circle it had once made around the enormous artificial horizon of the henge. As this was a time of momentous change, of new farming practices, technologies and ideas, the sky-watchers of Avebury may have wondered exactly what the relationship was between the events taking place in the sky and those taking place on the Earth.

It is important to remember that the Neolithic people stood at a watershed. Their lives were rooted in practices similar to those of their ancestors, but their monuments looked towards a very different future. They had left behind humanity's long established nomadic or semi-nomadic hunter-forager lifestyle, embarking upon lives of settlement and farming, in which they domesticated animals, developed trades and specialisations, built monuments and eventually instigated far-reaching technological innovations. In the future, there would soon be little space for the nomad, or hunter, or for many creatures, such as the bear, that were once central to their mythology. Instead, there would be increasing social differences, population pressure, deforestation, degradation of arable land, conflict over resources, violence and sometimes even war.

But the people of Avebury still looked to the Sun, Moon and stars, and what they saw there they incorporated into their great works of stone. They identified the constant and regulative seasonal paths of the great powers of the sky, the Sun and Moon. The megaliths gave a fitting form to what they saw as purposeful and divine. They identified the cosmic axis, the Milky Way, the stars and constellations, and by devotedly incorporating these features of the sky into their monuments, they showed that they wished to live in accordance with these powers. But the chief challenge of the Avebury sky-watchers was to respond appropriately to some extraordinary and unprecedented changes they saw taking place in the heavens, and relate these to the equally extraordinary changes they were experiencing on earth.

Acknowledgements

I have relied heavily on the archaeological work conducted on the Avebury monuments, especially the recently obtained dates for Silbury Hill and the Longstones Cove. I have also relied upon the work of pioneering archaeoastronomers: Alexander Thom, Gerald Hawkins, Edwin Krupp, John North, Euan Mackie, Aubrey Burl, Anthony Aveni, Robin Heath, Michael Hoskins and many others. Over half a century ago, when Alexander Thom extended his research to include stellar alignments, these were highly controversial. Today, however, just as a new generation of anthropologists is gathering detailed evidence of the stellar knowledge of aboriginal cultures, so archaeoastronomers are meticulously showing how this knowledge influenced the designs of prehistoric monuments.[2] While we cannot recover the precise meanings Neolithic monument-builders attributed to what they saw in the sky, it is now possible to include the stars among the celestial phenomena they were observing most closely.

As a result of leading archaeoastronomers helpful explanations of the rudiments of early visual astronomy, and anthropologists explanations of the dynamic relationship between indigenous people and the heavens, we no longer see the Neolithic monuments as observatories and their users as 'astronomer priests.'[3] The late historian of science John North, in his 1996 landmark book *Stonehenge: Neolithic Man and the Cosmos*, did not see the Neolithic monuments as astronomical observatories built "to discover the patterns of behaviour of the Sun, Moon or stars" but rather built "to *embody* those patterns, already known in broad outline, in a religious architecture".[4] North went on to show, in meticulous detail, how frequently alignments to the stars can be found in henges, long barrows, avenues, stone circles and other prehistoric, yet clearly "religious" monuments of Southern Britain.

Thanks to the work of researchers like Thom, Aveni and North, the question is no longer: *were* the Neolithic builders of Avebury henge watching the heavens, but rather: *who* were these people who intentionally "embodied" the patterns of Sun, Moon and stars into the building of Avebury? If we can begin to decipher these patterns, we can try to identify the missing language, narratives and the intentions of these extraordinary people.

The accuracy of this book is only as good as my ability to understand some very difficult topics and use some rather complex software. Although tramping through fields and close Ordnance Survey work was essential to this research, without theodolite surveys, the astronomical alignments must remain provisional and the diagrams are approximate not exact.[5] An ancient history and anthropology degree from University College London shaped my understanding of prehistory; yet a long-standing study of our native and ancient traditions, together with my own spiritual practice, has been just as important in deepening my respect and reverence for ancient British lore. The software I used in the preparation of this book was *Redshift* and *Starry Night Pro*. Dates are given as BCE, 'before the common era,' or CE, 'the common era' to avoid the confusion of BP, 'before the present,' and the implicit theism of BC and AD. I give distances in miles, yards and feet out of respect to naturally occurring measures and ratios used by ancient peoples. As celestial measures are given as *azimuths*, i.e., degrees clockwise around the horizon from north, I have had to consider the altitude of sky objects, the elevation of the horizon, calendrical and orbital changes, extinction angles and refraction—although I have not always stated this in the text.

As it is impossible here to provide a full picture, of either Avebury, ancient astronomy or the Neolithic era, I urge the interested reader to seek out the relevant texts, some of which are listed in the bibliography. Credit is due again to the excellent research on the part of the many specialists upon which this book depends, and above all, to the sustained contribution of Dr Philippa Berry. It is to her and our remarkable ancestors, the Neolithic star-watchers, that I dedicate this book.

1

Neolithic Astronomy

Archaic thought is cosmological, first and last…
De Santillana & von Dechend[1]

The Monument-Builders

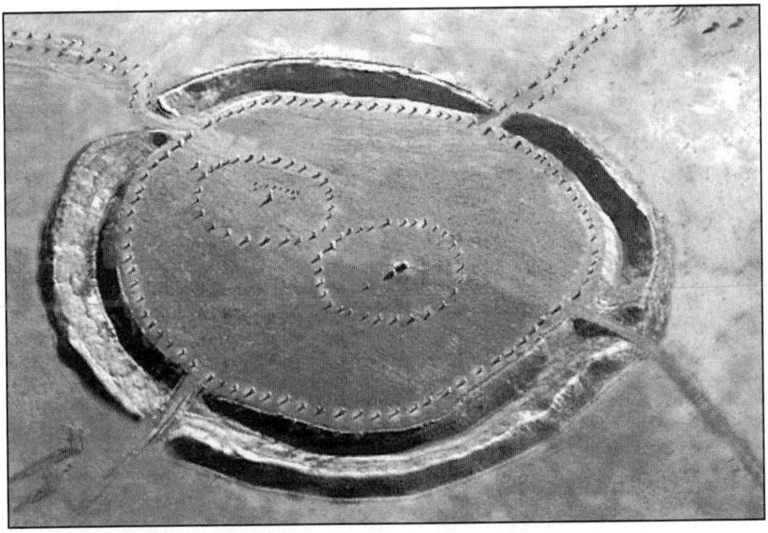

Aerial depiction of Avebury looking southwest, mid-third millennium BCE. The earthworks were much deeper and steeper at this time and when free of grass would have appeared chalk-white. Some details are omitted and the stone settings at the western entrance are unknown.

Despite the physical challenges, short lives and technical limitations of their time, the people who lived in Britain during the Neolithic era, from about 4500 to 2500 BCE, must have had a dynamic and exciting culture. A rich language, music and a vibrant oral tradition would have informed their complex

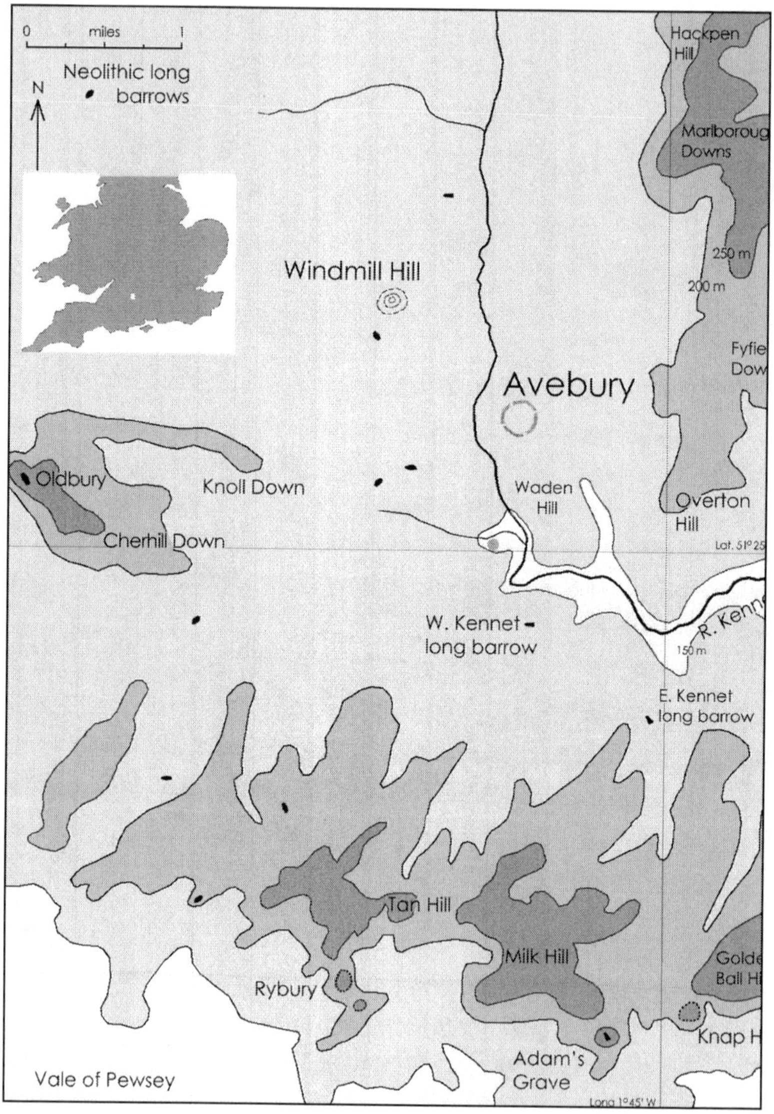

Figure 1. Map of the Avebury area showing high ground, Mesolithic campsites such as Hackpen Hill, Knap Hill, Oldbury and Rybury, and some early Neolithic long barrows.

planning and engineering skills. Their lives would have been full of stories, customs, lore and myth. These people first domesticated animals in Britain; they introduced pastoralism, and began the first farming on the island. They cultivated widespread resource and trading networks, greatly expanded the tool-kit of their Mesolithic predecessors, adopted new breeding practices, seed corn and forms of food storage, and had a vigorous sense of decorative design—an art they no doubt practiced on their bodies. They had an elaborate set of funerary practices, building sophisticated structures for their dead on a grand scale, often in stone. In the relatively new island of Britain, created by rising seas levels only a few thousand years before, the gradual and piecemeal movement away from the long-standing hunter-gatherer lifestyle of the Mesolithic era, into agrarian settlements, meant that by 4000 BCE Neolithic peoples were leaving a distinctive human imprint upon the land. As both their population and that of their herds increased in numbers, territories formerly visited only at certain seasons of the year gradually became permanent places to dwell.

In the Upper Kennet Valley in central southern Britain, one particular tribe or tribal network appears to have entered into a profoundly innovative relationship to their new territory. From the beginning of the fourth millennium (after 4000 BCE), this group began to create immense permanent monuments. They built long barrows for their dead, moved the first megaliths, and selected a nearby hill, Windmill Hill, as a place for episodic and seasonal gatherings. Eventually, towards the end of the fourth millennium, they set aside a large area of land below this same hill, and began to reshape it on an unprecedented and monumental scale.

The entire Avebury complex extends over several square miles. It consists of some of the greatest works by Neolithic builders anywhere in the world. With imposing barrows, banks and ditches, huge enclosures, megalithic circles and long avenues—including the largest stone circle and tallest mound in Neolithic Europe—the builders of Avebury dramatically and determinedly engaged with and reshaped their landscape. Despite subsequent attempts to destroy or remove most of its stones, a visitor to Avebury today can still gain a sense of the remarkable scale of this undertaking. All leave inspired by the extraordinary vision that it implies.

Avebury Astronomy

Stones of the Great Outer Circle in the southwest quadrant of Avebury henge. Some stones of the West Kennet Avenue are visible on the horizon.

The outdoor lifestyle of the Neolithic people, like that of their predecessors, depended upon the movements of the Sun and Moon. The light, warmth, directions and durations created by the solar and lunar cycles measured out the activities and the rhythms of their lives. While the Moon provided the most convenient marker of time, the warmth of the Sun determined when and where hunters could travel after the disappearance of the ice sheets at the close of the last Ice Age. Now, with domestic animals and light ploughs, solar cycles also affected when and where the new farmers could find good pasture and cultivate the soil. As old hunting practices declined and permanent settlements increased, the timing of seasonal agricultural activities became all-important; it is no surprise, then, that the Neolithic people incorporated soli-lunar cycles into the design of their new ritual sites.

While the movement of the Sun along increasingly well-marked local horizons provided our distant ancestors with a daily timekeeper and seasonal calendar, the movement and phases of the Moon charted not only the night, but also the weeks and months. The swift monthly cycle of the Moon as it passed along or near the *ecliptic*—the stellar path of the Sun and the planets—would have provided prehistoric peoples with a convenient measure of time. They could have measured the Moon against the stars of the ecliptic, the *zodiac,* counting off just over twenty-seven days for it to return to the same place, making in all about thirteen and a half lunar cycles a year. They could observe the *phases* of the Moon, counting off just over twenty-nine days from one full or new Moon to the next. Evidence from Palaeolithic find-sites of careful score marks on animal bones suggests that the first measures of time were highly symbolic calendars based upon these lunar periods.

The Neolithic people would have been entirely familiar with the annual rhythm whereby the winter full Moon rose in the same place on the horizon as the midsummer Sun, while the summer full Moon rose in the place of the midwinter Sun. (See Figure 50.) Indeed, evidence from many early-Neolithic sites has shown that their builders were already tracking the extreme positions of the Moon over its much longer 18.61-year cycle. Archaeoastronomers like Robin Heath and Gerald Hawkins have shown that by the fourth millennium BCE the people of the Wessex area had worked such a profound understanding of the movements of the Sun and Moon into their monuments that they would have known even the rudiments of the soli-lunar eclipse cycle. Some of their later monuments, most notably Stonehenge, would have helped them predict most solar and lunar eclipses with considerable accuracy.[6]

Yet a growing body of evidence gathered from the Neolithic monuments indicates that these early builders were not only following the passage of Sun and Moon against their local heavenly markers, but they also closely observed the movement of the visible planets, or 'wanderers,' along the ecliptic, as well as the nightly and annual passages of the 'fixed' stars.[7]

Probably the most important and easily noticeable attribute of the stars—apart from the direction of their revolution, east to west around the axis of the Earth—is that, due to the solar cycle, any individual star will always appear in the same *place* on any given horizon, and would always reappear, after a period of invisibility, at the same *time* each year. It was the stars, therefore, that provided ancient peoples with a reliable measure of the year, the seasons, the watches of the night, as well as directions for travel.[8] Individual bright stars and their constellations also formed an apparently unchanging backdrop in the sky, against which to observe the passages of the Moon and planets. Each consecutive night, if the skies were clear, ancient sky-watchers would have seen the Moon against a different backdrop of stars and guessed where the Sun was.

Once early star-names and star-patterns were established, the star-watchers could say that the Moon or Sun was in a specific area or 'house' of the sky just as astronomers and astrologers do today. The first records of this practice appear by the third millennium BCE in the Indus Valley and Sumeria. As early as 2700 BCE, the Sumerian temple of the goddess Nisiba, in Eres, was called the 'House of the Stars;' it is likely that a lapis-lazuli tablet sacred to this goddess—the 'tablet with the stars of the heavens'—was an early star-map.[9] But aboriginal identification of certain stars and constellations is certain to go back much further. For example, the association of Ursa Major with the bear may be more than 14,000 years old.

It was therefore individual stars and groups of stars, as well as the Milky Way, that provided the first recorded divisions of the sky. The star patterns that define the zodiac or the ecliptic—the pathway of the Moon and planets and the primary seasonal oscillation of the Sun—can be seen in lunar or solar terms, or both. We have long named these constellations or star groups for their resemblance to things on Earth. While the twenty-seven lunar mansions of early Vedic astronomers represented mundane and natural objects, as well as animals, the later, twelvefold, Greek Zodiac simply means 'circle of animals,' and borrows many of its now familiar star groups from those of ancient Mesopotamia.[10] Around 5000 years ago, for example, 'Chaldean' sky-watchers would have remarked that the Sun of spring rose in the place of the Bull; in the autumn, they would have noted that the full moons often rose near the stars of the figure whom we know as the Hunter, Orion, but they knew as the Shepherd or messenger of the gods. At the same time, both they, the Babylonians and the Egyptians were singling out the brightest star in the sky, Sirius; it marked the summer floods. The Egyptians considered Sirius or *Spdt* so important that its heliacal rising inaugurated the beginning of their New Year. Later they identified Sirius with the goddess Isis, and the stars of Orion with Osiris, her partner, as the source of the renewal of life. Unlike the Vedic Rishis and the Mesopotamian or Egyptian astronomers, the early British star-watchers have left us no written records, but I will show just how symbolically important certain star-figures, indeed all stars in general must have been for the Avebury monument-builders.

It is unlikely that the Neolithic people of Britain would have divided the ecliptic into the familiar, twelve-fold, solar Zodiac, but we shall see that it is very likely they divided it according to the Milky Way. They experienced the galaxy in all its glory as a perfect circle of densely packed stars and they saw it intersect with the path of the Sun, Moon and planets in two distinct places on opposite sides of the sky.

It is also likely that the meanings attributed to the celestial bodies by these new settled star-watchers influenced their perception of the landscape features over which particular stars or constellations rose or set. Thus, they would have seen some places as having a special relationship with the changing positions of sunrise and sunset throughout the year; others with individual stars that always vanished and reappeared in the *same* places on their local horizon. It is plausible that the monument builders would have selected particular stones for the henge because of the celestially imbued character of the locations from which they came. For example, at this latitude they may have treated stones from the north, the 'zenith' of the area, quite differently to stones from the south, the 'nadir,' and may have carefully distinguished stones of the stars from those of the Sun and Moon. A stone of the Cove, illustrated in this chapter, is marked with a circle and central hollow that faces a bearing to the Moon never obtained by the Sun.

I don't think I am overstating the case to say that the people of Avebury would have based their lives—their daily routines, their calendar, festivities, travel, buildings, monuments, ritual and agricultural practices—upon the light, meteorological conditions, visual phenomena and cosmic order provided by the changing sky. As the celestial bodies radiated light and heat, and generated wind and storm, as their radiant forms manifested eternal, regular and regulating powers, the relationship of this people with the heavenly sphere shaped not only their sense of space and time, but also their language, place names, cosmology, stories and mythology; in short, every aspect of their culture.

Neolithic Cosmos

For millennia, the ancient road known as the Ridgeway provided an entranceway into the high chalk lands of Avebury from the south. The Ridgeway passes below Adam's Grave Neolithic long barrow on the left of this picture on its way up to the hillcrest. The Knap Hill Neolithic enclosure is on the right.

Knap Hill from the northwest. An early Neolithic 'causewayed' enclosure, built mid-fourth millennium BCE.

There are several important points to make here. Firstly, the Neolithic people would have deemed it essential to maintain harmony with the order bestowed by the Sun, Moon and stars, by means of the correct spiritual or ritual observances. Their inherited attunement to numinous energies, including the 'spirits' of these bodies, would have involved specific rituals along with formal acts of recognition and divination. They may well have attributed any disasters or misfortunes, such as floods or destructive gales, to neglect of the correct spiritual observances—such as neglect of offerings to an ancestor. Surviving records from late Neolithic and Bronze age societies around the world show it was the ritual responsibility of all headmen, chieftains, kings and pharaohs to uphold the natural divine order. Chinese emperors, for example, were expected to be able to avoid the potentially calamitous effects of eclipses by observing the correct ceremonial procedures. Nothing was random in the Neolithic world; everything took place according to a divine purpose; thus, the order and timing of things had to be respected.

Secondly, as I noted above, it is likely that Neolithic peoples' knowledge of the stars had been accumulating for millennia. Their Mesolithic and more remote Palaeolithic forebears would surely have named the stars, and no doubt, developed and retold their stories. We know that the Aboriginal people of Australia have passed down a rich star lore over tens of thousands of years; for them, the stars are ancestral beings whose acts shaped the landscape and made things the way they are.[11]

Thirdly, anthropologists consider that naming things and telling their stories are the distinguishing hallmarks of what it means to be human. The Neolithic tribal people of Britain would have told and retold stories about the cyclical, regulating, spatial and temporal order of the Sun, Moon and stars as vital elements of an over-arching narrative, a rich memorial tradition largely inherited from their Meso- and Palaeolithic ancestors. They are likely to have sung parts of this narrative and to have retold it in stories for their children; these children would thus have been exposed from birth to a language that was grounded in an omnipresent spirit of life. They must have re-enacted this narrative in sacred locations, in dances and rituals that acknowledged the 'gifting' and abundant character of the Great Surround and the divine sources of creation.

Finally, as the Neolithic era progressed, ancient values, concepts and symbols slowly altered, because of humanity's increasingly fixed relationship to place. The first settled Britons would have conceived new stories: stories that expressed the difference of their way of life from that of their ancestors, including what it meant to live in a world of great megalithic monuments—of sacred, sanctified, man-made spaces. Thus while being inherently conservative, they would have been constantly reshaping their relationship to spirits of plants, animals, kin, ancestors and the world about them through new narratives that would have been prominent at their most meaningful moments of ceremony, especially fertility rites and the burial of the dead.

In an era when more than half the population died before reaching the age of fifteen, watching and following the recurring heavenly cycles would have given stability and regularity to lives that must often have seemed vulnerable, under threat, even chaotic.[12] In myths told around the fire about cosmic sources of healing, or great ancestors overcoming obstacles and gaining the secrets of life, the imagination of the storytellers must often have gone beyond their immediate world of forest, land and sea. Truly mythic narratives would have entered the cosmic landscape of the Sun, Moon and stars for their legitimation and authority. Such stories would have helped Neolithic people to feel more securely positioned within a divinely ordained order.

In their ambitious construction of vast monuments carefully aligned to the celestial sphere, the Avebury builders seem to have been searching for ways to deepen and intensify their experience of the cosmic order. In the new and unique monumental landscape they were creating, they could simultaneously bring their stories, their forms of divination and means of foretelling down to earth and look more deeply into the divinely regulated environment of sacred time and space. A profound piety drove them to look further into the heavens, in an attempt to understand and come to terms with great change in a world where nothing happened by chance.

When special knowledge came, as their great ritual monuments mirrored the movements of the heavens and provided information about cycles that could be predictive, it must have appeared as a revelation and a source of wonder to these people. Still deeply embedded in the natural world, they seem to have understood the stones as securing their harmony and communion with the heavens. They intended the cosmic narrative embodied in the enormous sarsens, banks and ditches to secure them plenty, fertility and well-being, through harmony with the myriad powers that ordered and governed their world. Under the great stones, in the awe-inspiring circle of the henge, at its central fires and its places of offering, the whole community could come together. Here they could understand shifting temporalities, mediate conflicts, maintain justice, foresee and avoid transgressions, offer sacrifices, arrange marriages, make sexual contacts, confirm tribal allegiances and inaugurate leaders. Here they could celebrate their shared sense of symbolic meanings and values on many different levels.

How the Neolithic people experienced this exactly at Avebury is unknown. There is little evidence from the interior of the henge. The builders scrupulously cleared antler, bone and shards away.[13] Nevertheless, it is easy to imagine strong sexual prohibitions as well as many social taboos, prescribed times for the hunt, for trade and exchange, prescribed methods of building, marital arrangements where husbands and wives spent as much time with their kinship and alliance groups as with each other, and strict codes that determined distribution of meat from the hunt and the herds to the young, the sick and the old. All such early codes inevitably derived their authority from some version of cosmic law, perceived in the cycles of the Earth and Sky. Without such a law, society could not function and disharmony would prevail. From this perspective, we can imagine early star watching at Avebury as shaping not only the origins of astronomy—that is, astronomy as divination or astrology—along with the beginning of theology and religion, but also the first statutes of law.

The star-knowledge and attendant wisdom obtained at Avebury also helped to shape new forms of identity, authority and power. Strong patriarchal trends begin to appear at this time among the cosmic powers of the influential Middle Eastern traditions. While the builders no doubt used Avebury and other sites like it for ceremonies that celebrated tribal identity, different forms of emerging political authority began to guide the successive stages of monumental construction at the henge, especially by the time of the Bronze Age. The final chapter explores changing forms of power and authority at Avebury. Yet ultimately, the Neolithic people built their monuments to help locate themselves within the world. Through their reverent actions, especially through the highly ritualised process of constructing their extraordinary monuments, these tough, lean, sophisticated and self-reliant people defined themselves securely within an immense and still mysterious cosmos.

A Relative Chronology

Writers on the Neolithic period of Avebury have long lamented the lack of an accurate chronology to compare the monuments and set them in their appropriate context. Past excavators of Silbury Hill, for example, had always obtained a wide range of dates for their finds, although, chiefly due to the lack of re-grown turf, they settled on a short length of time for construction. Recent excavations, however, have shown that the construction of Silbury Hill was protracted, going on in several stages after 2450 BCE. Unfortunately, the situation is not as clear for other sites in the area.[14]

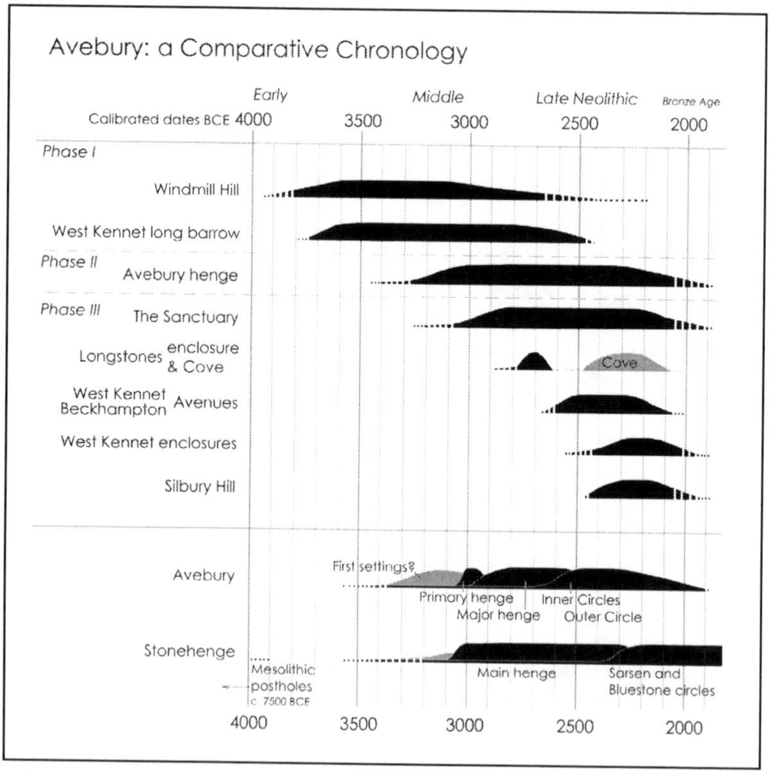

Based upon recent archaeological reports, the dotted lines on the accompanying chart show the earliest and latest dates for activities on a site, while the heavy lines show the most likely time of construction and use. As the same evidence can be interpreted differently, the lines are very broad indeed. Aubrey Burl, for example, is willing to push the erection of the primary stone settings at Avebury back as far as 3400 BCE, but most interpreters prefer 3000 BCE.

The chart suggests three main phases of activity. Phase I, defined by seasonal occupation at Windmill Hill and the erection of West Kennet and other long barrows, is Early to Middle Neolithic, a prolonged period subject to little change similar to the Mesolithic. Phase II, defined by the creation of Avebury henge, the Sanctuary and the Longstones enclosure—together with the first phase of Silbury Hill—is later, but still characterised by durability. Phase III, defined by the completion of Silbury Hill, the avenues, the Longstones Cove and the West Kennet Palisade enclosures, is Late Neolithic and relatively brief. The chart also compares the different phases of Avebury henge and Stonehenge but, as an example of the uncertainty, the Stonehenge Bluestones may have arrived on the site much earlier than the carved sarsens.

2

A Sky-Watcher's Paradise

On the island is a magnificent sacred precinct of Apollo and a notable temple adorned with many votive offerings and spherical in shape. They say how the Moon viewed from this island appears to be but a little distance from the earth… the god visits the island every nineteen years, the period in which the return of the stars to the same place in the heavens is accomplished.

Diodorus Siculus, II

Avebury Henge

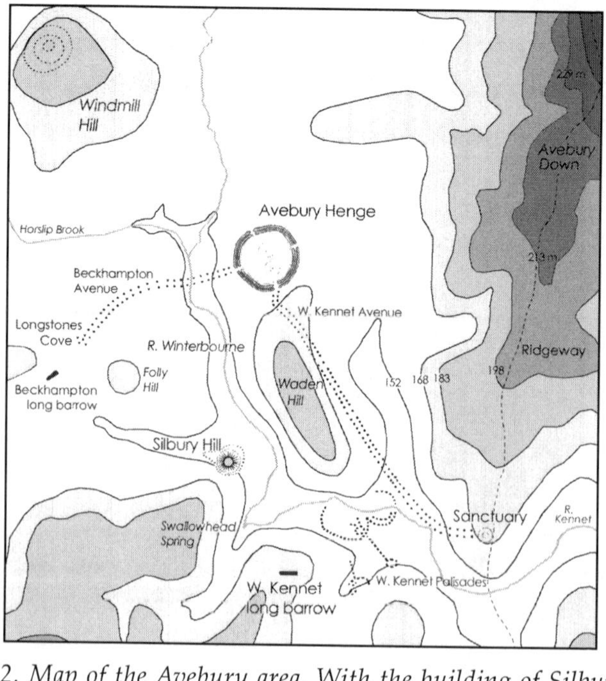

Figure 2. Map of the Avebury area. With the building of Silbury Hill

after 2500 BCE, any visitor to the area, perhaps entering by the Ridgeway or the Kennet valley, would have been struck by the number, variety and immense scale of the monuments (not all shown here)—some of them already over a thousand years old.

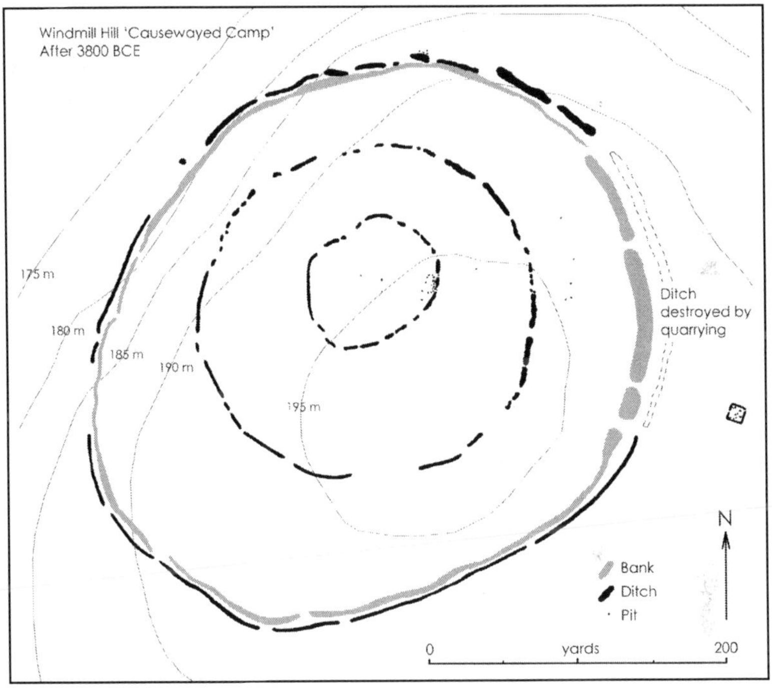

Figure 3. Plan of the three concentric Early Neolithic enclosures on Windmill Hill, most likely built in a sequence from inner to outer to middle in the centuries after 3700 BCE. Made up of segments, and broken by causeways that provided access from all direction, the ditches reached considerable size in places and contained thousands of votive or sacrificial deposits.

Avebury henge lies in the upper valleys of the River Kennet, below a circle of flint-rich chalk hills. These hills provided resources and campsites for Mesolithic nomads as they moved across the land after the last Ice Age. Before the first Britons began to settle, this area was covered by relatively light, open woodland. It was also littered with glacially deposited 'sarsen' stones (sarsen = Saracen or pagan stones), and criss-crossed by several important tracks or 'Ridgeways.' These upland paths allowed grazing animals and people to move about freely in a climate warmer and more favourable than that prevailing in Britain today.

Some time after 3800 BCE, a group of these people cleared away trees and vegetation on the summit of Windmill Hill, just above Avebury, and began to build three concentric rings of earth works. They would occupy and use this multi-purpose enclosure seasonally for many hundreds of years, working a mixture of imported and local flints, herding animals, processing food and holding large, festive gatherings. This group or tribe remained largely migratory; they gathered on the hill only on an episodic basis: to work together, trade, socialise, and, when resources allowed, to feast and make what seem to have been thank-offerings to their gods or guardian spirits. This latter practice usually involved placing innumerable joints of meat—sometimes whole carcasses of mainly beef or pork—in the deep pits or ditches of the enclosures.

This 'causewayed enclosure' of the Windmill Hill people, although neither the first nor the last built in this area, has been deemed one of the most significant in social terms, playing a vital role in the development of the Neolithic era in central southern Britain.[1] Distinct from the wide-ranging world and transitory campsites of the Mesolithic nomad, the three huge enclosing rings on the hill determined what lay both inside and outside of the tribe's boundaries. Windmill Hill therefore represented a new desire for a fixed symbolic centre, however temporary: a place where people could gather in large numbers to affirm shared traditions and community—and from where they could look out in all directions, over the wooded hills and valleys to the sky beyond.[2]

At some point in the second quarter of the fourth millennium

BCE, not long after the establishment of their great enclosure, the Windmill Hill people selected another low hill lying to the south of Avebury, just above the River Kennet, for the construction of a long barrow. This was an elaborate stone-roofed earthen mound, with a central chamber at the end of a stone-lined passageway flanked by four smaller side chambers. The people were to build several other long barrows in the area, although not always on the same scale. After they had performed funerary ceremonies, probably in the forecourt to the barrow, they placed the often deliberately disjointed bones of a group of their dead inside these chambers. They appear to have revisited these special ancestral bones at chosen times, sometimes removing them temporarily or permanently. As the first megalithic ('large stone') monument in the Avebury area, West Kennet long barrow marked a shift from wood to stone, predating by as much as a thousand years construction in stone in dynastic Egypt.[3] The Windmill Hill people ended their long and complex relationship with the West Kennet long barrow about 2500 BCE, when they filled and closed the monument with huge blocking stones. Just before the era of Windmill Hill and the long barrows ended, however, work had already begun on the finest piece of monumental architecture ever conceived by the Windmill Hill people or the people of Britain: this was Avebury henge.

Avebury henge lies on the low chalk dome that extends from the northern end of Waden Hill. This hill may not seem particularly striking to modern visitors to the area, but it evidently had a particular significance for these Neolithic people.[4] The archaeologist Alasdair Whittle described Windmill Hill itself as a "massive ceremonial arena," but at Avebury, the builders would take ideas inherent within both the early Neolithic causewayed enclosure and the long barrow to an even higher level of complexity and magnitude. The overall structure of the Avebury monument was to be immense: hundreds of posts and stones, many as great as forty tons, some weighing more than sixty (one in the Cove estimated at one hundred tons is believed to be the largest standing stone in Britain) were arranged in large circles and avenues, several miles in extent.[5]

To create the megalithic element of the monument, the builders erected sandstone sarsens that may have already been on or near to the site and brought many more in from several miles away. They accomplished this difficult work periodically, over hundreds of years, perhaps over a thousand years. The result was a stone circle over 360 yards in diameter, made up of around one hundred stones, and approached by two large avenues of stones. By the time it reached its final form, the Great Outer Circle contained two further stone circles, timber posts and circles, a stone row and other enormous megaliths. The Avebury builders enclosed and unified all these features within a colossal ditch and bank—the henge itself—that exceeded a quarter of a mile in diameter. To create the extraordinary, almost obsessive, depth of the ditch of the henge, they had to dig into the chalk subsoil painstakingly and laboriously, using simple antler pickaxes and bone shovels, then carry the spoil onto the bank using woven baskets.

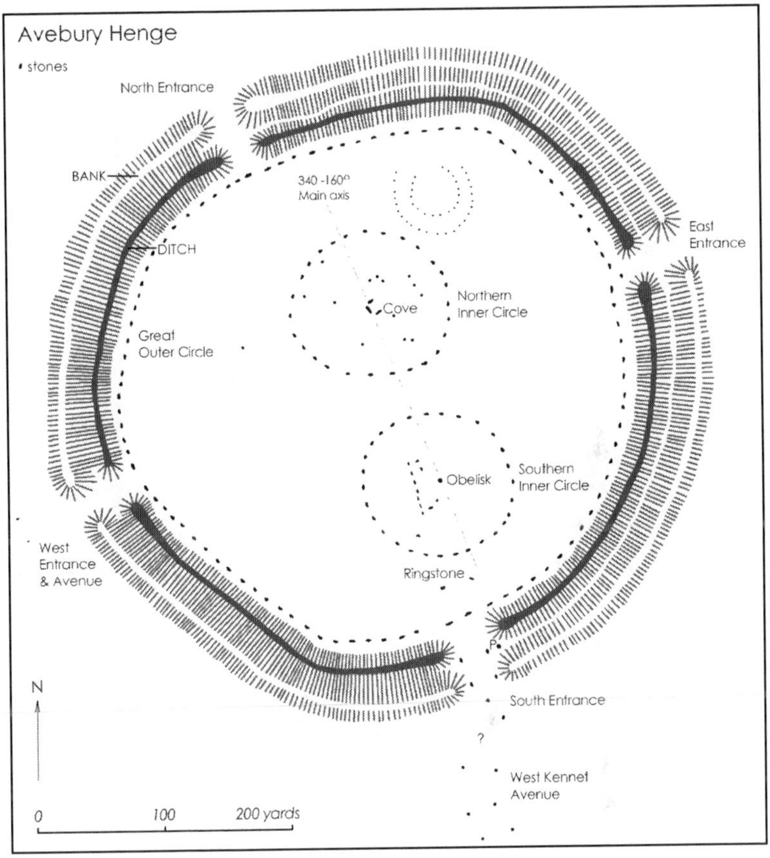

Figure 4. Plan of Avebury henge, mid-third millennium BCE, showing the henge with stones intact. There were approximately 98 stones in the Great Outer Circle, 27 in the Northern and 29 in the Southern Inner Circles. The 'Obelisk' once at the centre of the Southern Inner Circle was the tallest stone at over 18 feet. At the centre of the Northern Inner Circle stood a 'Cove' of three huge stones. Postholes in the circle's northeast quadrant suggest additional internal timber circles. Within the henge, the ground drops away slightly on either side of a line drawn through the centre of the two circles, the main axis of the monument.

Based on recent excavations, a possible construction sequence is as follows: the Cove, the Obelisk and other NNE and SSW stones and posts before 3000 BCE; the first enclosure circa 3000 BCE; the inner ditch and outer bank circa 2800 BCE; the Inner Circles between 2800 and 2500 BCE. The builders completed the Outer Circle and the Avenues after that time, in a period of intense activity that also saw the erection of the Longstones Cove, the West Kennet enclosures, Silbury Hill and the stones of the Sanctuary. The posthole, P, at the southern entrance, however, may be extremely old indeed.

Dating Avebury

Although this thesis is not yet generally accepted, it is entirely plausible that its builders could have erected the first stones of Avebury as early as the second half of the fourth millennium BCE, between 3500 and 3000 BCE, most likely in the last quarter of the millennium. Archaeologists now consider that the Obelisk, the Ring Stone, the D feature, the Cove with the largest stone on site, and the great stones at the southern and northern entrances to the henge, which appear different in size and arrangement to later stones, were the first megalithic features.[6] What will prove to be the crucial astronomical orientation in this vast structure, between the two main groups of these early stones, the Obelisk and the Cove, lies at 160° south, 340° north. It seems likely that the builders first constructed the Outer Circle, then the ditch and bank of the henge itself later, making an irregular and vast circle around clusters of already existing megaliths.

The steeply sided ditch of the henge eventually reached over thirty feet in depth. Its high bank, once slightly higher than today, was created outside of the ditch, from its chalk spoil. The fact that the builders put the bank *outside* of the ditch is what makes it a henge, a 'ceremonial' site. The erection of an inner bank and outer ditch, as on Windmill Hill, would have implied defensive purposes (this in spite of Whittle's comment about the Hill's additional ceremonial function). Archaeologists now think the Avebury builders began their work around 3000 BCE, creating a primary earthwork of turf and chalk that, while not very deep or high, broadly laid out the size and shape of the henge. Not long after, perhaps within decades, at most a few centuries, their descendants proceeded to implement the immense second, and final, stage. These builders gave especial emphasis to the four entrances to the henge. They flanked the wide entrance causeways with carefully graded banks that dropped into deep ditches. Water partially filled these ditches at certain times of the year.[7] At this stage, any freshly cut or scoured chalk on the banks would have appeared brilliant white.

From the surprisingly small amount of archaeological evidence found on the site it appears that this second group of builders did not place many of the stones in the Avenues and the Circles until quite late in the henge's main period of use: that is, between 2600 and 2000 BCE. For example, they may have built both the Southern Inner Circle, centered upon the Obelisk, and the Northern Inner Circle, centered upon the Cove, after 2600 BCE, long after the ditch and bank. However, other evidence suggests that the placing of these stones could have been contemporary with the building of the henge itself. The exact dates of this phase, and almost every other stage of the monument are therefore unclear.[8]

What is clear is that although only fragments remain, the two Inner Circles were majestic creations. The builders appear to have selected the immense stones for their distinctive shape and weathered character, placing them in the ground to best display these features. They set up the stones with their flattest under-sides facing the centre of the circle, and aligned each carefully to its neighbours in order to emphasise the continuous and containing character of the ring. These stones typically have either a lozenge-like, diamond shape; a phallic, columnar shape; or a zoomorphic, animal form. To hold the stones in place the builders brought in smaller sarsen packing stones and sometimes special soil. Marks from wooden levers indicate their methods of construction. These Inner Circles seem reasonably geometrically exact: the southern one of twenty-nine stones is a circle, the northern one, perhaps originally of twenty-seven stones, may have been deliberately egg-shaped. Archaeologists now think stones were added to the early and immense entrance stones to form the sections or arcs of the Great Outer Circle well after the Inner Circles, probably after 2400 BCE. Marking an exact centre of this circle is impossible.

It is likely that the builders would have completed some parts of the work quite quickly. Self-organised teams defined by their regional or tribal affiliations could have dug out their section of the primary or final ditch within a few years. But archaeologists think that in general this phase of the building at Avebury was ongoing. Sometimes a squat stone may have been set in a shallow hole with minimum effort; overall, however, the amount of labour required for digging the pits, making ropes and hauling the huge stones must have been enormous. At times, especially for the largest stones, the work would seemingly have required a contribution from the entire available labour force of central southern Britain. Yet at other times, sometimes spanning whole centuries, there was much less activity; in some periods, there was apparently no building at all.[9] While bones and antlers have been found in the ditches, but little evidence has been found in the henge itself, some archaeologists have read this as a sign of 'ritual cleanliness.' Although there are a few burials beside stones, these were added later and no foundation burials have been found; in other words, the individual has virtually vanished from the site. Some scholars have speculated that the builders saw the task of construction, especially the setting up of stones, as significant in its own right, so that no further rituals would have been required. I think this is unlikely; yet of course, Neolithic Britons were building many other monuments throughout this period. Almost twenty miles away due south, the first phases of Stonehenge also date to around 3000 BCE. The exact relationship between these two sites is unclear, but up to eighty massive sarsen stones used for the final stages of Stonehenge came from the Avebury area.

While carbon-dating methods have greatly improved, archaeologists have found it extremely difficult to interpret the diverse features of the entire Avebury complex. Stones, post-holes, ditches, bones, flints and sherds may be there in numbers, but such finds do not give up their secrets easily. Scholars agree that the monuments were more than just a territorial or tribal marker, and undoubtedly held great social and political as well as ritual and symbolic meaning. Yet they also say that what exactly those meanings were will remain enigmatic.[10] After all, the Neolithic builders were part of a complex culture that left no written records, their language is entirely unknown and their material vestiges often confined to burials. The prevailing view, therefore, is that just as it is hard to imagine what the Avebury builders actually did in their henge, it is impossible to establish what their intentions were in building it. But can archaeoastronomy help to develop this incomplete picture?

Stones & Foresights

The Cove at the centre of the Northern Inner Circle, looking northwest. Originally a third stone stood in the background making a loose arrangement open to the northeast—azimuth approximately 50°, to midsummer Sunrise or midwinter full Moons. The base of the stone to the left extends over ten feet below ground; this megalith weighs about 100 tons.

Its outer bank forms an artificial horizon around Avebury that is rather like the rim of an immense open bowl. By allowing the tops of sarsen stones to rise above this rim, the monument-builders greatly facilitated their view of the sky. This regularly divided artificial horizon of the henge-bank, along with the more distant horizon (Waden Hill to the south, Avebury, Fyfield or the Marlborough Downs to the east, Beckhampton or Folly Hill to the southwest and Windmill Hill to the northwest, all sources of sarsen stone), provided the Avebury builders with invaluable

Three of the remaining stones of the Southern Inner Circle, named in the text from left to right as the 'South Stone,' the 'Silbury Stone' and the 'Crucis Stone.'

sets of astronomical foresights. The challenge for the archaeoastronomer today is in finding the corresponding backsights; these are the places where Neolithic sky-watchers would have stood within the huge area enclosed by the henge.

Suitable backsights are everywhere among the inner rings of stone: at their centres, along their edges, and across the whole. The exact centre of the whole henge is not easy to identify, however, even on a reconstructed plan. In his 1967 survey, Alexander Thom placed the centre of the henge in the area between the two internal circles—a location that is now unfortunately crossed by a road and surrounded by houses.[11]

From both the Obelisk and the Cove, which mark the centres of the two Inner Circles, the Avebury sky-watchers could have sighted accurate and permanent astronomical alignments, using at least one stone of the Inner Circles and an additional stone of the Great Outer Circle, to the artificial and natural horizon. Over such distances, and on such a scale, Avebury henge was capable of providing astronomical accuracy as good as if not better than an ancient Babylonian or Egyptian temple.[12]

Four entrances mark the perimeter of the monument. Offset 15-20° counter clockwise from north, south, east and west, these entrances may have represented the many sets of four points observable in the sky: the solstitial extremes, the lunar extremes, the cardinal directions or the four great quarters of the celestial sphere. The builders may have planned a third inner circle, the same size as the two internal circles and to the north of them on the same 160° axis. If so, this remained incomplete or was removed when the henge was built.[13] Another circle, a double one, perhaps of wooden posts, once lay in the northeast sector, but this feature remains uninvestigated. Further features may lie hidden elsewhere.

Returning to the centre of the henge, the next challenge is to place what we see today in its original context, when this is so very different to the one that prevails today. The people who built and used Avebury would have seen the sky-alignments as an integral part of their experience of inhabiting a world of purposeful immanent powers. For them, a life-force pervaded plants, animals, humans, rivers, stones and place, as well as the cycles of the Sun, Moon and stars. The builders would have carefully located and created any ceremonial site in such a way as to honour this 'Great Surround,' its diverse inhabitants and powers. Such sites were places for rites of passage, prayers, offerings, appeals, thanksgiving and contrition. While Avebury was many things to many generations of people, it seems obvious that its builders viewed it as the means of connection and communication between different worlds and states of being. Anthropologists such as David Lewis-Williams and

Gerardo Reichel-Dolmatoff inform us that in all aboriginal cosmologies there are worlds above and below the plane of human existence. At ancient places like Avebury, it is highly likely that a vertical earth-sky axis complemented the horizontal axes of the site; the Neolithic people would surely have understood this distinct vertical axis to be multi-layered.[14]

Like other tribal peoples worldwide, the Neolithic people of Avebury would also have seen the tiered Otherworlds as occupied by what was other-than-human: mythologised ancestors, animal spirits, giants, malevolent agencies, benign forces, gods and world-creating powers. In most indigenous and traditional cosmologies, the beings of the Upperworld reside upon mountains, in the Sun, the Moon, and the upper and starry regions of the sky. In contrast, the beings of the Lowerworld reside in caves, deep earth or water, the dark regions of the sky, below the ecliptic, or entirely below the horizon. Tribal songs and myths name these beings, tell and retell their stories and describe their position in the cosmos. Yet Avebury is so complex, and on such a scale, that it seems the intention of its builders was not to privilege any single story, any one divine power, or any one astronomical cycle or alignment, but rather to include *everything* within the structure's multiple dimensions. The people who made the great henge intended it to make an inclusive and comprehensive statement about their relationship with the cosmos. Although we will never understand all the implications of that statement, Neolithic Avebury must have been a storyteller's, a shaman's and a sky-watcher's paradise.

In sum, the Early Neolithic people of the Upper Kennet Valley had conducted ritual observances on the open summit of Windmill Hill to honour the earth and the heavens for hundreds of years. As they cleared woodland, improved farming techniques, gradually settled, and achieved grain and livestock surpluses that allowed them to extend their activities, they apparently decided that by setting up megaliths on the valley floor they could express their relationship to the terrestrial and heavenly spirits more profoundly than on the summit of Windmill Hill. Together with a colossal artificial horizon marked by monumental stones, Avebury's distinctive natural horizon offered them many more symbolic and meaningful possibilities. They could have used only the great sarsen stones already scattered around the Avebury site—but no, it is evident that the builders wanted their monument to make a very big and elaborate statement.

Inner Circles of the Moon

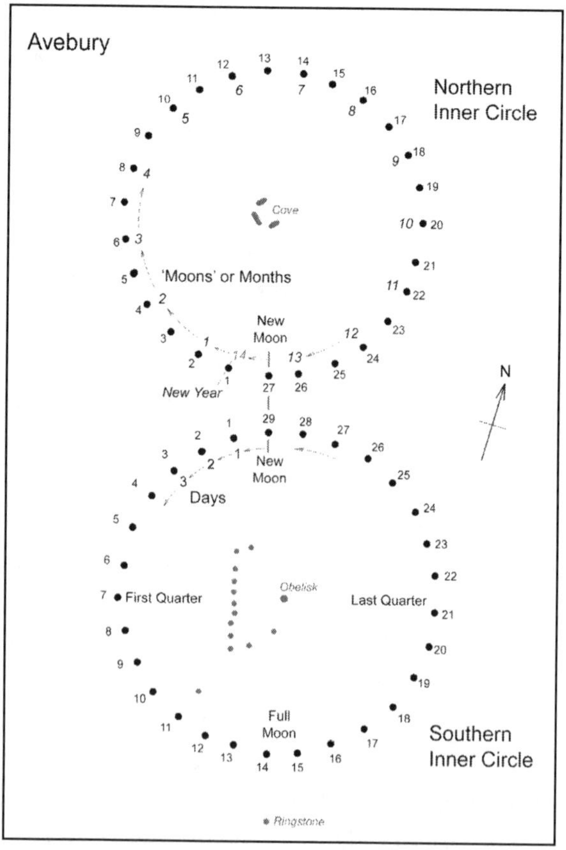

Figure 5. Lunar Avebury: The two Inner Circles of Avebury as lunar

indicators. Select the two stones of the Inner Circles nearest each other as your starting points, marked stones 27 and 29—the likely number of stones in each circle—and begin at the new Moon. (Note: it doesn't matter where you start or which way you go or at what phase of the Moon, it all comes out the same in the end.) Move daily to the next stone in each circle as shown—after fourteen days the Moon will be full. After twenty-nine days (actually 29.53 a synodic month), you will have made one complete circuit of the Southern Inner Circle and the Moon will be new again. The southern circle thus counts off the lunar phases (its anomalous stone settings, such as the Ring Stone, could have taken the half day into account).[15] *The completion of one circuit of the northern circle marks the twenty-seven days (actually 27.32, a sidereal month) needed for the Moon to return to the same position in the sky from which it started the cycle. But as the Northern Inner Circle has just twenty-seven stones, you will advance in your tracking of the twenty-nine lunar phases two further stones, to stone 2. This marks the beginning of the next lunar cycle, the next new Moon, or 'month 1'. Advance again around the two circles. On completion of the next cycle of phases, you will arrive at stone 4 or 'month 2'. And so on. It will take you thirteen and a 'half' lunar cycles, or almost one year, to come around to your starting point, stone 27. 13.5 moons x 27 = 364.5 days or one year. Begin the next year where you ended on stone 1 (or 'month 14'); you will need to advance around the northern circle for twenty-seven years before stone 27 again marks a new Moon.*

If a system like this was in operation, the Avebury sky-watchers could have used the stones of the two Inner Circles to count days, lunar months (both synodic and sidereal), years and groups of years. Instead of decades or centuries, the sky-watchers could have used 'lunaries.' As well as marking or 'holding' the day and the lunar month, each stone could have been seen as a 'lunary'—a keeper of great time cycles. Each lunary consisted of twenty-seven years, or 364.5 moons, a figure remarkably close to the number of days in the year. Thus, both circles counted off the days, the southern circle counted off each cycle of phases, the northern circle counted off the complete number of lunar rotations in a year, the year of 364.5 days, and the years in counts of twenty-seven, or 364.5 Moons. The sky-watchers would have had to make adjustments in the order of three days every four years against the alignments to maintain accuracy, just like our leap year, but small adjustments to the regular ticking of the southern lunar month circle would have kept things running smoothly. A system like this also could have helped determine the 18/19 year lunar cycle, the cycles of the lunar nodes and thus the chances of an eclipse.

The Neolithic people of Avebury went to great efforts to select individual megaliths or sets of stones to represent certain astral bodies, cycles and events in the sky. The great stones set upright and aligned against the horizon, reminiscent of animal forms, brought the presence and power of the Sun, Moon, stars and planets down to the Earth. It is not hard to imagine skilful teachers initiating a novice by instructing them to observe the movement of a celestial body using a certain set of stones until they understood the cycles, powers, myths, omens, observances, divinatory practices and songs that went along with it.[16]

The alignments and the circles would have enabled these sky-watchers to monitor durations or periods: hourly, daily, monthly, annual and multiples of soli-lunar movements. Novices could have quickly acquired a comprehensive, visceral, understanding of the cycles represented by the multiple circles; but learning the detailed knowledge of the complex (and sometimes retrograde) movements of the planets, and the movements of the stars, would have taken longer. Evidently it took time to understand the knowledge the stones contained. The stones themselves would have provided the hands-on exercises in counts, ratios, figurative geometry and, of course, the understanding of calendars and time keeping. The stones were the notation; their alignments connected them to the heavens, while their shadows operated as informative gnomons or sundials. But more important to the dutiful sky-watchers would have been the manner in which they experienced and revered the divine powers that the stones embodied.

The numbers of stones in the two Inner Circles strongly suggest that by the mid-third millennium BCE, a dedicated ritual observance of the cycles of the Moon was at the heart of Avebury. See Figure 5. The builders may have intended the twenty-seven stones of the Northern Inner Circle to represent the days (27.32) the Moon takes to orbit the Earth and return to the same place against the stars—known as the sidereal month. They may have intended the twenty-nine stones of the Southern Inner Circle to represent the days (29.53) for the Moon to complete one cycle of phases, to go from full to full, or from new to new Moon—known as the synodic month.[17]

Imagine a world without our weeks, months, 365-day years and leap years; a world in which the Moon is the main method of keeping time. You might say, for example, let us meet in a Moon, or when it is next full or new. No one has to count; you just look at the sky. There is good evidence that such lunar calendars were in use from a very early time. The problem for those who depend closely upon the seasons is how to say, let us meet at the same time next year, as the lunar and solar cycles do not follow each other. Although apparently tied to fertility, periods of gestation and menstruation, the lunar cycle does not follow the seasons. Which cycle do you prioritise? Or do you, like many ancient cultures, try to run and align lunar and solar calendars simultaneously?

The Neolithic megalithic monuments may have been attempts to reconcile the cycles of the Sun and the Moon, so that a fixed number of lunar cycles fitted into the solar cycle, or the seasons always began with a certain Moon. There are several ways to do this, involving both the sidereal and synodic cycles, and using circles of 27, 28 and 29 stones or their multiples. The builders could have used alignments to the solstitial extremes (summer or winter solstice) to calibrate the lunar calendar. They may have noticed that periodically adding a synodic month, for example every three years, brought solar and lunar cycles back into alignment. Figure 5 suggests one method of counting the lunar cycles that uses the two Inner Circles to name, track and calibrate different counts. The stones could have represented days or phases of the lunar cycle, and the circles complete cycles, that is, 'Moons' or months. These in turn could have nested within longer cycles, years or groups of years, perhaps represented by the many stones of the Great Outer Circle.[18]

Knowing and agreeing upon the durational cycles—when they began and when they ended, what they were called and how they were represented; knowing the exact number of days until the next round of ritual, festive, pastoral and agricultural activities—would have helped Neolithic farmers plan their lives and make appropriate decisions and preparations. They could put cattle out to pasture, bring in the bull, count ovulation cycles and length of pregnancy, prolong or end lactations, give animals away or slaughter them—all according to the cycles of the Moon and Sun. They could also order their lives: hunting, planting, harvesting, coming of age, sexual encounters, marriages, pregnancies, cohabitation, child rearing, fasts, funerals and feasts, in the same manner. Yet the scale, geometry and beauty of Avebury's Inner Circles suggests their builders did not need them just to mark the soli-lunar cycles for calendrical purposes (these were already closely followed) so much as they wished to deepen their veneration for these cycles that determined the most meaningful aspects of their lives.

Time Stones

The Neolithic sky-watchers of Avebury could have worked with the repetitive and easily followed solar cycle using combinations of the assembled sarsen stones. From the central Obelisk, for

The great ditch and bank (the henge proper) of the southeast quadrant of Avebury, seen from the southern entrance.

example, they could have tracked the Sun's annual passage using the stones of the Southern Inner Circle without difficulty. Sets of stones to the east and west broke the double horizon provided by the bank and the distant horizon (the two often seem to track each other) and threw long shadows at dawn and sunset. One of the surviving stones in the southwest part of the circle (stone 105 on the official plan) could have provided a setting for activities around midwinter Sunset. These stones would have enabled the sky-watchers to follow the solar year against the monthly lunar sequence, the great 18/19 year lunar cycle and even longer cycles. They may even have seen the named and storied stones as 'containing' these cycles of time. A skilled sky-watcher could have told an enquirer exactly how much or what kind of 'time' a stone or combinations of stones contained, whether in days, months and years, or in auspicious mythic etymologies and ancestral genealogies. Thus these megaliths were quarried as much from time as from geology and culture; they literally were selected to contain the nature and quality of the durational sequences or cycles of time.

The Avebury sky-watchers could have bundled up the years in relationships of cycles, each characterised by names, aspects, myths and pedigrees, which when read against the durational sequences embodied in the stones gave them considerable accuracy. The caption to Figure 5, for example, proposes a 'lunary' of twenty-seven years or 364.5 lunar rotations, to replace the decade or century as a long unit of Neolithic time. The sequences could have reached so far back in time that, just like our histories and dating systems today, they were characterised entirely by mythology—perhaps by a great conjunction, or a time belonging to a primordial ancestor. The sky-watchers could have measured the cycles by simply moving around a suitably calibrated circle. Each circle might keep a different count, but in general, their 'time stones' would have defined sets of favourable and unfavourable days, and identified events and periods for certain activities. Both the twenty-seven and twenty-nine stones of the Inner Circles at Avebury and the fifty-six Aubrey Holes at Stonehenge appear perfectly arranged for this kind of activity.[19]

Apart from the benefits of having such an accurate calendar, Neolithic sky-watchers would have found that the megaliths gave a monumental expression to their understanding of the cycles of time. Almost certainly they would not have seen time as we do, as a linear passage from a random event in the past to an end in an impossibly distant future. Although they may have seen time as having begun with an event, perhaps even ending with an apocalypse or a new world, they were far more likely to have seen time as a quality and as a recurrence, defined by repeating cycles. Against the durational sequences—days, moons, years or 'lunaries,' perhaps perceived as gifts of the Sun and Moon—the Neolithic sky-watchers could even have begun to follow the slow-moving and often retrograde cycles of the visible planets: Venus, Mars, Jupiter and Saturn. Their stone circles, found all over the island of Britain, would have helped them better anticipate and agree upon times for many different events, from spring ploughing to autumn ceremonies. At their most complex, these circles marked the 18.62 year cycle of lunar extremes and thus the cycle of the lunar nodes—the intersection of the solar and lunar paths. These defined when eclipses were most likely to occur, and the nineteen-year 'Metonic Cycle,' when the Moon returned to the same place in the sky. This is what Diodorus seems to be describing in the quotation at the beginning of the chapter.

Assembling Avebury

It appears likely that the builders initially used wooden posts to assist them in setting up the stones. The Sanctuary consisted of timber settings for many years before the builders introduced the stones. Chapter 5 will describe the usefulness of the postholes found beside 'D feature'. There is a posthole marked by a concrete post by the southern entrance and no doubt, there are more postholes in this area, probably beneath the road surface. In the same manner as the entrance to the early phases of Stonehenge, the Avebury builders may have employed fan-shaped sets of wooden posts for use as extrapolation devices, although none have yet been found.[20]

It seems that only after the builders had confirmed a horizonal alignment to the relevant astral body, its path or cycle—and most likely marked it out by posts—would they have selected the appropriate stones. Clearly, they chose certain stones from among the 'grey wethers,' the sarsens of the nearby hills and valleys, for their unusual size, shape and already established significance in their place of origin. These stones must have been viewed as living beings that commanded respect. Then teams of people would have levered the immense sarsens onto rollers with great effort before dragging them several miles to the henge—an exceedingly difficult and dangerous task (probably aided by oxen), accidents must have happened and lives lost. The arrival of each stone at the henge must have been a tremendous event. As discussed in Chapter 10, the builders had to make each aspect of the henge congruent or integral to the symbolism of the whole; a lot of thought would have gone into the placement of each stone. It had to harmonise with its neighbours, in size, shape and arrangement; and it had to be part of a grand purposeful cosmology. As the monument slowly grew in size, the assembling of the stones—each embodying a cycle of time, each with its particular celestial, ancestral and mythic power, each perhaps with its own rite and song—must have allowed the Neolithic people to feel that their henge encompassed the entire cosmos.

A basic feature of this early 'astronomy' is that there was no need for abstract notation or complex mathematical knowledge. The monument-builders set complex cycles within their circles in direct accordance with what they saw in the sky. While this process no doubt conferred not only knowledge and predictive abilities but also power and prestige, the intentions of the builders were far more spiritual and symbolic than scientific. They were essentially holding their knowledge in the form of an oral, collective, memorial spiritual tradition, one which required devout and comprehensive observances and that culminated in extraordinary monument building. The stones were set up so the people could deepen their experience of and engagement with the surrounding inspirited world. Thus, the stones they set up to the Sun, Moon and stars only incidentally provided the sky-watchers with calendrical and what we would call astronomical information. What they actually provided the builders with was a connection to the powers of the cosmos: to the recurrent cycles of time, fertility, rebirth and life itself.

In the world of the Neolithic monument-builders, Avebury would not have been seen as a calculation device—a table or a chart that indicated that on such and such a date the Sun would reach its lowest point, or a new Moon occur, or Venus reappear as the morning star. To them, the heavenly being they knew as the Sun renewed the year at the Winter Solstice, its lowest point on the horizon. The mysterious lunar entity, so often veiled in shadow, waxing and waning, was also reborn during a time of darkness, ushering in a new, but qualitatively different cycle. The primal being who revealed itself in the wandering star Venus, renewed the season on the first day of its return. And so on. They patiently incorporated these events into their monuments; their purpose was to honour and engage with these celestial beings down to the finest points of detail—details that, once discovered, entered their songs, stories and now their stones.[21] The stones were thus records of life and time, gifted by the heavens, and measured in mythic narratives and genealogies.

This was not observational science. It was a symbolically loaded, conservative, spiritual and tradition-driven practice with serious outcomes. The main advantage of this system, unlike modern time-keeping devices and calendars, that need constant re-calibration to keep them in tune with the durational sequences of the Sun, Moon and stars, was that the henge-builders based their lives as well as their monuments upon a direct experience of the celestial bodies. As a place that must have been revered as 'Keeper' or even as 'Generator of the Cosmic Cycles,' Avebury henge would have needed no re-calibration. The immediate, real-time, dedicated and sweaty work of the monument-builders meant direct participation in the great, divine, regulating and mythically charged cycles of

Earth and Sky.

In sum, through using especially selected stones to mark out the movements of the heavenly bodies, the Neolithic sky-watchers of Avebury found a permanent and distinctive manner in which to participate with the cosmos. Their ancestors' long experience, knowledge and veneration of the cosmos had generated a rich astral-lore rooted in the patterns of life. Their encoding of this laborious and mythically driven process—however symbolic and subject to the requirements and perceptions of their time—would not only have increased their knowledge and improved their agricultural calendar, it would also have kept 'history,' that is, time itself. Thus, the stones themselves were the means of notation. They acted as 'containers' for lineages; as cultural record-keepers. The megaliths stood waiting to regenerate the durations they held. By holding the past, they also guaranteed the future, facilitating better social relations and socio-political stability. By setting up the stones, the people could regulate every aspect of their lives according to the divinely ordained cycles of the sky.

Idealised view from the northern bank of Avebury henge, circa 2300 BCE.

The Impact of Avebury

The Avebury monument-builders established numerous and permanent alignments to the celestial bodies as part of a dedicated work of representing the rich spiritual and mythic content of their lives. The monuments could have counted off the cycles of the Sun, Moon and stars in terms of a venerated, conservative and ancient memorial tradition that dealt in names, qualities, aspects, powers and provenances. They may have named the solar and lunar cycles, for example, after the passages of deities through different worlds. The arrival of the midwinter Moon in a particular house of the stars might have been auspicious for the lineage of a particularly powerful ancestral headman or woman, or simply have been good for spring sowing. John North describes all the alignments between the main stones at Avebury and Stonehenge as having either solar or lunar correspondences; a description complemented by the work of Robin Heath and Lionel Sims.[22] The builders could easily have followed the cycles of Sun and Moon with selected megaliths; when these soli-lunar cycles repeated, these particular stones released the unique qualities of 'time' they held.

As it is highly likely the Neolithic people linked lunar and menstrual cycles, the Moon may have governed traditions and practices of male-female relations: coming of age ceremonies, the timing of sexual relations, marriages and pregnancies. Thirteen Suns may have defined coming of age ceremonies for both sexes. Nine Moons or stones of the Northern Inner Circle defined a pregnancy. Twenty-seven Suns, or a 'lunary' of 364/5 Moons of both circles, may have defined a generation. The Moon may also have governed the nearly universal taboo of contact between menstrual women and men engaged in the hunt and all its ritual activities.[23] Without any direct evidence apart from the stones, we have to work hard to imagine the living people involved in these scenarios, but the astronomy provides important clues.

Another purpose of the Inner Circles may have been to estimate when the mythically charged eclipses were likely to occur—the recurring times when the solar and lunar cycles intersected.[24] Eclipse events may well have been central to the tribes mythic narrative, requiring anticipation and proper propitiation. Such functions, combined with the ongoing task of observing the heavens for omens, would have encouraged the designation of 'favourable' and 'unfavourable' days for undertaking social or economic activities. It would have been auspicious, for example, for a clan or tribe to undertake a certain type of activity at a time that was beneficent to their lineage. Some favourable cycles would have repeated quickly, some turned around much longer durations—but might therefore have been seen as belonging to a more primal and powerful force. Such knowledge would naturally have granted status and power to those able to establish and deliver it. The stage is therefore set for complex acts of divination, for astronomy as astrology, and for star-diviners to receive rewards and status for their specialist services. I describe prehistoric observance of the Moon, especially the symbolically rich eclipse cycle, in Appendix 3.

Once Avebury's main mythic and spatial co-ordinates were established, its soli-lunar axes set up and running, its sky-watchers would have been working on so accurate a scale that they would have been capable of distinguishing small movements of time and space. They could read the messages encoded in the stars and stones with precision and ease. Some alignments to the seasonal stars would have been benign, some malefic; solar and lunar extremes would have been particularly auspicious. The dark areas of the night sky and the stellar regions traversed by the Sun and Moon were quite likely regions of specific fortune or misfortune, good or evil. The reappearance and disappearance of certain stars and star figures over certain stones would have marked different times of year and governed the activities of the season. As said, the monument granted the means to regulate social affairs, provide pedigrees, 'remember' alliances and correctly time activities, thus increasing prosperity, ensuring the future of the people and generally preserving political stability.

Consequently, as will be explored later, the small but surprising precessional movement of the stars—1.5° a century—may ultimately have become a cause for concern. The Western world dates knowledge of precession from the Greek astronomer Hipparchus in the second century BCE, but fragmentary and elusive archaeological evidence hints at awareness of this phenomenon by other civilisations at the Neolithic stage of their development: for example, in Sumeria, China, India, Polynesia, Olmec and Maya culture and in ancient Egypt.[25] If the pre-literate Neolithic sky-watchers of Avebury had not yet grasped the details of precession, because of the permanence and long usage of their monuments they were at least moving toward this understanding by the end of the third millennium BCE.

There can be no doubt that a huge amount of new information entered Neolithic society because of all the parts that made up Avebury. The Avebury complex would have enabled proud lineages of builders and users to access much more extensive knowledge than they had obtained from the earlier causewayed camps, cursuses and long barrows. Avebury was a unique sacred centre filled with the presence of heavenly aligned stones, against which a group of accomplished men and women could measure themselves and so determine their place within the cosmos. Its function was to maintain harmony with the divine, spirit worlds, and enable its people to communicate between them. Critically, Avebury allowed observance of the divinely regulated natural order, and so helped time procedures and determine protocols for avoiding any transgressions of that order. At the same time—as explored in the final chapters—it is likely that the gathering of the resources needed to build and develop the sites, and the control of their use by a growing elite, would have begun to create a society very different to the one that had first initiated and built Avebury. Making, using and maintaining these awe-inspiring structures would have made considerable impact upon the people of the time.

3

Windmill Hill & the Mystery of the Moving Stars

In the earliest periods during which structures were oriented on the heavens, directions seem to have been toward the risings and settings of a handful of bright stars rather than toward the Sun and Moon.

John North

The First Settlers: Windmill Hill

Early in the fourth millennium BCE, a large group of people, probably members of a regional tribal network, built an enclosure or 'causewayed camp' upon the broad summit of Windmill Hill, about a mile and a quarter northwest of Avebury henge. Many seasons of excavation have shown these people gathered in the enclosure on a seasonal basis, when they would have built or repaired existing shelters, worked, ate and lived together. They most likely gathered in the autumn when the local springs and streams were flowing freely again, then dispersed over the course of the winter when dwindling local resources compelled them to move elsewhere. Over several centuries, the people of Windmill Hill carved out three massive concentric rings of ditches in sausage-like sections, the outermost ring almost 400 yards in diameter. They also dug numerous pits on the hill. Into these ditches and pits they put thousands of bones, entire animal remains, worked stones, food and numerous other objects. Some of these objects were simply discarded; others were carefully placed in the earth. Windmill Hill gave the people, the tribe, a defined and protected area for

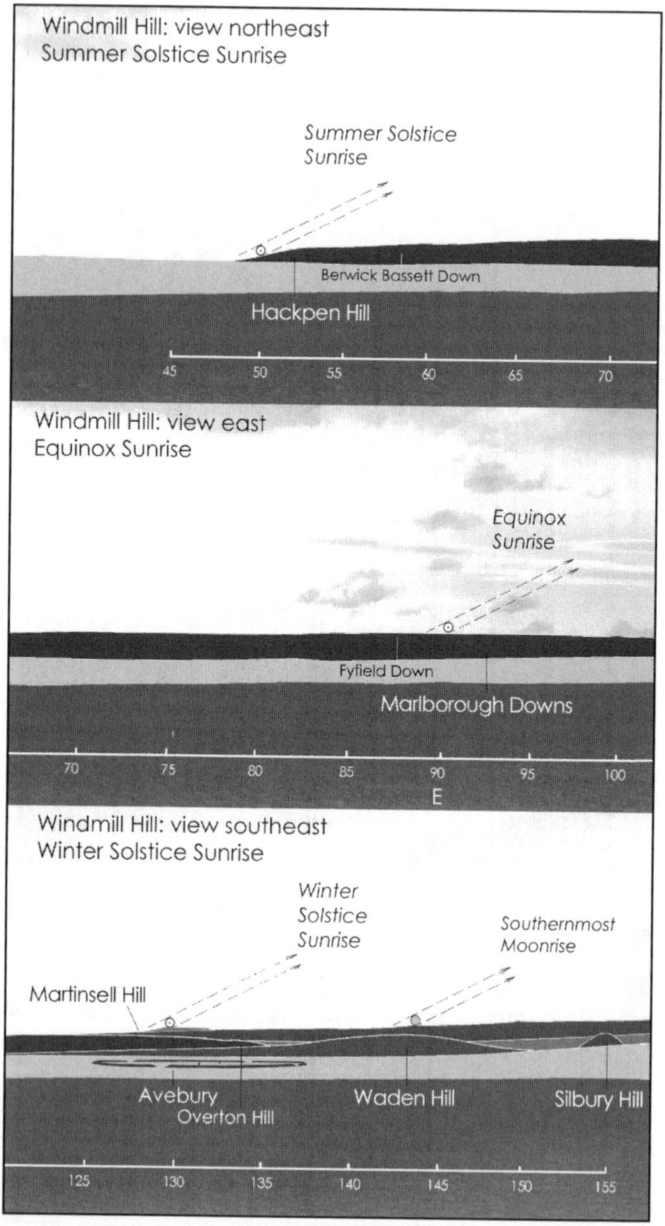

Figure 6. View from Windmill Hill. The midsummer Sun rises at the base of Hackpen Hill and Berwick Bassett Down at the northern end of the Marlborough Downs. The Sun rises due east at the equinoxes

over Fyfield Down. These alignments have changed little since 3500 BCE, although trees were likely to have covered the skyline. The midwinter Sun rises at the southern end of the Marlborough Downs over Martinsell Hill, one of the highest points on the Wessex Chalk escarpment to the south, azimuth 129-130°. Below Martinsell Hill are Overton Hill and Avebury henge. Also shown is the southernmost rising Moon c.3000 BCE.

Figure 7. Detail of the previous figure showing the midwinter Sun rising over Martinsell Hill, Overton Hill and Avebury from Windmill Hill at the beginning of the third millennium BCE. The primary henge and some stone settings are likely to have been in place at Avebury. Martinsell Hill was the site of a traditional ball game where "boys take their positions at intervals in a line from the base of the hill to its summit, and using hockey sticks knock the ball in succession up the hill."[1]

their gatherings and general activities as well as for other more formal and complex pursuits: the burial of the dead, the making of offerings, ritualised feasting, story telling and sky watching. The Windmill Hill people also flourished, partly due to rich

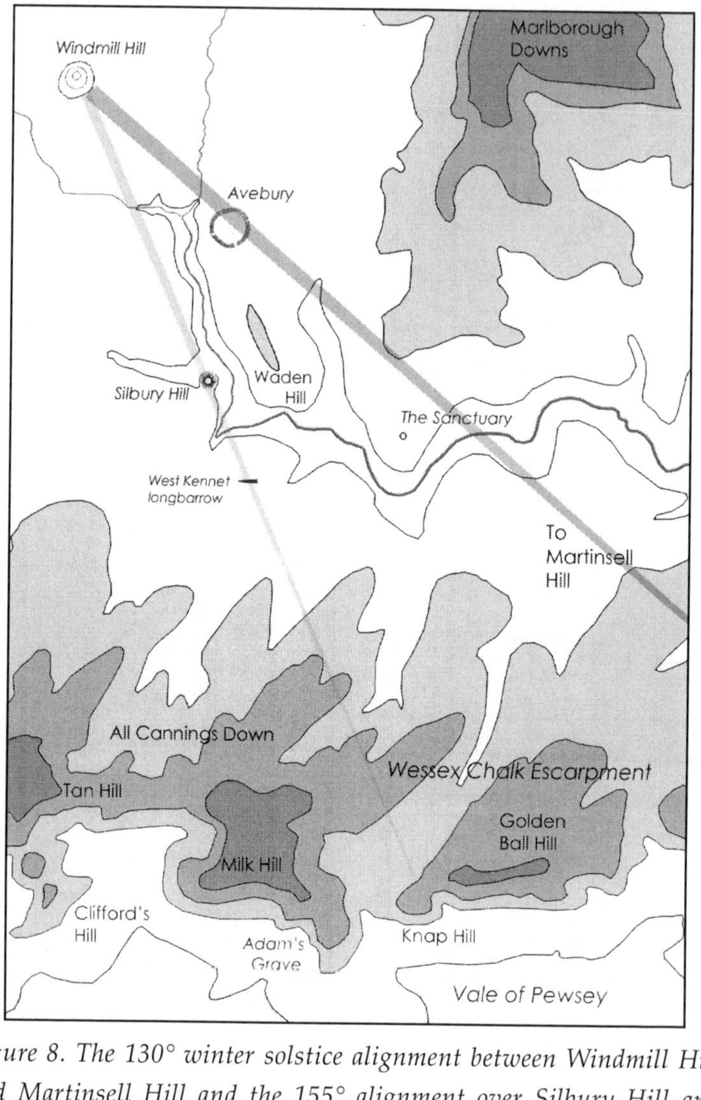

Figure 8. The 130° winter solstice alignment between Windmill Hill and Martinsell Hill and the 155° alignment over Silbury Hill and West Kennet long barrow to Knap Hill (not directly visible—below the horizon).

local resources, and partly due to the influence they exerted over a widely spread resource network of goods, authority and information.[2]

Imagine groups beginning to gather on Windmill Hill in the autumn. There should have been plenty of food, the springs were beginning to flow and their herds of cattle, pigs and goats could fatten on the local pastures and woodland. The farming settlements nearby would have produced cereals, hay and other resources. As the people could not take all their animals through the winter, they would have butchered many, dried their meat, cured their hides, taken fat, sinews and other useful materials. Some years would have been feast years, but others would have been lean. On several occasions, these people conducted rituals where they carefully laid out half or whole cattle in deep pits.[3] Offerings like this reveal a wish to propitiate, to give thanks to and perhaps divine the wishes of the natural and supernatural forces perceived to control the world. For as we shall see, this was a people that wanted to communicate with these powers, and determine which activities were beneficial and which were not.

Like ancient and tribal societies all over the world, the Windmill Hill people would have believed that through the right kind of ritualised intervention, they could affect the surrounding world in their favour. They needed to maintain a good relationship with its spirits, especially those plants and animals they depended upon and had domesticated. The animating force of life may have been revered in all its many forms, but it is quite likely these people also believed in unifying, transcendent powers: creative forces or spirit deities of water, lightning and fire—all of which had to he honoured and placated. It is easy to imagine a strong moral dimension under-pinning their activities. They should not offend these spirits, or misfortune would follow. Kinship ties to enforce the prescribed rules of behaviour and reduce intra-group conflict would have been very strong. It appears the tribe would have accompanied all their economic activities: husbandry, hunting, foraging, breeding, slaughtering and so on with ritual prognostication and divination. As was later recorded in the religious practices of the ancient world, they would have read auguries from the sky, from the appearance of birds and wild animals, as well as from the death throes, bones and entrails of their slain animals. As part of their wish to maintain the right relationship with the surrounding world and its spirits, the people would also have listened carefully to their dreams and visions, especially those of their shamans.[4]

Above the wooded landscape, broken here and there by farming settlements that were often little more than a clearing or a hilltop kept open by grazing animals, the people of Windmill Hill looked out towards a horizon marked by several prominent landmarks. These landmarks helped them to observe and mark the changing patterns of the sky. Interestingly, a number of them were closely connected with the nomadic pathways of their Mesolithic ancestors. As shown in Figure 6, they knew that when the Sun rolled up the northern flank of Hackpen Hill at the northern end of the Marlborough Downs it was the Summer Solstice. Their ancestors had used Hackpen Hill for sourcing and making implements from flint throughout the Mesolithic era. The Windmill Hill people would have seen the Equinox Sunrise over the centre of the high ground to the east, and when the Sun rose from the southern end of the Downs—over Overton Hill, and beyond it, Martinsell Hill—they knew it was the Winter Solstice. They would also have seen the Sun set into the southern flank of Cherhill Down, another important Mesolithic site, at midwinter. See Figure 15. The lack of any corresponding feature in this landscape for midsummer sunset, together with the greater intensity of the ritualised deposits in northeastern pits and ditches, suggests it was midsummer sunrises, midwinter moonrises and midwinter star rises in the northeast that most concerned the people of Windmill Hill.

The Midwinter Sky

The midwinter night skies of the time were certainly highly distinctive. At this season, beginning in November, the nightly spectacle of several first magnitude stars in the south must have been dramatic. In this era, alpha Centauri, the third brightest star in the sky, along with its companion beta Centauri, then the tenth brightest star, as well as the four brilliant stars of Crux, all rose close together in the southern skies. (See Figures 10 and 11.) Due to precession, these radiant stars, embedded in the southern portion of the Milky Way, had been visible each winter in the high northern latitudes for many thousands of years. As Crux, the Southern Cross and the pointer to the hidden South Celestial Pole, rose on the southern horizon, then rotated westwards on winter nights, it would have suggested to the people on Windmill Hill the existence of a hidden pivot to the world axis: an underworld 'root' to the invisible Lowerworld, where more brilliant stars might be hidden. The south, after all, was the place where the Sun went each winter—it therefore must be a place of fire and light.

On the other side of the horizon, the Northern Cross—named Cygnus the Swan by the Greeks and a goose in Celtic star lore—pointed to the place of the North Celestial Pole. Its extended wings pointed to the other end of the *axis mundi*: the North, the visible Upperworld, the place the Sun approached every summer, but never reached. (See Figure 12.) The perceptible relationship of the northern circumpolar stars with the mysterious southern stars, apparently allied to a hidden lower world, helped define a conspicuous axis or 'axle' through the Earth, around which the entire sky turned.

From the summit of Windmill Hill, the Neolithic people would have seen some of the greatest hills in the area in a line along the striking Wessex Chalk escarpment that formed their southern horizon. As shown in Figure 8, Martinsell Hill, the rising place of the midwinter Sun, lay seven miles away. Golden Ball Hill, Knap Hill, Milk Hill, Tan Hill and their adjacent hills lay at a distance of about five miles.[5] Tan Hill lay due south, with Rybury camp beyond it. The Mesolithic ancestors of the Windmill Hill people had used these hills. Their ancient names possess a long tradition in local lore. These hills provided the people of Windmill Hill with excellent horizonal indicators of the rising and setting positions of the remarkable Crux-Centaurus stars over the winter months. Due to the lengthening or shortening days, the hills allowed the people to track the annual first and last appearance and disappearance of the stars at dawn and dusk. From the beginning of November, until their disappearance in May, the heliacal rising and setting dates of the Crux-Centaurus stars would have provided a precise and accurate stellar calendar to accompany that of the Sun and Moon.

West Kennet Long Barrow & Alpha Centauri

The West Kennet long barrow; view from the northeast. Completed by 3600 BCE, the blocking stones were put across the entrance by 2500 BCE.

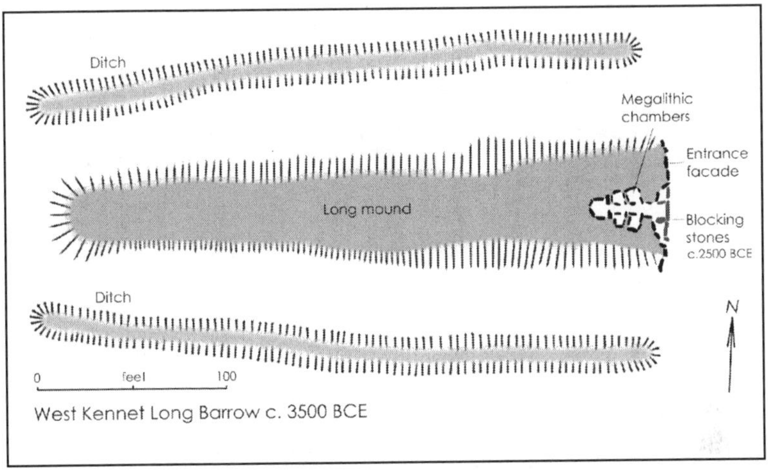

Figure 9. Plan of West Kennet long barrow. In use for the deposition of mortuary remains for over a thousand years, the long barrow was filled with earth and the entrance closed by stones in the mid-third millennium BCE.

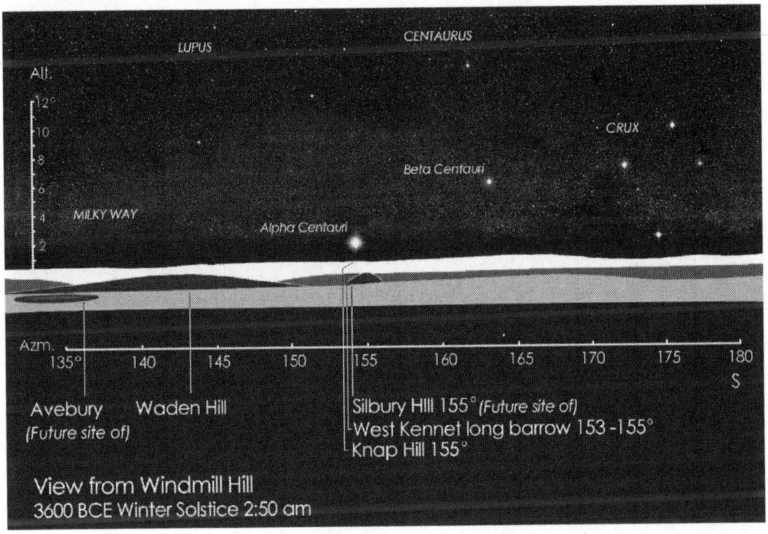

Figure 10. View south from Windmill Hill, midwinter circa 3600 BCE. The Crux-Centaurus group of stars had dominated the southern winter skies for thousands of years but were now beginning to fall below the horizon. As Crux, the Southern Cross, approached its

culmination due south, and the Milky Way began to level around the horizon, alpha Centauri rose over the alignment to Knap Hill. These first magnitude stars appeared in the sky above West Kennet long barrow, circa 3600 BCE. The highest star of the group, gamma Crucis, left the barrow about a thousand years later. Note: Although Silbury Hill is also on the 155° alignment, it was built circa 2450 BCE long after Windmill Hill and West Kennet long barrow were in use, so its stellar associations will be explained later.

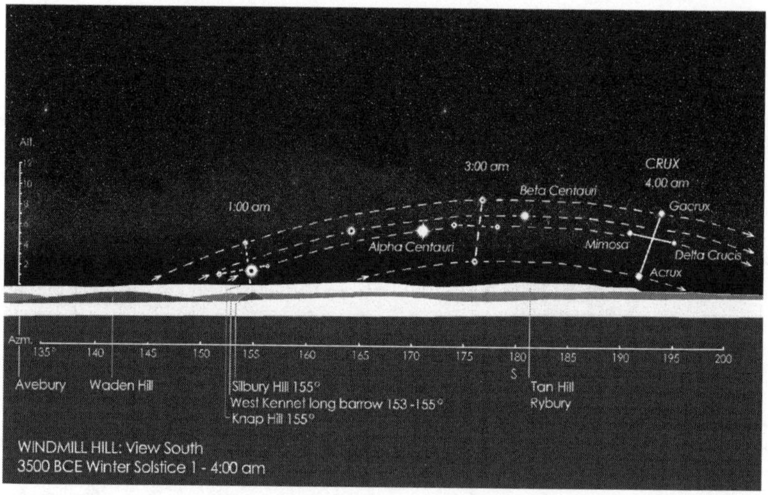

Figure 11. Time-lapsed view south from Windmill Hill showing the paths taken through the night sky by the stars of Crux, alpha Centauri and beta Centauri at 1:00, 3:00 and 4:00 am, in midwinters circa 3500 BCE.

***1:00 am**: the upper stars of Crux rise over Knap Hill and West Kennet long barrow, closely followed by beta Centauri.*

***3.00 am**: alpha Centauri rises over the barrow; all the stars of Crux become visible.*

***4:00 am**: as Acrux sets over high ground to the southwest, alpha Centauri becomes the brightest star in the sky. Alpha Centauri would have been lost in the atmosphere by 2600 BCE. (Note: The extinction angle of these first magnitude stars was often less than two degrees—especially for alpha Centauri.)*

At some point, not long after the transitional Mesolithic-Neolithic people first arrived on Windmill Hill, between 3700-3600 BCE, they constructed a significant long barrow for the burial of some of their dead. They had already built several of these monumental long barrows, and were to build more, including those at Horslip, South Street and Beckhampton or Longstones, but this new barrow was going to be unusual. They would build it in stone in a location just below the *rising point* on the southern horizon of the Crux-Centaurus stars, viewed from Windmill Hill. Only alpha Crucis, the brightest but lowest star of the Southern Cross, rose further south over Milk Hill at this time. As shown in Figures 10 and 11, the location of this important long barrow marked the rising point of one major, first-magnitude southern star constellation and one major asterism (star group), within which the giant star alpha Centauri would have been especially prominent.

Alpha Centauri, the alpha star of the huge constellation of the Centaur, is the star closest to our Sun. It is a multiple star, known as Rigel or Toliman to Greek and Arab astronomers, a binary system of two yellow/orange stars that orbit each other every eighty years, plus a red dwarf only two degrees away known as Proxima Centauri.[6] As Canopus was not visible in the northern hemisphere in the fourth millennium BCE, and Arcturus was not as bright as it is today, once Sirius had set each night, alpha Centauri would have become the brightest star in the sky for the people of Windmill Hill. As alpha Centauri reappeared each year in early November, at dawn, and then rose earlier and earlier before being seen for the final time at sunset in early May, the Crux-Centaurus stars would have appeared as the stars defining winter.

With its nightly appearance always heralded by the four stars of Crux, as well as by its companion beta Centauri (all among the twenty brightest stars), alpha Centauri would undoubtedly have stood out in the southernmost sky. But that was not all: *these stars are embedded within the low band of the Milky Way, which at that time was visible in its entirety, wrapped around the horizon.* In this era, throughout the winter months, the galaxy ringed the horizon for an hour or so. The event took place for the first time in early November before dawn, and for the final time before dusk in early May. With the two crosses embedded within the Milky Way north and south, this must have been a magnificent spectacle for the people on Windmill Hill, even if an extinction angle of 2° or more on some nights meant that many of the stars of the Milky Way would not have been visible down to the horizon.[7]

Their ancestors, the Mesolithic hunter-gatherers, must have been very familiar with the Crux-Centaurus stars as they rose and set over the winter months, heralding the brilliant band of the Milky Way. These majestic stars had been visible at the latitude of Windmill Hill since the twelfth millennium BCE, the end of the Ice Age (a time when Britain was still joined to the Continent, and a huge plain, rich in game, still lay in the area of the North Sea). By about 6000 BCE, the Crux-Centaurus stars had fallen to the south, but from there ushered in the first complete views of the Milky Way around the horizon. Early people would have used these southern stars to guide them on the north-south trails of Europe before Britain became an island. The extraordinary appearance of these brilliant southern stars would surely have entered the stories, spiritual practices, rituals and cosmology of the people of Windmill Hill.

For many millennia, the Crux-Centaurus stars and the encircling Milky Way had served as a visual link, a pointer and a gateway to a hidden southern realm. Together with the stars of the north, they defined the vertical axis of the sky and the uniquely visible circle of the galaxy. They must have been the quintessential stars of winter and the power that lay in the Underworld—the place of the midwinter Sun. After the eighth millennium BCE, however, things began to change. Due to the slow precessional rotation of the Earth, the Crux-Centaurus stars and the Milky Way once again fell to the south. As the Crux-Centaurus stars continued in their descent towards the south over the fourth millennium BCE, did the people of Windmill Hill come to wonder if their ancestral stars were disappearing forever?

It seems entirely plausible that the Crux-Centaurus stars inspired the Windmill Hill people to locate West Kennet long barrow according to the rising position of the group's greatest star. When viewed from the central enclosure of Windmill Hill, alpha Centauri rose over the location of the long barrow between 3700 and 3500 BCE, exactly the time of its construction, at an azimuth of 153°-155°—allowing for the extinction angle—the length of the barrow.[8] The builders must also have been aware that Knap Hill, another significant early Neolithic causewayed enclosure, lay on the alignment beyond the long barrow, on the other side of the Wessex Chalk escarpment.

By 3450 BCE, due to the southward precessional movement of this portion of the sky, alpha Centauri no longer rose precisely over West Kennet long barrow. The star had sunk further south and on hazy nights would have been lost from sight. By 3100 BCE, beta Centauri and beta Crucis no longer rose over the long barrow. By 2800 BCE only the topmost star of Crux, gamma Crucis, was visible rising above it, while the lowest and brightest star of Crux, alpha Crucis, had completely vanished from view. However, the length of the long barrow meant that for the people of Windmill Hill, the last star of the group, gamma Crucis, did not entirely leave that portion of the sky until after 2500 BCE. Remarkably, these dates coincide exactly with the building of the long barrow, circa 3600 BCE, with its period of use, and with its slow closure by infill and eventual blocking by 2500 BCE.[9]

Early Sky-Watchers & the Stars

As human settlements gradually became permanent, and more local markers were established, early sky-watchers would have noticed the subtle movements and patterns in the heavens. A circle of posts would have been a simple way to see that the midwinter Sun rose diametrically opposite the setting place of the Sun at midsummer, while the rising midsummer Sun opposed the setting place of the Sun at midwinter. A continuous timber palisade circle built at Goseck in Germany as early as 4900 BCE opened in three places: the north, and the southeast and southwest, marking the Polar axis and the rising and setting points on the horizon of the midwinter Sun.[10] With time, the Sky-watchers would have observed that the Moon not only followed the path of the Sun (the midsummer full Moon rising in the place of the midwinter Sun, and the midwinter full Moon rising in the place of the midsummer Sun), but also had its own distinctive path, reaching extremes in relation to the Sun over a fixed cycle of 18/19 years. These horizonal patterns determined the primary divisions of time and space, defined the calendar, and, over the cycle of the year, created spatial co-ordinates and axial symmetries that emphasised their now sedentary experience of living at a location often understood (for them, at least) as the centre of the world.

As early sky-watchers saw the Sun and Moon rise and set against the divisions of the horizon over the course of a year, they would have realised they could also divide time and space according to the stars.[11] They could mark the paths of the Sun and Moon as well as the less obviously regular movement of the planets on the ecliptic against the backdrop of the stars (the cycles and times of the disappearance and reappearance of Venus being especially conspicuous). But unlike the planets, Sun and Moon, the stars follow a fixed course in their daily journey east to west, they always rise and set in the same place on the horizon, they never stop or go back. Early sky-watchers would have realised that they could observe everything against the stellar background of the celestial sphere, which evidently turned about the central axis or spindle of the world suspended between two poles. From a very early time, people would have used the stars to watch the position of the Moon and to gauge the seasonal position of the Sun. They would also have looked for the *first* annual reappearance and *final* annual disappearance of stars—their heliacal and acronychal rising and setting times, defined in this note.[12]

Just when and how early humans began to do this is unknown. We do know that a lack of notation or writing does not prevent oral traditions from transmitting complex information. The dates of coherent astronomical traditions are slowly being pushed back into the Mesolithic and even the Palaeolithic eras.[13]

The Northern Pole

The first sky-watchers would have observed the rising of the celestial bodies in the east and their setting in the west. They would have seen the rising Sun and Moon move along the eastern horizon over the course of the year, and set correspondingly in the west. The daily passage of the Sun, followed by the Moon almost every night, would have been among the first heavenly phenomena to enter the cognitive experience of ancient peoples. They could have used the shadow of a simple device, a stick or *gnomon*, to determine the cardinal directions, divide the day, and measure the seasons. Modern astronomers now use celestial great circles as their key markers, but we should bear in mind that the astronomy of the first sky-watchers was Earth and horizon-based. It employed the visible circle of the horizon as its primary marker; and supplemented it in the Neolithic era with artificial horizons constructed from mounds,

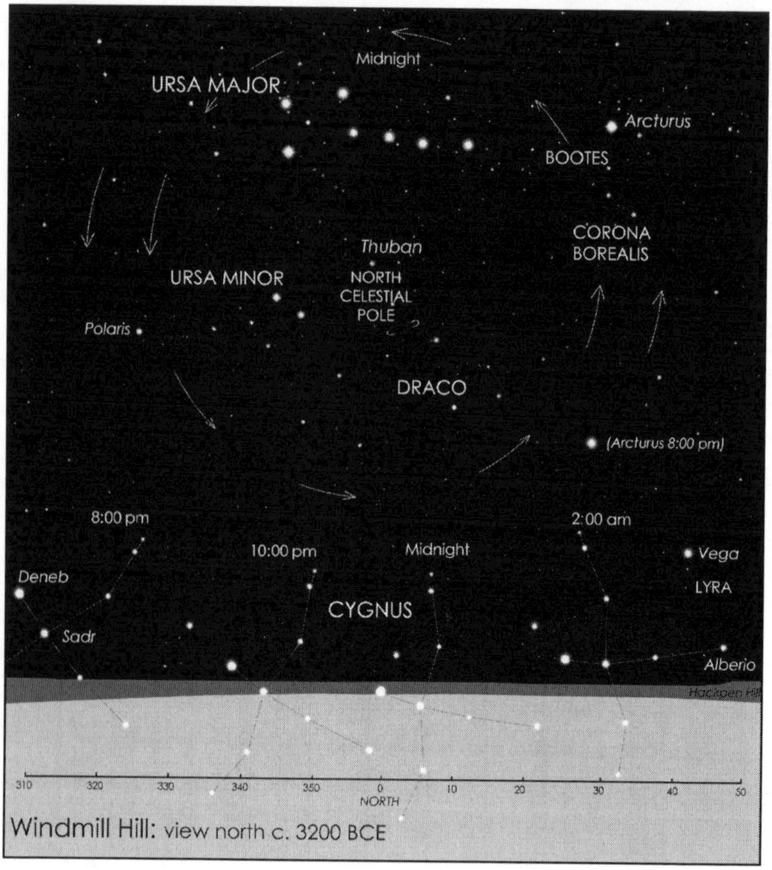

Figure 12. View due north from Windmill Hill circa 3200 BCE showing Ursa Major and a time lapsed passage of Cygnus. The circumpolar constellations rotate around the North Celestial Pole, at that time marked by the star Thuban in the constellation of Draco. The levelling of the Milky Way accompanies the reappearance of Cygnus upon the horizon. Ursa Major, the Great Bear, balances the passage of Cygnus on the other side of the Pole—the constellations aligned north-south at midnight. Arcturus, 'Protector of the Bear', one of the four brightest stars in the sky, rises as Cygnus began to set.

cursuses, barrows, dolmens, henges and timber or stone circles (all of which cast significant shadows). The horizon itself may have been sacred; in the Babylonian creation myth, for example, the horizon represented the rim and thus the meeting place of heaven and earth. The revolutions of the Sun and Moon and the rotation of the stars around the horizon all pointed to the presence of a central primary vertical axis, the *axis mundi*—with the *gnomon* at the centre. The horizonal orientations and divisions of space thus formed a bounded landscape measured east-west, north-south, engaged in a rhythmic, daily and seasonal relationship to an above, a centre and a below.

Thus, for the Avebury sky-watchers, the never-setting stars of the north rotated in full view around the Northern Celestial Pole, which at that time was near the star Thuban in Draco. The stars of Cygnus passed half under the horizon, marking the north, as opposed to the Crux-Centaurus stars on the other side of the horizon half rising above it, marking the south. Remarkably, the stars of Cygnus, the Northern Cross, were embedded in the Milky Way in a similar manner to the stars of Crux, the Southern Cross. As Crux rose to point to the hidden Southern Pole, Cygnus rose to point to the visible Northern Pole, but the stars of Cygnus first *set* then rose with the entire Milky Way, while the stars of the Southern Cross *rose* with the Milky Way before setting. This distinction will turn out to be important.

The true northern circumpolar stars and their greatest constellations such as Ursa Major and Minor never set at all for viewers in the northern hemisphere. The Greeks saw these constellations as bears turning about the Northern Celestial Pole, assisting in the rotation of the *axis mundi*. At the same time, certain stars may have been understood as permanently 'hidden' below the horizon even in distant prehistory—never appearing at all. Only if a traveller journeyed far enough south might they see and speak of them on their return home. Thus, the early sky-watchers may have seen a primary vertical axis divide the sky even without any knowledge of a spherical earth or sight of a Southern Pole.

The horizon would seem to divide this axis into an 'above' and a 'below,' an Upper and an Underworld, with this world as the Middle. The stars above the Zodiac, the stars against which the Sun, Moon and planets travel from east to west in the Zodiac, and the stars below the Zodiac could also have helped define a tripartite cosmos. In a cosmos of three realms: an Upperworld defined by the Northern circumpolar stars, a Middleworld defined by the Zodiac and an Underworld of the briefly seen southern stars, what was the nature of stars that passed from one world into another? What would happen to those stars that vanished apparently permanently?

An Axial Centre

Distinguished historian of religion Mircea Eliade observed that the earliest, most ubiquitous and fundamental spiritual act is always the establishment of a centre. Defining the centre allows the measurement of all things. By honouring a special landscape feature, constructing an altar, lighting a fire, planting a pole as a *gnomon*, creating a medicine wheel, or by engaging in some other form of ceremonial activity, the shaman defines the sacred centre around which the world of their tribe can be oriented. Establishing the centre brings spiritual order and drives away negativity or evil spirits. The centre embodies the sacred order, manifests the group's identity and traditions and maintains them over time. The circular enclosures on Windmill Hill may well have functioned in this manner; providing a location for seasonally timed ceremonies, whose formal and sacred nature, among other things, helped foster social integration and reduce potential conflicts. Eliade described how ancient shamanic peoples—into which category we can surely place the Windmill Hill tribe—invariably saw a vertical axis extending from or through this centre. This *axis mundi* or 'Axis of the World' ran through the centre of the three worlds as a wooden pole, a spindle, a tree or a mountain, or as some kind of cosmic pillar. A ladder or a rope is often attached (or even nailed) to the northern Pole Star.[14]

In the ancient star lore of the far northern hemisphere, the northern stars frequently belong to an 'Upperworld'—an eternal realm of immortal beings—while those of the south belonging to an 'Underworld'—a world of the dead. However, the ancestors can belong to either of these, or their directional meanings can appear reversed. In many shamanic traditions, the three worlds have further tiers; often there are three or four levels above the central human realm and three or four below it. In some aboriginal cultures, anthropologists have reported up to twenty-seven levels.[15] Figure 50, which looks out from the centre of Avebury, suggests a cosmos divided into different tiers by the horizon and sets of stars. (A preview of Figures 48 might also be useful at this time).

The three great enclosures of Windmill Hill may reflect a tripartite cosmology, while the north-south polarity of the stars observed from there could have meant its people held a tiered celestial axis. While they may have held that mysterious beings and great powers: mythologized ancestors, deities, giants and supernatural creatures, or aspects of these beings, dwelt in all the worlds, their cosmology probably saw those of the Underworld as being particularly challenging. The shaman frequently acted as a guide to the souls of the dead through this region to their proper place in the cosmos; otherwise, they will not rest and trouble the living. Only by reaching the place of the ancestors, could a soul become safe and venerable, even oracular and a provider of guidance. The shaman can access great healing, fertility and wisdom through contact with or journeying to the Otherworlds, but also, potentially, great harm, even evil. Shamanic traditions therefore teach the shaman to treat the beings in the many worlds with the utmost respect, and with the correct ritual observances, for example, by indirectly naming their spirit-helpers.[16]

Eliade and others have shown that the traditional role of the shaman was to visit the Otherworlds, divine the future, seek wisdom, abundance, healing and guidance, make offerings and generally mediate between the spirits and this world. The shaman guided the souls of the deceased, found out what was required to avoid sickness and misfortune and sought the favour of the gods and the spirit world. The shaman invariably accomplished this through journeying to the Otherworlds by the means of the *axis mundi*. Typically, the shaman climbed a pole, went up a mountain, or passed through an Underworld entranceway. Through correct ritual observance of the great powers, such as the making of offerings to the appropriate celestial forces, the shaman established the centre, the sets of horizonal directions, the world axis and the path between the many layers of the cosmos. He or she also defined time by their observations of the Moon, Sun and stars. Any act of defining the centre, space and time, according to Eliade, banished the impurities and chaos of the profane world, allowing a "break-through in plane" to the sacred.[17] The process of defining the centre renewed the primordial order of things, via an "eternal return" to the divine source. This involved a suspension of profane time in the eternal order: recapturing a time, for example, when there was unity between humans and the world, and people shared the language of the animals. Finally, the process ensured the safety and return of the shaman on their journey between the worlds.

It appears that the early Neolithic people of Windmill Hill were intensely interested in the symbolism of the centre, the circle, the horizonal axes and the vertical axis, whose Poles were determined by the northern and southern stars. The location of their most significant long barrow, West Kennet, lay just below the rising point of the southernmost stars. This suggests that the

Windmill Hill tribe held a characteristically shamanic sense of the *axis mundi*. They may have perceived their place, their enclosed hill, as tiered and bounded, specifically centralised, and astronomically oriented: in other words, they focused on an 'axial centre.' The alignment to the long barrow suggests that the people of Windmill Hill wished to place themselves in a special relationship both to the *axis mundi* and to the Milky Way. The movement of the key stars of the Milky Way, particularly the Northern and the Southern Cross, may have shown them how the path of the Milky Way emphasised certain temporal and spatial divisions. As the galaxy rotated around their horizon on midwinter nights, most especially, as it levelled with the horizon and several highly distinctive first magnitude stars upon the north-south axis came into view, the Milky Way drew a shimmering circle of stars around their *axis mundi*, circumscribing its boundaries and defining the centre of their new world.

More speculatively, the cosmology of the Windmill Hill people may have held that their dead, some of whose bones they had carefully arranged in the West Kennet long barrow, could only enter the difficult passageway through the Underworld at certain key points in time and space—most probably at midwinter, when certain stars illuminated this passage. If they envisaged the cosmic axis as a World Tree, West Kennet barrow could have symbolised an entranceway to its 'root.' The Neolithic people who used West Kennet barrow, as elsewhere, put its ancestral bones through many processes of inhumation and exhumation: bringing them in, taking them out, organising and finally sealing some in the chambers. Sun, Moon and stars would have determined the times of funerary rites, of communication with the ancestors. In the winter months, the southern stars may have marked or held open a gateway, a road to the south and entrance to the Underworld that extended to the depths of the *axis mundi*. Alternatively, these stars may have opened a pathway around the rim of the horizon, briefly but spectacularly illuminated by the Milky Way. Did the disappearance of these key southern stars due to precession, after 2500 BCE, render this long barrow non-functional or otherwise inauspicious, and prompt the Windmill Hill people to seal it, end its period of use and turn their ritual attention elsewhere?

Sirius: Star of Fertility & the Winter Solstice Sun

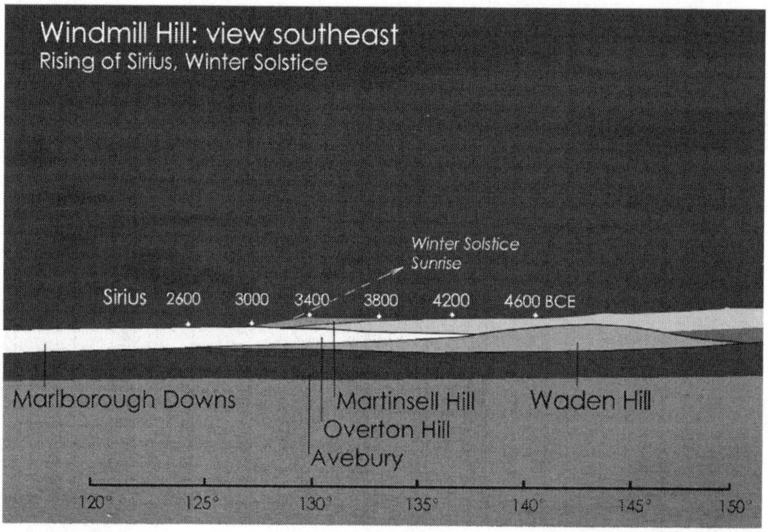

Figure 13. View from Windmill Hill at twilight showing Sirius as the heliacal rising star. Sirius rose further eastwards over the millennia, until by 3300 BCE the star rose on the same path as the midwinter Sun, rising over Martinsell Hill at an azimuth of 129°.

As the brightest star in the sky, the 'Dog Star' Sirius would surely have had an especial importance for the Avebury sky-watchers. Technically a southern star, Sirius had become visible at Avebury during the mid-seventh millennium BCE, before which time it had not risen at this latitude for several thousand years. Sirius accompanies Orion the Hunter, one of the greatest and most easily recognizable of constellations, and was viewed

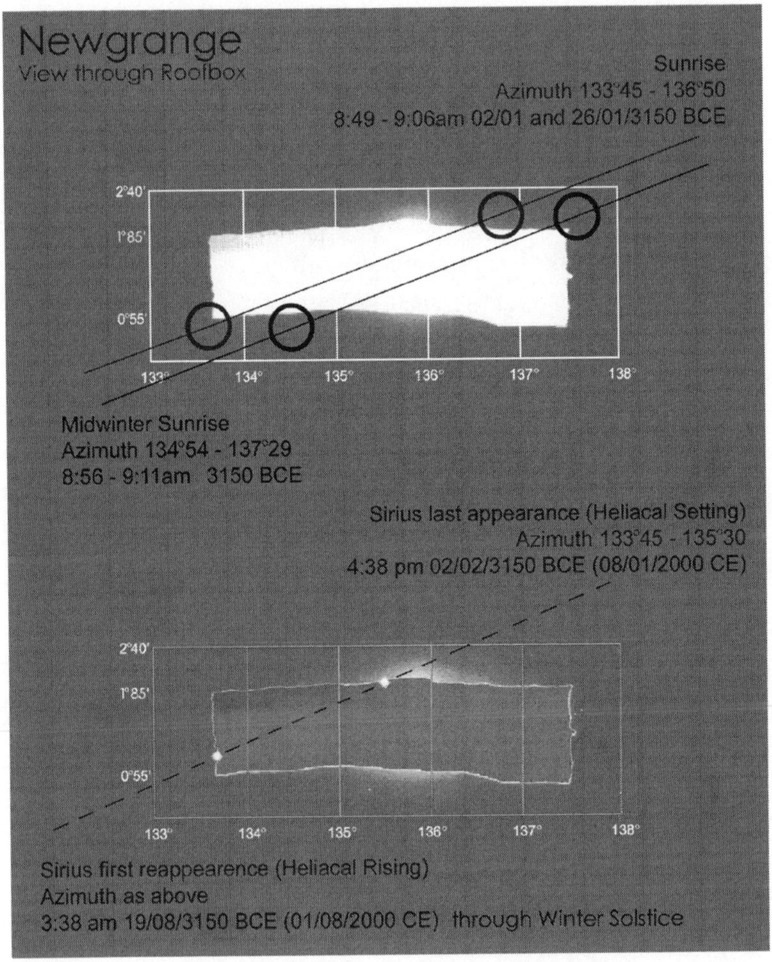

Figure 14. The builders of Newgrange constructed this famous chambered mound so that light from the Sun entered the central chamber along a passageway through an aperture, or roof-box, at the Winter Solstice. The upper diagram shows the movement of the Sun across the Newgrange roof-box in the last quarter of the fourth millennium BCE. The lower diagram shows the movement of Sirius across the roof-box in that era, the first and last dates of its appearance and their equivalents today. The elimination of solar glare and the precision of the alignment allowed for close observation of both the Sun and Sirius. Although the exact coincidence of the path of Sirius

and the winter solstice Sun took place at the latitude of Newgrange about 3400 BCE, it is shown in 3150 BCE. The Egyptians employed similar apertures, aligned to stars circa 2500 BCE, to orient the Great Pyramid.[18]

by the Greeks as the alpha star of Orion's hound. Significantly, for early farmers, it disappeared annually at the time of planting in early April, reappearing at the time of the harvest in early August. Although several ancient peoples considered Sirius a wolf or Dog Star, in ancient Egypt its link with the annual fertilising of the land (via the Nile flood) was paramount. Thus in Neolithic Britain, as in several other ancient cultures, it may have had a dual significance, as connected both with animals important for the hunt and also with the grain and harvest so important to the first farmers. When this luminous blue star vanished, it would have been time to plant; when it reappeared, it was time to harvest, and probably time too for ceremony that celebrated the land's fertility.

Over the course of time, generations of Mesolithic and transitional Neolithic people would have become aware that Sirius was gradually reappearing at a slightly later time in the solar year than the time observed and most probably memorialised by their ancestors; it was also rising higher and slightly further to the east. This movement was very slow, imperceptible in a single lifetime. Yet over the centuries, as shown in Figure 13, the difference would have been quite enough for Neolithic skywatchers at newly fixed centres like Windmill Hill to note that the rising point of Sirius had moved significantly eastwards against their horizonal markers; in this case, toward the horizonal marker of the symbolically all-important midwinter Sun. The brightest star's rate of precessional progress over the course of the fourth millennium meant it would have become obvious that *the nightly path of Sirius would eventually coincide with the path of the Sun at the winter solstice*. Although these two events happened at different times in the year, careful star-watchers would have observed that both Sirius and the midwinter Sun occupied the same rising and setting points on the horizon and followed the same path through the sky.[19]

Like their hunter-gatherer ancestors, the new farmers and pastoralists all across Northern Europe observed the winter solstice Sun, and marked it upon the ground using increasingly permanent and monumental markers. The Winter Solstice event, perhaps above all others, embodied the symbolic importance attached to light, fire, and also, by implication, to the regeneration and rebirth of the midwinter Sun. Now Sirius was about to converge with this solar path. Could the convergence of the paths of these two celestial bodies have held such symbolic importance for the Neolithic people that they built megalithic monuments specifically to mark this event? It is certainly interesting for example, that the building of Newgrange in Ireland, in the last quarter of the fourth millennium BCE, coincided with the occupation of the same position in the sky of the path of Sirius and that of the midwinter Sun. (See Figure 14.) At different times of the year, Neolithic Irish sky-watchers could thus have viewed the rising of both Sun and star along the passageway of the immense chambered mound. The long passageway would have particularly enhanced their ability to watch the annual first and last (heliacal) appearances of Sirius.[20]

Observers gathered on Windmill Hill would have seen Sirius move across the sky each night, from approximately August to April. The star was bright enough to break through the extinction angle and appear upon the horizon. The heliacal rising (first annual reappearance) of Sirius took place just before dawn in late July, early August, when the star briefly appeared on the eastern horizon before being lost in the light of the Sun. As the nights grew longer, Sirius appeared for an ever-greater length of time. At the time of harvest in August, observers on Windmill Hill would have seen Sirius reappear briefly above

Martinsell Hill at an azimuth of 129 – 130° (also just over the nearer Overton Hill, the future location of the Sanctuary). As shown in Figures 6, 7 and 13, and as described in the next section, over the following weeks and months they would have seen the star climb higher into the sky, passing over the future location of Avebury henge.

The people of Windmill Hill would have seen Sirius rising on the alignment over Martinsell Hill for the last time just after the winter solstice. The star appeared higher and higher in the night sky at each succeeding dusk before finally vanishing into Cherhill Down. As shown in Figure 15, Sirius would have appeared for the last time over Cherhill Down at dusk in early April, the time of its heliacal setting. At 230 – 231°, Sirius was now setting in the same place as the midwinter Sun—a location on Cherhill Down that led up to what is now the site of Oldbury Castle, but had once been one of the oldest and longest used Mesolithic sites in the area. Then the star vanished from the sky for almost 120 days (the time of the planting and the growing of the grain), reappearing at the time of the harvest. I will consider Sirius as a possible harvest star again in Chapter 7.

Their creation of seemingly permanent horizonal alignments gave the Neolithic people the potential to mark the precessional movement of the stars. Some of the symbolism of the slow stellar change could conceivably have already entered the mythic traditions of early Neolithic peoples, and may even have contributed to the nature and timing of certain ceremonies at the great ritual centres. As explained, the people of Windmill Hill could not only have seen Sirius rising higher in the sky over the thousand years they occupied the site, but they also could have noted other southern stars gradually falling lower below their horizon. While there is no direct evidence of this, and thus the details of Neolithic observation of the midwinter Sun and Sirius alignment from Windmill Hill may elude us, one small but tantalising crumb of evidence remains.

Midwinter over Martinsell Hill

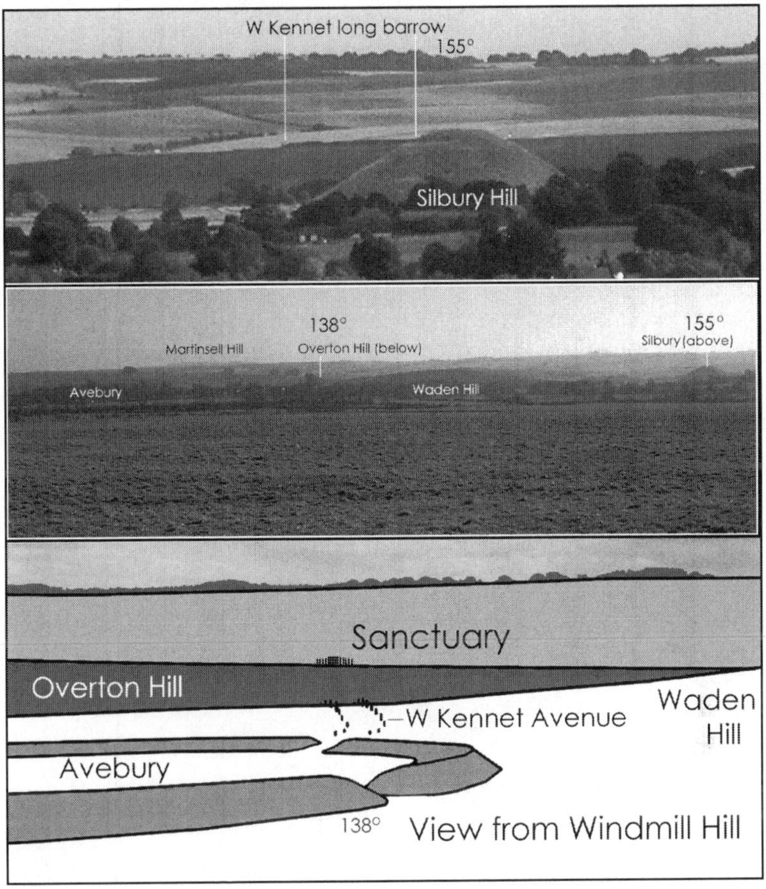

View south from Windmill Hill. Centre: View toward Waden Hill from Windmill Hill. Martinsell Hill is to the left on the horizon, above Avebury. Upper: West Kennet long barrow is visible behind and just to the left of Silbury Hill. Lower: The Sanctuary is visible above the stones of the Kennet Avenue.

Seven miles from Windmill Hill, at a bearing of 129-130°, Martinsell Hill forms one of the highest points on the Wessex Chalk escarpment, a ridge that dramatically marks the northern boundary of the Vale of Pewsey. Distinguished by an Iron Age fort and a promontory running southwest that bears the Giant's Grave, an ancient enclosure, Martinsell Hill is the most distant point on the horizon visible from Windmill Hill. See Figure 7. As described above, observers gathered in the great triple enclosure on Windmill Hill would have seen the Sun traverse the Marlborough Downs, from Hackpen Hill in the north—the place of the summer solstice rising Sun—to Martinsell Hill, just above Overton Hill at the extreme southern end of the Downs—the rising place of the midwinter Sun.

Each year, as the days became shorter, the nights colder and longer, the Windmill Hill people would have seen the rising Sun edge increasingly slowly towards Martinsell Hill. When the Sun finally reached the hill it was the winter solstice, that is, the furthest point south that the Sun reached before 'standing still.' A few days later, the Sun then turned and rose higher in the sky. The Sun always moves so slowly at this time that it is easier to see when it starts to return than when it stops, then count back to determine the exact solstice date. At an azimuth of 130° from the centre of Windmill Hill, the top rim of the midwinter rising Sun would have first appeared at the base of Martinsell Hill. The Sun then rose fully over the summit of the hill.

As described above, Sirius would have appeared at dawn in the same place from early August. As the year advanced, the star rose progressively earlier each night until, on the winter solstice, it was rising over Martinsell Hill for the final time almost at the same time as the Sun set in the southwest. As the midwinter Sun and Sirius repeated their climbs into the heavens (at an inclination of approximately 26°), at their respective times and seasons, both would have appeared above Overton Hill and over the future Avebury site (centre 132°) over the course of the second half of the fourth millennium BCE—the time of the Windmill Hill people. It is quite possible they set up the first stone or timber markers at Avebury at this time. The megaliths of the Obelisk and the Cove may belong to the third quarter of the fourth millennium, their exact locations preceded by wooden posts.[21] Yet, there is no midwinter marker at Avebury as prominent as that visible from Windmill Hill to Martinsell Hill.

Now, Martinsell Hill preserves a folk tradition of an unusual local ball game. "People still meet on the top of the hill... and a curious game is played on the steep slope," wrote Alice B. Gomme in *Folklore* 1907. "A number of boys stand one above the other, and the one at the foot starts a ball, which is hit up the hill with hockey sticks, each of the players passing it to the one above him, until it reaches the top boy, when it is allowed to roll down, and the game is begun again."[22] The game took place on Palm Sunday in the nineteenth century, but the name of the hill suggests an earlier medieval association with St Martin at Martinmas, November 11. Martinmas traditionally marked the day cattle were slaughtered and salted, the beginning of winter and a period of fasting lasting forty days—about the time of year the Windmill Hill people would have been ensconced upon the Hill. The ball game is strikingly suggestive of midwinter solar symbolism. The struggle to get the ball to the summit may allude to the midwinter Sun as it edges towards its pivotal point of standstill and return on December 21, forty days after Martinmas—as viewed from Windmill Hill over Martinsell Hill. The hill also has a strange association with wolves: seventeenth Century antiquarians wrote of "Wolf Platforms" being attached to the site.[23] Might these Martinsell Hill traditions preserve a memory of long ago when Sirius, the wolf or Dog Star, was seen rising over the hill on the same sky-path as the midwinter Sun?

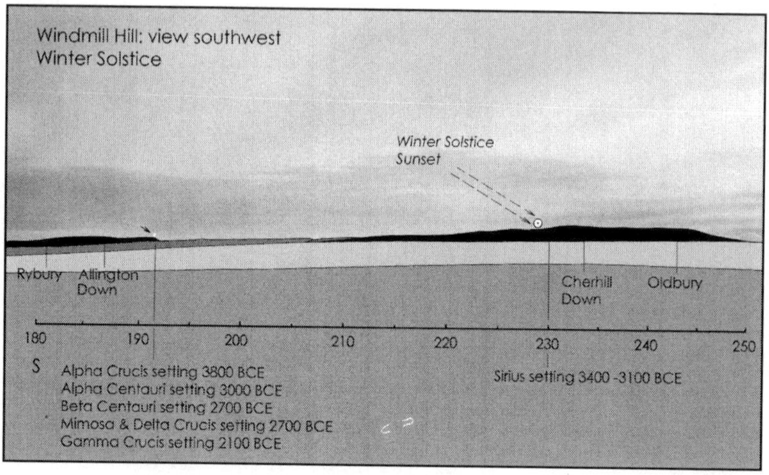

Figure 15. View southwest from Windmill Hill showing the Winter Solstice Sun setting into Cherhill Down at an azimuth of 230°, an alignment the Sun shared with Sirius in the latter half of the fourth millennium BCE. The western end of the Wessex Chalk escarpment marked the setting of several, now invisible, first magnitude stars, most of them at dawn.

A Prologue to Precession

Precession is a slow rotation of the axis of the earth over a cycle of approximately 26,000 years that gradually alters the view of the stars in the celestial sphere as observed at any fixed point and time. Appendix 1 provides a full definition. Because of precession, new stars appear and old stars disappear, the position of the Milky Way itself changes dramatically, and, perhaps most significantly of all, the Sun rises in a different part of the celestial sphere at a different time of year. Thus, every 13,000 years the spring equinox will have moved 180° in relation to the stars of the celestial sphere, while the winter solstice will occur in the place of the stars that once marked the summer.

From another perspective, the polar axis of the Earth tilts toward and away from the galaxy, periodically reaching the

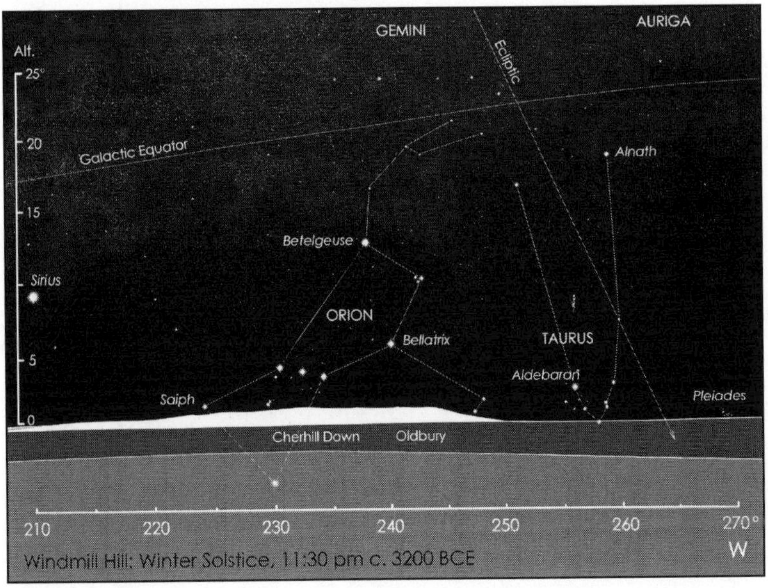

Figure 16. View of the previous figure showing the constellation of Orion setting into the length of Cherhill Down, midwinters, fourth and third millennia BCE. Sirius set along the back of the Down over the course of the third millennium BCE. Today, Sirius sets at an azimuth of 243°. Note the intersection of the ecliptic (the path of the Sun and planets) with the Galactic Equator (a line drawn through the galactic plane), and the manner in which Orion and Taurus indicate this point.

greatest extremes of the ecliptic and the galactic equator over each cycle of precession. Circa 4500 BCE, the beginning of the Neolithic, as the equinoxes aligned to the galactic crossroads, the combination of the 60.2° tilt of the ecliptic to the galactic equator and the 23.5° obliquity of the Earth, a total of nearly 90°, meant the galaxy appeared at one extreme. To viewers in southern Britain the Milky Way moved from vertically overhead toward the horizon over the course of a long winter night, until by 3000 BCE the Galactic Equator and the horizon coincided. The Sun would have been on the crossroads of the ecliptic and the level Milky Way almost a month after the equinoxes.

Precession is so slow—one degree in approximately seventy-two years—that its effects over a single lifetime are infinitesimal. One degree is equivalent to the distance between two standing stones twelve paces apart when observed from a mile away. But over the centuries of Avebury's occupation the precessional shift involved would have progressed sufficiently—on average about fourteen degrees in 1,000 years—to become strikingly apparent. Also, stellar precessional movement at this latitude appears greatly magnified when viewed against a conveniently sloping southern horizon. This may explain why the sky-watchers of Avebury built their key alignments to a horizon where precessional movement was happening almost twice as fast—one degree in less than forty years in the case of alpha Centauri over Waden Hill.[24]

The earliest hint of recorded knowledge of precession does not appear until late in the second millennium BCE, in Babylon, when astronomers described measuring the Sun against the stars. The Greeks did not describe it until the second, possibly the fourth century BCE. But many archaeoastronomers contend that prehistoric peoples must have noticed the slow but inexorable precession of the stars if their ancestral lore involved any reference to star positions.

When visible, the stars, unlike the Sun and Moon, appear to rise and set in *exactly* the same position on the horizon every night. The two Poles of the celestial sphere, north and south, also appear to occupy permanent positions in the sky. The bright star Polaris currently occupies the position of the Northern Celestial Pole. Due to the rotation of the Earth, the 'fixed' stars appear to rotate around the Poles, rising and setting in the same place on the horizon (if they rise or set at all) depending upon the location on the Earth of the observer. Thus, the visibility of each star is determined by its magnitude and by the light of the Sun.

The stars of the Zodiac mark out the ecliptic, that is, the path taken by the Sun and the planets through space. The traditional division of the Zodiac into 360° and 12 'houses' of 30° provides a convenient manner of dividing the celestial sphere, but it is not the only method. Vedic astronomers employ the *nakshatras*, the twenty-seven lunar 'mansions,' as do the Chinese, to divide and define the celestial sphere. The Babylonians originally started with eighteen regions before adopting twelve. The ancient Egyptians employed a thirty-six fold division, calling each 10° segment a *decan*. Each decan governed a ten-day period and the addition of five intercalary days made up the year. Each annual round of decans began with the annual heliacal reappearance of Sirius, which, crucially for the Egyptians, coincided with the beginning of the inundation of the Nile.

Now, the Sun would always rise in the same constellation on the same calendar date every year—the winter solstice rising Sun would always rise in Sagittarius, for example—were it not for the fact that due to a slow secondary rotation of the Earth's axis the Sun appears to be slipping backward around the Zodiac. The Zodiac is precessing, i.e. moving forward, in relation to the Sun. Due to precession, the winter solstice Sun that is currently rising in Sagittarius will next rise in Scorpius, while the spring equinox Sun will move from Pisces to Aquarius.

This slow movement is due to an additional rotation of the Earth like that of a spinning top or gyroscope. The axis of the Earth draws a circle in the sky, and in so doing redefines the position of the Poles against the stars. It is difficult to track the movement of the Poles, but this did not stop the Egyptians from aligning a shaft of the Great Pyramid to Thuban in Draco—at that time, circa 2500 BCE, the star closest to the Northern Celestial Pole. The precessional movement of bright stars on or near the horizon is greater, and their rising and setting points easier to track against fixed features on the horizon.

Early observation of precession is by no means a new

question. The highly skilled surveyor and mathematician Professor Alexander Thom showed how megalithic builders, for example at Mid Clyth near Caithness, employed parallel and fan-shaped rows of stones aligned to distant landmarks to create markers that would have enabled those builders' successors to observe stars precess over several centuries. Thom identified the main stellar focus at Mid Clyth as Capella, a first magnitude star prominently positioned near the Milky Way, which changed at this latitude from being a setting and rising star to being a circumpolar star, one that never set below the northern horizon.[25] Such dramatic precessional effects could have been seen anywhere stone alignments had been in place for several hundred years. More recently, distinguished polymath and historian of science Professor John North saw observation of precession as a given for experienced Neolithic sky-watchers whose descendants used the same sites for a millennium. Lastly, in *Hamlet's Mill,* published in 1969, controversial historians of science Giorgio de Santillana and Hertha von Dechend gathered mythic data from Finnish sagas to Sumerian epics, that they proposed only made sense as attempts to describe great and inexplicable changes in the order of the cosmos.

Having become familiar with one particular view of the relationship of Sun, seasons, stars and Milky Way, and having encoded that relationship within their seasonal calendar of activities, worldview, memorial tradition, symbolic narratives and finally within their permanent monuments, the Neolithic sky-watchers noticed a subsequent shift away from this relationship in the heavens. Through sharpening their attention by the means of their monuments to the small changes in the positions of the stars against the wheel of the year, and especially through close observation of the loss of crucial southern stars embedded in the Milky Way, the sky-watchers at Avebury became able to identify a shift away from the traditional order. Even though they lacked the notation, arithmetic, physics and the cosmography to define or explain its cause, the cycle of precession would have appeared to them, as it did to later astronomers, as the greatest visible observable cycle, a veritable 'Cycle of the Ages.'

If the monument-builders had incorporated the slow movement of the fixed stars against the solar year into their monuments, then they may have seen this movement in the same manner as other early astronomers—as an indicator of social change. Vedic astronomers marked out a precessional cycle of 24,000 years with different ages known as *yugas*, of generation and degeneration. Some aspects of Vedic star-lore can be traced back to the third millennium BCE and even beyond. The Greek astronomer Hipparchus thought that at the end of the Platonic or a Great Year of twelve Zodiacal ages, lasting in total 36,000 years, the primordial heavenly order would be restored. Early Greek and Vedic astronomers were both wrong about the numbers; but like these astronomers, the Avebury sky-watchers may have viewed precession as a cycle, rather than as a departure from a foundational time of beginnings that they needed to maintain.

Exact Calendars

Both because of their well-marked horizon, and because of the transmission of knowledge across generations, it would have become apparent to well-trained Neolithic sky-watchers that the 'fixed' backdrop of the stars, against which the cyclical movements of the Sun, the Moon and the planets took place, was not fixed at all, but was itself subject to change. Once they had marked in stone the seasonal movement of the solar and lunar cycles against the apparently fixed stars on specific local horizons, the people of Avebury had, perhaps unwittingly, developed the means to become aware of subtle changes in the 'background order' of the heavens; changes that were only discernible over very long periods of time.

Unlike the broad alignments from Windmill Hill and the long barrows, the many features of the Avebury complex would have provided its builders with their first really precise information about the heavens. The consequent development of exact calendars would have given people a means to stay in favour with the divine powers. As was described both in the writings of the eighth century BCE Greek author Hesiod and by the second century BCE Coligny Calendar of the Celts, and in countries such as India which reserve ancient astronomical traditions today, the Neolithic people of Avebury would almost certainly have designated some days as 'bad' and others as 'good.' They would have seen certain heavenly conjunctions, lunar phases and above all eclipses as auspicious or inauspicious, fortunate or unfortunate. Babylonian omen tablets dating from the late-third millennium BCE treat the heavens in exactly this manner. This applied astronomy has close affinities with astrology—an integral beginning that many modern astronomers want to forget. The improved Neolithic calendar would have allowed hunting, building, agricultural, ritual, social, and all other activities to take place at times deemed in most accordance with the natural and divine order.

As the sky-watchers gradually acquired more complex celestial information, this would not only have provided them with practical benefits, but also with a greater sense of their unity with the divine order or will of the cosmos. They may have seen any actions that went against the complex spiritual order defined by a calendar as the cause of misfortune. Neolithic society would have tightly prescribed agriculture, hunting, trade, travel and warfare, and even or especially marriage and sexual relations, because of the apparent link between lunar and menstrual cycles. There is considerable evidence among surviving tribal peoples of the belief that if they do not practice activities at the correct times with the appropriate speeches, songs, offerings or artifices, then the natural order itself will fail.

For example, if they do not honour the Sun and Moon in the appropriate manner, the celestial bodies will not behave as they should, and retribution and misfortune, perhaps in the form of drought or storm, swiftly fall upon the community. Religious traditions, usually involving gifting or offerings, Sun salutations and so on, accompany this sort of belief. Even modern city dwellers can be heard asking what they did to deserve bad weather on their vacation and even what they might do or give, quasi-magically, to change it!

The central goal of Neolithic shamans, monument-builders and elders would have been to keep human affairs closely aligned to the order of the heavens, and thus regulated through correct divination and ritual observance of the Earth and Sky. But at Avebury, their unique monuments could also have enabled them to discover that a great change was slowly taking place in the skies: an event that was not part of their traditions and over which they had no control. It may have dawned on the Neolithic keepers of ancestral star-lore that at some point in the future the summer Sun would rise at the time of the stars associated with the winter, and the winter Sun at the time of the stars associated with the summer. The same would be true of the Moon. To cap it all, many of their beloved southernmost stars would soon not be visible at all.

The Question of Precession

If the monument-builders were aware of such changes, the question is how might they have responded to the evidence that seasonal events in the sky—events to which they had permanently aligned their monuments—had now moved elsewhere? What could have been their response to the news that the stars which were a vital part of their calendar, which had provided an aid for agriculture, navigation, the watches of the night, a crucial component of their social narrative, and their charters for ceremony and the ritual year, were gradually rising in another season—or worse, vanishing altogether? Would they have been alarmed by this shift, or merely interested by it? Would they have seen these events as ill-omened?

In the winter months, for example, when they went to a special mound or stone, such as the Avebury Cove, and ancestral traditions informed them that the midwinter Sun and Moon should rise with a particular pre-dawn backdrop of stars, and this had changed, did they see this as inauspicious? Ovid's *Fasti*, a Roman calendar written some 3000 years later, makes it clear that auguries, oracles and divination techniques relied upon such an order. New Kingdom Egypt depended upon the Sun rising on the path of a heliacally rising star. Chapter 8 describes beta Taurus heliacally rising before the Sun in spring at the Sanctuary in 2300 BCE.[26] Just when early British sky-watchers had built the "notable temple" described by Diodorus, and literally set in stone a model of the sacred centre—a temple whose alignments allowed them to participate directly with the divine order of the cosmos—just at that point, the divine order changed.

Whether they tried to explain these changes in the sky with a new set of explanatory or 'just so' stories, or whether they tried to mark or even prevent the changes with a new and massive monumental undertaking (perhaps on the assumption that if the skies were changing, then at least the Earth and stones might provide them with an anchor, a fixed and unchanging base) can never be known. With that point conceded, some today will still say that the Neolithic people could not have noticed precession at all, on the basis that the astronomical component of their megalithic sites was insignificant or only rudimentary. This also must be conceded for some parts of Britain.

Yet, although it is unlikely that the exact timing of procession was known to them, if the lineages of keepers of Avebury henge had learned anything from centuries of experiencing the sky, it was that everything proceeded in cycles. If all else did, why not the stars? It was the periods and the relationships between things that would have intrigued them, even if the numerical aspect of these relationships eluded them. The astronomically sophisticated Avebury sky-watchers may even have had the idea that, like the cycles of the Sun and the Moon, the vast star-cycle of precession would turn back upon itself, but would not have been able to determine *when* this would happen. Von Dechend and Santillana describe how later Indo-European cultures consistently likened the slow rotation of the Poles to the movement of a mill. No one was quite sure how quickly the grinding stones turned or what forces made them do this; all they knew was that they turned. The megalithic monuments may have been enigmatic when it came to crunching the numbers of precession, but as we have seen with the lunar cycles, their very permanence pushed their builders into a close engagement with the cosmos where they could discern even the smallest changes.

The Milky Way

This chapter proposed that the Neolithic people of Windmill Hill observed the movement of Sirius in relation to the Winter Solstice Sun and the movement of the Crux-Centaurus stars in the Milky Way against the southern horizon—both events due to precession. We will see in the next chapter that the significance of the 'main alignment' of Avebury through the centres of its two internal circles, is that it provided the sky-watchers with a finely tuned marker against which they could continue to track the lowest possible passage of the stars closest to the Southern Pole over the enormous period from 3300 to 2000 BCE.

We will also see that the Avebury monuments-builders would have been aware of the two points where the ecliptic—the path defined by the Sun, Moon and planets, the Zodiac—

crosses the Milky Way. Although we have no direct information about how the Neolithic people saw the Milky Way, it is inevitable that the band of stars formed by largest cosmological body in the sky would have meant a great deal to them. The most dramatic feature in the sky is the galaxy; its division of the celestial sphere and especially of the Zodiac must have figured large in their mythology, as it does in many others.

In essence, at a time when the Milky Way was visible around the entire horizon, the Windmill Hill and Avebury sky-watchers would have used a variety of key reference points to symbolically divide and map out the heavens. The Northern and Southern Cross and the two crossing-points of the ecliptic at that time divided the Milky Way into four distinct parts, north and south, east and west. The Northern and Southern Cross pointed to the Poles and thus to a vertical axis, the *axis mundi* or World Tree, around which the stars, indeed, the entire firmament, turned. The two points where the ecliptic crossed the Milky Way, in Gemini and Sagittarius, provided them with markers east and west. The great circle of the Milky Way around the horizon would have deepened the sky-watchers' sense of Avebury being the axial centre of the cosmos. Indeed, I will argue in the next chapter, that the builders intended Avebury to *be* the Milky Way, and that the four-fold division of the Milky Way inspired the four-fold division of the henge.

Finally, their elaborate and permanent monuments enabled these sophisticated North European sky-watchers to see the Sun change its seasonal place against the stars. During the era from 3500 to 2400 BCE, not only would the Sun have moved over fifteen degrees against typical stars, half a Zodiacal house, but the annual path of the Sun would also have crossed the galaxy some fifteen days sooner in the seasonal year! People who employed permanent markers such as the line of sight from Windmill Hill to West Kennet long barrow or from Windmill Hill to Martinsell Hill could not have missed these sorts of astronomical events. As the Milky Way fell to the south, as some of its brightest stars were entirely lost from the sky, and as the Sun rose at midwinter over a prominent landmark marked by a different set of stars than Sirius, what repercussions would this have had upon the symbolically defined and astronomically regulated world of the monument-builders?

4

Avebury: In the Image of the Milky Way

This circle (the Milky Way) is to sidereal what the ecliptic is to planetary astronomy – a plane of ultimate reference, the ground-plane of the sidereal system.

Sir John Herschel[1]

The Great Henge

Two massive sarsen stones define the southern entrance of Avebury henge.

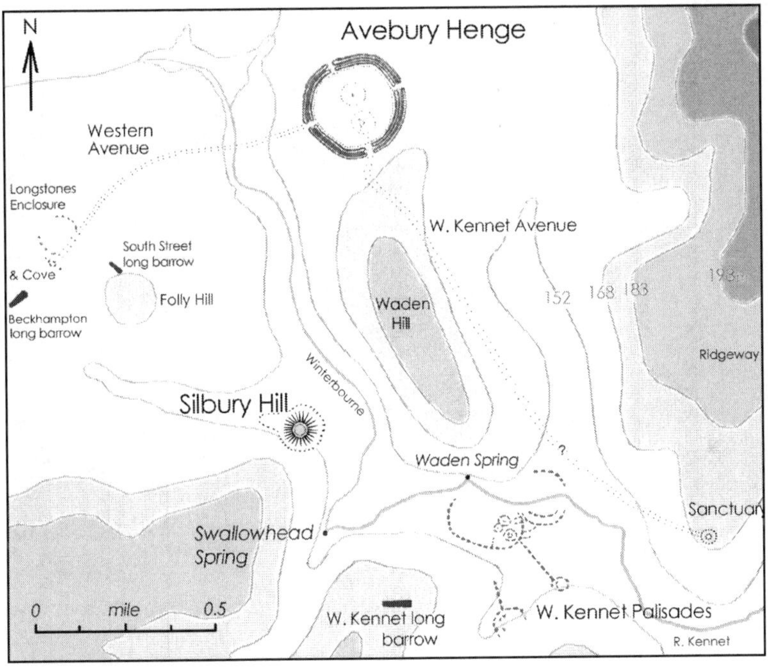

Figure 17. Detail of the area around Avebury henge in the third millennium BCE.

My central argument turns around the events that took place in the night sky for the Neolithic people of Avebury. Ever since Britain had become free of ice, the southern half of the galaxy had been visible in the sky. In the warm period known as the Holocene Climate Optimum, Mesolithic hunter-gatherers could have moved further north each summer and then south in the winter, following the game and the stars. At this latitude, the southern part of the Milky Way had reached its highest around 8000 BCE and then had fallen back towards the southern hemisphere. In the centuries after 4000 BCE, when the Crux-Centaurus stars rose in the small hours, the Milky Way became entirely visible around the horizon. This midwinter event was technically exact around 2800 BCE, when the henge of Avebury was either complete or under construction.

Figure 18. Idealised reconstruction of Avebury circa 2500 BCE. To reproduce the Milky Way, the builders could have scoured the white chalk of the banks. A line drawn through the centres of the primary stone settings has an azimuth of 160/340°, a line from the Cove passes through the 'D feature' at 166°. These are stellar alignments crucial to the entire Milky Way. Note: not all known features are shown.

The elevation provided by the outer bank of Avebury and the clear night skies of the time helped to eliminate the extinction angle, ensuring that the Milky Way shone brightly immediately above the whole white chalk rim of the henge.[2] With trees removed, the horizon was sufficiently distant not to impede the view. This winter passage of the Milky Way accompanied by its many, highly distinctive first magnitude stars, must have been an extremely moving spectacle—especially in the deep south.

As shown in Figures 23 and 48, sky-watchers at the Cove saw the Southern Cross rise over the Obelisk and ascend Waden Hill over the southern entrance. Crux stood upright due south and, just as it began to set, the Milky Way appeared around the entire horizon. It was accompanied by the rising of alpha Centauri, at that moment the brightest star in the sky, and, in the north, by the rising of Cygnus and the ascent of Ursa Major.

This winter levelling of the Milky Way would have made the Avebury sky-watchers acutely aware of the axis of the Earth's rotation about the Celestial Poles. They would have had a strong experiential awareness of the north-south axis, the *axis mundi*. The stellar pointers to the Poles, the Southern and the Northern Cross, embedded in the Milky Way, sometimes diving under or appearing just above the horizon, divided the cosmos north and south, defining the upper and the lower worlds. The sky-watchers also would have been aware of the ecliptic, east and west, where the paths of the Sun, Moon and planets crossed the Milky Way in two fixed places: once against the stars of Gemini and once against the stars of Sagittarius. As the Milky Way formed a brilliant circle of stars, the Avebury people must have felt their sacred place was the axial centre of Heaven and Earth.[3] The geographically auspicious location of Avebury, together with the enormous white chalk ring of the henge and its four causeways, brought them into alignment with every aspect of the cosmos.

The builders made the first henge at Avebury, the primary ditch and bank, at some time around or not long after 3000 BCE, exactly the time the Milky Way was approaching its most level elevation around the horizon. Archaeologists agree that during the following centuries the builders deepened the ditch and made the bank much higher, greatly enhancing the visual impact of the henge.

A truly remarkable quantity of pure white chalk came from the deep ditches. The builders could have scoured the surface of the bank around the henge on a regular basis to keep it clean. Avebury's vast outer bank would have shone against the stars and on moonlit nights. The builders of Stonehenge, Marden, Mount Pleasant, Durrington Walls, and other henge monuments on the chalk downlands of southern Britain worked in a similar manner. Like the builders of the great causewayed camps before them, they hewed out chalk from great depths with antler picks and ox spatulae to build immense circles of white on the ground. If their intention was to mirror the great circle of the galaxy, then it is as though the builders of Avebury wished to either transform the chalk itself into the heavens, or take the Milky Way in some way into the ground.

Avebury henge gave its builders many opportunities to observe and incorporate the events unfolding in the sky into its forms. Aligned to the rotation of the stars, marking the cycles of the Sun and Moon, and encircled by the brilliance of the galaxy during the midwinter months, its builders evidently wanted the chalk, the stones, the circles and the other features of the great henge to contain all that took place in the heavens. Its lunar Inner Circles, key solar and stellar stones and stellar boundary all reflected the heavens, mixing water, earth, stone and light. Yet just as it must have seemed to the Avebury sky-watchers that they had observed the cosmic patterns, made them the subject of myth, worked their mysteries and their calendar around them, told them in stories to children, and embodied them forever in their immense earthworks and standing stones, the very permanence of the henge would gradually have compelled them to realise that the established order was, in fact, changing.

As Sirius progressed slowly further east, away from the Winter Solstice alignment, those who kept the knowledge of the star-alignments—astral lore that they presumably passed down over generations—would have noticed a significant change. The Milky Way, the Great or Silver River, Road of Souls, Semen of the Gods, the Milk of the Goddess, *Via Lactea*, to give it its ancient and universal names, continued to fall towards the south. After thousands of years of visibility, the stars that heralded the complete appearance of the Milky Way were slowly vanishing from the sky. By 2800 BCE, Acrux had completely vanished (if not before, due to the extinction angle), while alpha and beta Centauri, as well as the remaining stars of Crux, were lost to the sight of the monument-builders not long after.[4] By the third millennium BCE, 2500 BCE, the southern portion of the Milky Way was clearly falling from the sight of the Neolithic sky-watchers.

In sum, over the course of millennia, the permanent alignments of Avebury henge allowed succeeding generations of Neolithic people to integrate their lives with the cosmos—to extend their awareness far into the skies. The sight of the entire, or at least the upper part of the Milky Way, divided four-fold by its two crossing-points with the ecliptic and the Southern and Northern Crosses, appears to have stimulated the structure and design of their principal monument. This defined the main alignment in stone as well as the great ditch, bank and four causeways of the henge. Yet over the third millennium BCE, the very alignments that secured their integration with the heavens also allowed the people to see that the galaxy was no longer making a great circle in the winter skies around the horizon. They could plainly see that significant southern and northern stars, the pointers to the Poles, were shifting their position, while those in the south were becoming entirely lost from sight. As the established order of the sky slowly changed, and the great monument that held and mapped the key cosmic axes and reference points became no longer true to the heavenly events whose stories it told, what did its builders decide to do about it?

Silbury Hill & the Southern Stars

A massive mound, the largest of its kind in Neolithic Europe, demanding more physical effort than any other project undertaken at that time in Britain, lies about two-thirds of a mile south of Avebury henge. Silbury Hill is an over 120 feet high, conical, flat-topped and somewhat stepped artificial mound. Unlike the transportation of the four-ton Preseli bluestones to Stonehenge, which being by boat posed mainly technical problems, or the

Silbury Hill. Probably built in three main phases after 2450 BCE, construction of this immense mound may have continued as late as the early second millennium BCE. This period corresponds with the slow descent and eventual loss of the three upper stars of the Southern Cross due to precession, as observed from Avebury.

audacity of dragging forty-ton sarsens from Avebury to Stonehenge, building Silbury was just plain hard and dirty work. Archaeologists now think construction took place in several phases, known as Silbury I, II and III. The builders began phase 1, a small primary mound, after 2450 BCE, slowly adding to it over a number of years before beginning a much larger, more rapidly built, second mound. The final push on the third and greatest phase, may have taken place not long after that, possibly within a generation, at the very latest by 2100 BCE, more likely a hundred years before.[5] The builders appear to have returned to work each autumn when food surpluses were present, but the springs in the surrounding chalk valleys were

Figure 19. View showing beta Centauri reaching culmination over the north-south axis of the henge, and the upper stars of the Southern Cross setting over the future location of Silbury Hill, circa 2500 BCE. Compare with Figure 10.

likely to be low or even dry.

The seventeenth-century antiquary John Aubrey wrote in his *Monumenta Britannica*: "No history gives any account of this hill; the tradition only is, that King Sil or Zel, as the countrey folke pronounce, was buried here on horseback, and that the hill was raysed while a posset of milke was seething." Other local traditions recorded in the nineteenth century, told that King Sil was either buried upright on a golden horse or within a golden coffin, that he wore golden armour or that he and his horse were solid gold, and that he occasionally rode around the hill. The gold, the circular character of the mound, the perambulation and the name Sil or Sul (the Latin for Sun is *sol)* have suggested solar associations to many. A goddess known as Sul or Sulis, with underworld, water and solar connotations was honoured in Roman Britain not far away at the thermal springs of Bath.

Many think a goddess, perhaps of the springs, should be associated with the mound. The questions raised by these legends with their mythic associations, and the issue of whether or not the mound was solar, will be discussed in Chapter 6.[6]

Silbury Hill is visible from many points on the main axis of Avebury henge, but it vanishes south of the Obelisk. To the viewer standing beside the Obelisk the summit of Silbury lies about ten degrees west of south at 189-191°. From the location of the Obelisk, from as early as 3300 BCE, the magnificent star, alpha Crucis would have risen upon Waden Hill, well over the extinction angle, to stand upright with its sisters over the future location of Silbury Hill. Alpha Crucis or Acrux, the thirteenth brightest star in the sky, is the lowest star of the Southern Cross. From that date onwards into the third millennium BCE, alpha Crucis would have only briefly cleared the distant horizon, only just emerging from Waden Hill before setting at the point where the summit of Silbury Hill eventually was to intersect the horizon. For viewers at the Obelisk, a large stone of the Southern Inner Circle described here as the 'Silbury Stone,' would have marked this setting location by the mid-third millennium BCE. See Figure 21. Another important stone lay precisely south from the Obelisk, thus I call it the 'South Stone.' A third stone, called here the 'Crucis Stone,' marked the point where the upper stars of Crux—as well as beta Centauri—were setting at the beginning of the third millennium BCE. All three stones are intact today.

To explain how Avebury and Silbury Hill are linked by the southern stars, imagine standing beside Neolithic sky-watchers at the Obelisk on a clear winter night. You would see the stars of the Southern Cross emerge from Waden Hill on the 160° main alignment of the henge. You would see the stars rotating and rising up due south over Waden Hill, crowning the horizon along with the Milky Way. The elevation of Waden Hill, at two degrees plus, meant the rising and culmination of Crux was clearly visible. As shown in Figures 26-27, from the end of

October, through the winter solstice until late March—for a period lasting well over a thousand years until about 2800 BCE—sky-watchers at or beside the Obelisk would have seen Crux rise up over Waden Hill. The compact constellation rose just to the east of south, stood upright upon the southern horizon, then set where Waden Hill met the horizon just west of south—*exactly in the area where the builders were to locate Silbury Hill.*

In the millennium prior to 3000 BCE, alpha Crucis, or Acrux, the base of the Southern Cross, became the heliacal setting star at the winter solstice; that is to say, the constellation of Crux stood on the horizon and vanished in the dawn light at the winter solstice at the western foot of Waden Hill. Crux provided a marker of the rising and falling Milky Way and was a 'pointer,' an indicator of the otherwise hidden Southern Celestial Pole around which the stars of the southern skies appeared to turn—a southern fulcrum of the sky. But alpha Crucis was also the first really important star to disappear, as the slow movement of precession after 3000 BCE began to turn upside down what would have been for the Neolithic people an extremely long-standing and no-doubt spiritually important order of the heavens.

In fact, the time of building Silbury Hill, between 2450 – 2100 BCE, coincided exactly with the era when the long-visible southern portion of the galaxy, marked by its all-important south-pointing constellation, Crux, finally dropped below the southern horizon. Throughout the Mesolithic in Britain, the galaxy had always risen high in the south; it had taken a long time to decline, but now the order of the heavens was changing.

Whereas before 3000 BCE the entire constellation of Crux had been visible due south from Avebury henge, after this time its lowest star Acrux became lost to view. As shown in Figure 19 and 22, only the three stars of the upper half of Crux emerged from Waden Hill on the main 160° alignment to form a triangle low on the horizon.[7] Critically, the triangle formed by the upper three stars of the Southern Cross then set *over the exact location of Silbury Hill* from about 2800 BCE as, one by one, each of them replaced Acrux as the heliacal setting star at the winter solstice. This triangle of stars mirrored the conical shape formed by the great mound; or the shape it would have achieved if the builders had intended the mound to reach a point.[8]

By 2400 BCE the two central stars of Crux, as well as beta Centauri, were as low over the location of Silbury Hill as they ever would be, before they became lost to sight in the atmosphere above the horizon. Yet, if conditions were favourable, the sky-watchers could have seen them travel down to the horizon in the centuries thereafter.[9] By 2100 BCE, Silbury Hill was almost certainly complete. By this time, as shown in Figure 23, only gamma Crucis remained to set upon its summit—as seen from the Obelisk of Avebury henge. By 1900 BCE, due to precession, the Southern Cross had entirely fallen from the sky. Gacrux had vanished into the area now marked by Silbury Hill, and the galaxy had long fallen away from encircling the entire horizon.

Given this remarkable coincidence, what was in the minds of the builders of Silbury Hill? Were they trying to check the fall of Crux, the Southern Cross, as seen from Avebury henge? By building a colossal mound that rose into the triangle formed by the three falling stars, were the builders hoping to arrest the descent of the constellation? Alternatively, was the building of Silbury Hill simply an attempt to represent a celestial movement or moment by the transitional Late Neolithic-Early Bronze Age monument-builders?

As we will see in Chapter 6, Silbury Hill with its remarkable springs appears as the primal mound, the multi-tiered World Mountain, the ultimate symbol appropriate for a world centre and *axis mundi* between the worlds. Silbury Hill crowned the horizon in the place where the stars of the Southern Pole had entered the Underworld. Its builders marked the Great Axis of the sky and the many layers of the cosmos itself, bringing them down to Earth, and honouring, or perhaps propitiating its cycles in a great work: the largest mound ever seen in Europe, comparable even to the contemporary pyramids of Egypt. Yet remember, when viewed from Windmill Hill, Silbury Hill appears on the original alignment to West Kennet long barrow and Knap Hill, the alignment on which the Silbury Hill builders' ancestors had watched the rising of the southern stars over a thousand years before. Thus, surely by intention, the mound that received the *setting* stars when seen from Avebury henge was located in such a manner that its builders were also acknowledging their ancestors' reverence for the *rising* of the same stars.

Crux: the Southern Cross in the Northern Skies

View south from the Obelisk today. The concrete marker in the foreground, the pointed stone at centre and the socket of a missing stone beyond it lie on the north-south alignment of the henge. Were the henge-builders aware that West Kennet long barrow lay beyond Waden Hill on this alignment? The summit of Silbury Hill is

concealed by the stone right of centre. A concrete post marks a posthole at the base of the trees above the remains of the fallen Ring Stone on an alignment of 166°.

The Obelisk to Silbury. Silbury Hill is just to the left of the Silbury Stone, which hides Silbury Hill when the viewer stands closer to the Obelisk.

The constellation which vanished from the view of sky-watchers at the northern 51st latitude during the third millennium BCE, and which marked the southern portion of the Milky Way, is known today as Crux or the Southern Cross; but this was not always so. When in 1501 CE, the Italian explorer Amerigo Vespucci became one of the first Europeans to see the Southern Cross after it had been lost to view in Europe for many thousands of years, he did not identify it as a cross; rather he described its pattern as a 'mandorla,' that is, as almond or vesica shaped. It is plausible that the early British sky-watchers also saw it in this manner; perhaps identifying its four stars with an entranceway, a threshold, an ancient symbol of the divine feminine, the vulva of the goddess, in the manner of the later Celtic *Sheila-na-gig*.

This remarkable constellation, the most compact in the sky, the 'pointer' to the South Celestial Pole, located in the Milky Way in the southernmost region of the sky, must have made a great impression upon prehistoric sky-watchers for the thousands of years it was visible in the northern hemisphere. Alpha, beta and gamma Crucis were, at that time among the twenty brightest stars visible from Britain in the sky and Acrux was in the top ten. Similarly, the area of the sky near beta Crucis or Mimosa is so exquisite, even to the naked eye, that it was named the 'Jewel Box' in the nineteenth century. The stars in this constellation include double stars, pulsating stars, and red and blue-white super-giants of such beauty that Dante Alighieri imagined its four 'holy' stars as representative of the highest virtues, belonging to the world before the Fall:

> Meseemed the heavens exulted in their flame –
> O widowed world beneath the northern Plough,
> For ever famished of the sight of them![10]

Dante saw the stars as belonging to a virtuous realm of lost ancestral greatness. Due to the precessional cycle, the stars of

Crux were lost to view from the 51st parallel of latitude over the course of the third millennium BCE, having been visible in the sky for close to thirteen thousand years. They continued to be lost to sight in Europe, vanishing from Palestine at the time of the Christ.

It is intriguing to note that many of the Avebury stones are similar to the shape of the Southern Cross. The builders appear to have carefully chosen and set up four-pointed, lozenge-shaped stones with their longest point in the ground. Did these stones mimic the diamond pattern of the four-star Southern Cross, with 'lost' Acrux at its base, from 2900 – 2300 BCE? This is speculation of course, but the time of the constellation's visibility is certainly within the main period for the erection of the standing stones, both within the henge and the avenues.

A Bear Mother Cult?

Paul Shepard argued in *The Sacred Paw* that the universality of a Bear Mother myth across the Northern hemisphere showed its extreme antiquity.[11] In the myth, a woman marries a bear and 'bears' children, a Bear Son or twins, there are several variations.[12] The root of the Latin for bear, *ur-*, betokens primal forms, while the Greek for bear, *art-*, belongs to powerful deities such as Artemis. The name Arthur, *arth* is Welsh for 'bear,' combines both roots. Looking north, the Great Bear, Ursa Major circles the Northern Pole (in Vedic tradition, its seven stars are the seven *Rishis,* wise men) while the Bear Son as Ursa Minor follows, ascending and descending the polar axis. Thus, the Southern Cross may point to the hidden Southern Pole, representing the womb of the Bear Mother or the entrance to her cave or den at the root of the *axis mundi.*

The pregnant bear, as *Ursus arctos*, the Brown Bear, the 'bear of the north,'enters her den, when the Sun is furthest south in midwinter, to semi-hibernate. She miraculously emerges in the spring with her cubs. In some versions of the Bear Mother myth, including one by Aristotle, she has licked them into being and shape.[13] The Polar Bear, *Ursus maritimus,* emerges from an ice cave with her young. The bear—often identified with the shaman—is capable of climbing trees; like the shaman, it can enter the root of the World Tree but also climb to its crown. At the time of Avebury, the Southern Cross appeared in the south as the constellation of Ursa Major reached its culmination high overhead.

An ancient Bear Cult may at one time have defined and distinguished the two Poles of the *axis mundi* in terms of a World Tree. The cult gave a primal form to Great Mother worship and described the pathway between the worlds. As the Bear Mother emerged from her cave at the roots of the World Tree, she bore with her the fertility of the primordial core of the world, represented to the Neolithic people of Avebury by the southern stars. Ancient traditions from the northern hemisphere tend to link the hibernating bear together with migrating waterfowl and the winter solstice as the primary symbols of death and regeneration.[14] As the bear could hear all human conversation, it was customary to never name the bear and only address it indirectly, such as the 'Old Man,' 'Honey Paws' or the 'Golden King.'

In some Siberian versions of the Bear Mother myth, the Bear Father, often linked with the Pole Star, is usually slain by the woman's kin in a set of highly ritualised acts that end with the appropriate distribution of the bear's parts. The soul of the Bear Husband goes to heaven upon the path between the worlds to give a report of the quality of the ritual observances of the people to the gods. The Bear Father, lately appearing as Beorn, 'bear,' in Tolkien's *The Hobbit,* turns the axis of the stars. Alternatively, her offspring, the Bear Son goes down into the Underworld then ascends the *axis mundi* in search of the honey, the food of the gods, the immortal nectar, representing the blessings, wisdom and order of the heavens maintained in the place of the Bear Father.[15] The early Avebury monument-builders also would have seen Arcturus, 'protector of the bear,' companion of Ursa Major and Minor, reach its zenith, north and directly overhead, just as the Southern Cross began to set and alpha and beta Centauri rose to lie due south over Waden Hill.

The stellar dance around the spindle of the Poles that was so spectacular at the time of Avebury may thus find a myth in the ancient legends of the bear. Echoes of this myth are everywhere in fairy tale. In Britain, Arthur, the primal bear king, is said to sleep in a cave, waiting the hour of greatest need. Such myths must have passed through a Neolithic phase in Britain, whose greatest monuments at Avebury appear fascinated by the passage around the Poles.

The Fall of the Milky Way 4000 - 2000 BCE

Figure 20. Idealised view south from the Obelisk showing the southern entrance in the mid-third millennium BCE, the missing stones of the Southern Inner Circle and timber posts, suggested by the known post-hole. More postholes may plausibly exist. The orientation of the henge to Waden Hill was clearly fundamental to its symmetry.

Figure 21. View south from the Obelisk showing reconstruction of known stones. The 'Post Stone' complements the 'South Stone' on either side of the southern entrance. The assumption is that the missing stones were similar in size to existing stones. Other posts may have existed, or were replaced by stones as their settings became permanent. The Sun, Moon, stars and planets reached culmination over the South Stone.

We can better understand the significance of both Crux and Silbury Hill to the monument-builders by imagining ourselves once again standing beside the Neolithic sky-watchers on a typical midwinter night at Avebury. Some readers may prefer to return to the astronomical details later, or to follow the outline in the diagrams and summaries.

During midwinter as twilight increased, Orion and Taurus, with Gemini above them, would initially have dominated the southern sky, as they still do today. The galaxy would have formed an arch vertically overhead along the henge's main 340 / 160° alignment. Arcturus and the Corona Borealis would have appeared low in the northern sky; later the fifth brightest star in the sky, the brilliant Vega, would have joined them. This had been the winter star dance for as long as people had been in the area, and for longer. But as the Great Hunter, Orion, triumphed in the south, closely followed by Sirius, not all in the heavens was as it had appeared to the first builders.

Sirius may well have been making her bright passage across the south—over the summit of Waden Hill on the path of the midwinter Sun. But Cygnus was diving fast toward the northern horizon on the main axis of the monument, and the Milky Way was bearing down hard upon the heels of the Hunter and Sirius. Towards midnight, the great southern constellations were already departing from the skies, while the Milky Way was pressing down onto the western horizon. Even the passage of Vega low over the northern skyline could not disguise the fact that Cygnus, its brightest star Deneb below the horizon, had become all but lost from sight. Moreover, the amount the Milky Way had been falling in this manner had increased so much over the centuries that it must have seemed to the star-watchers that something was driving its southernmost stars from the sky. This was not the pattern that earlier generations of star-watchers had observed and memorialised.

But shortly after midnight, a 'miracle' occurred. As Cygnus reappeared in the north, the constellation of Crux rose out of Waden Hill (at 160° in the south) to stand upright upon its summit, heralding the appearance of the Milky Way along the eastern horizon. The galaxy had not fallen after all! It was still there—albeit lower in the sky. As the Milky Way set toward the west, in fact, it had risen in the east, to form a majestic, if low circle around the entire horizon. Although appearing later in the night, many beautiful stars, asterisms and constellations known to their ancestors, especially those within the body of the galaxy, still came into view for the Avebury monument-builders.

In the final act of this sky-drama, as Cygnus climbed into the sky in the north (accompanied by Ursa Major and, as will be shown, Capella), and while the stars of Crux departed from their culmination in the south, the Milky Way began to lift upwards in the east to reveal alpha Centauri. At that moment, alpha Centauri became the brightest star visible in the sky. Thus over the millennia, although the stars of the south slowly had slowly fallen back below the southern horizon, they had brought with them one final gift: the astonishing sight of the Milky Way wrapped around the entire horizon. For thousands of years the Crux-Centaurus stars and the Milky Way had been visible in the southern skies at this latitude. But as the precessional rotation of the Earth caused them to fall from sight, the entire ring of galaxy would have encircled viewers at the latitude of Avebury, giving the sky-watchers at the Obelisk a final gift, a wave goodbye from the departing sky-pattern.

Although an interpretation of these events is obviously being offered here it is necessary to be cautious. An alternative reading might be that Orion and Sirius, Gemini and Taurus, positioned at the other crossroads of the ecliptic and the galactic equator and their planets, were seen as *leading* the Milky Way towards the west; they were not being "pressed down" by it at all. Perhaps as Deneb of Cygnus dipped below the northern horizon this was not seen as signalling a difficult underworld passage, but rather an important calendrical and celebratory event; associated, perhaps, with the homecoming of the winter wildfowl. A further reading suggests that as Cygnus left the Upperworld and entered the Lowerworld it may have mediated between the two Poles—the cave and the stars of the Bear Mother and Father.

5

The Crux-Centaurus Stars

...I turned, and fixed my mind
Upon the other pole, beheld four stars, the same
The first people saw...
Dante[1]

Alpha & Beta Centauri

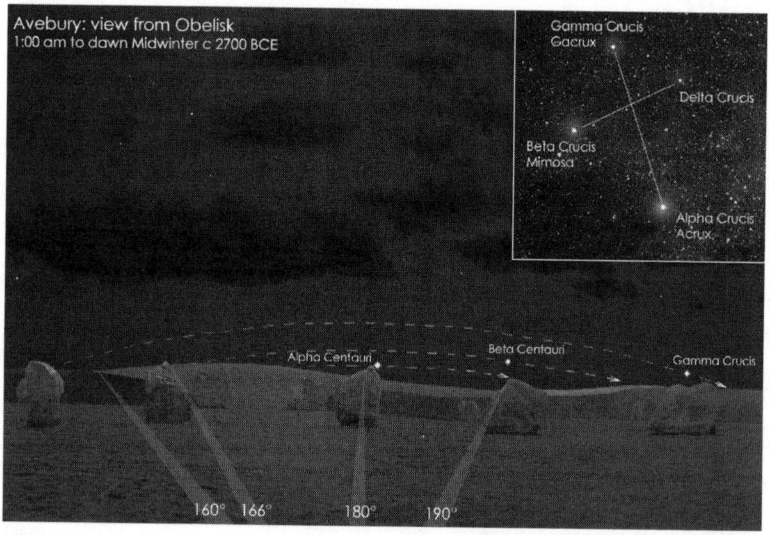

Figure 22. View south from the Obelisk showing some critical azimuths, the passage of stars over Waden Hill and a newly constructed southern entranceway to Avebury henge, circa 2700 BCE. The ditch and bank are complete; the stone circles are in place. The huge and carefully selected new stones of the Southern Inner Circle conceal the possibly earlier Ring Stone and its likely partner. They may have replaced wooden posts. Alpha Centauri is setting (for the final time) over the 'Silbury Stone'—so called as it marks the future location

of Silbury Hill—at 190°. The other stars of Crux and beta Centaurus will set here in succeeding centuries. The inset box shows the stars of Crux, the Southern Cross.

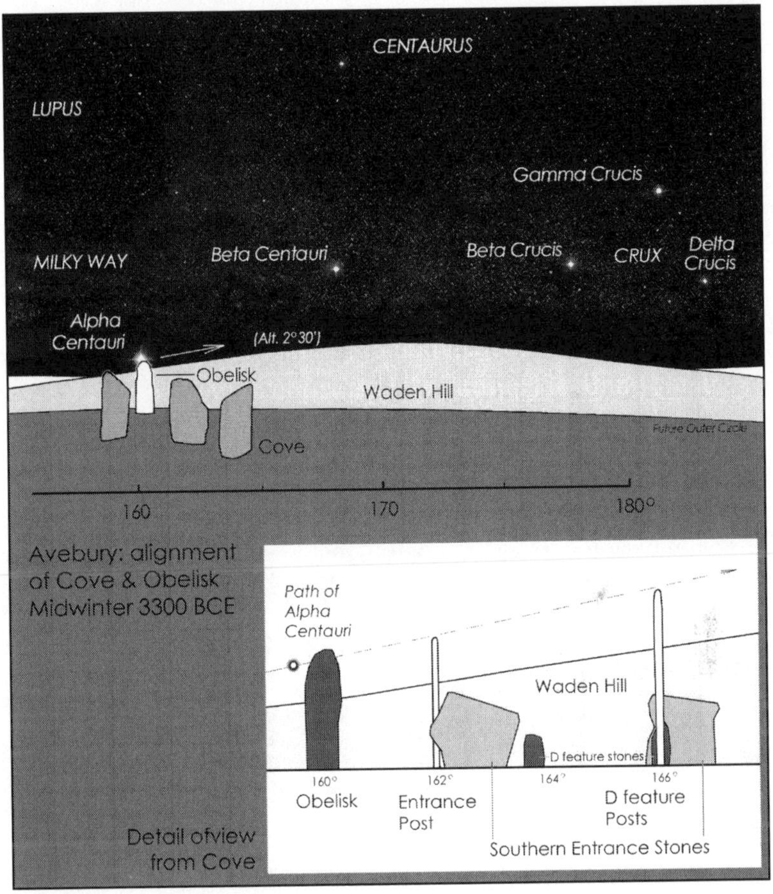

Figure 23. Alpha Centauri rose over Waden Hill when observed from the main axis of Avebury henge, Cove and the Obelisk, in the fourth millennium BCE—azimuth approx. 160°. A minimum elevation of 1° and a maximum of 2.5° meant Waden Hill was well above the star's extinction angle. By 3300 BCE, the star was rising almost upon the profile of the hill. By 2800 BCE, alpha Centauri had long gone (as had alpha Crucis), only beta Centauri, beta and delta Crucis were skimming the hill. By 2000 BCE, only gamma Crucis was rising on

160°. Sky-watchers at the Cove could watch the critical first appearances of these stars over a variety of posts and stones—only the earliest stones and known posts are shown here. An observer on the ground at the centre of the henge would have seen many more stones break the skyline (see Figure 18).

Alpha and beta Centauri came to the attention of Mesolithic hunter-gatherers at this latitude as they were the brightest stars in the southern skies—outside even the southern extremes of the Sun and Moon. The nomadic people may have had stories of coming from the south as the climate warmed and seas rose, or they may even have retained contact with their cousins on the Continent who could still see these southern stars. It appears the two stars subsequently remained important to the early Neolithic occupants of Windmill Hill; the Wessex Chalk escarpment that formed the southern horizon would have leant itself to their observation.

In the period 3700 – 3500 BCE, West Kennet long barrow was built below the rising point of alpha Centauri and other southern stars as viewed from Windmill Hill. John North was the first to note this crucial astronomical detail.[2] It appears that the rising and setting of alpha and beta Centauri, as well as the spectacular stars of Crux, drew the attention of early sky-watchers at the Obelisk or the Cove of Avebury henge. These magnificent stellar giants rose initially over the eastern flank of Waden Hill on the main alignment of the henge between these stones at 160°.

Obviously not all the people of the era would have been aware of all the meanings and stories held by the stars; but universally, we identify the stars with all those who can soar to the heavenly realms. The Celtic story in the *Mabinogion*, for example, of the struggle between Gywnn and Gwythyr for Creiddylad, the "fairest woman in the isles," can arguably be set among the stars. Gwynn appears as Orion, the hunter, and Scorpius as Gwythyr, the hunter's nemesis. The scorpion bites the heel of the hunter as the constellations, located upon the two crossing points of the ecliptic and the Milky Way. They chase each other across the sky, one triumphing in winter and one in summer. As Crux lies at their centre, the vesica-shaped constellation may once have been identified with Creiddylad, who thereby can be read as a remnant of an ancient astral goddess, for whom twin gods, an 'Earth Son' and a 'Star Son,' a Winter and a Summer King, compete.[3]

It is, however, impossible to connect this legend with Avebury. Aside from the traditions of Martinsell and other hills in the area, the two wyverns on the font in Avebury church and the legend of King Sil, to be discussed shortly, there appear to be no legends attached to Avebury. If any trace of a tradition could be found, however slight, it would help to illuminate the ancient cosmological narrative, the significance and especial sanctity held by the ancient Neolithic people for Avebury.

Stars & Stones: the View from Avebury

Figure 24. Gamma Crucis rising at 166° over Waden Hill. View from the Obelisk circa 2300 BCE. This star would have been the last of the

Crux-Centaurus group to have made this passage; dropping below the 166° alignment during the following century. Beta Centauri, beta and delta Crucis rose here circa 2700 BCE; alpha Centauri circa 3000 BCE; alpha Crucis circa 3500 BCE. The setting positions of these long-visible and surely highly significant stars could also have been closely marked.

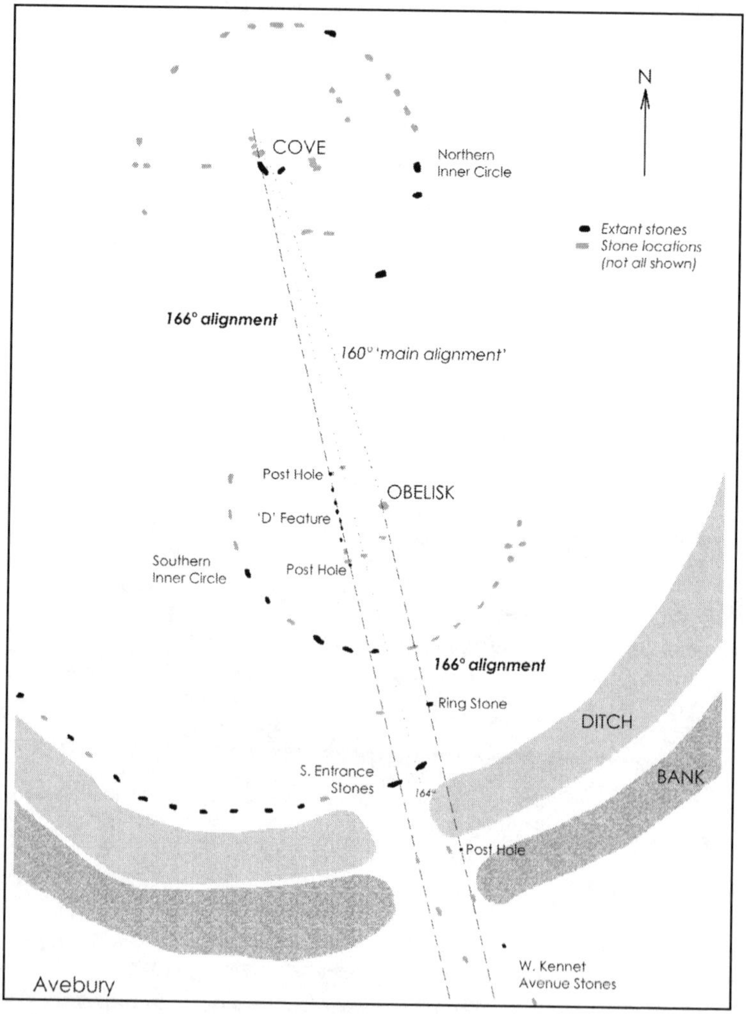

Figure 25a. Plan showing extant standing or fallen stones, the location of some, but not all, of the missing stones (marked by concrete posts), and known postholes. The primary 166° alignment between the Obelisk

and the posthole beside the southern entrance includes the Ring Stone. The second 166° alignment between the Cove and the southern entrance includes the D feature linear stone setting, two postholes, the Devil's Chair, and the partner of the Ring Stone—more stones than any other alignment on the site. All the stones mentioned are among the earliest erected, while the postholes may be even older. Alpha Centauri, beta Centauri and the stars of Crux rose and skimmed over the profile of Waden Hill on these alignments from 3600 to 2100 BCE; most of these stars rising in the middle of that period.

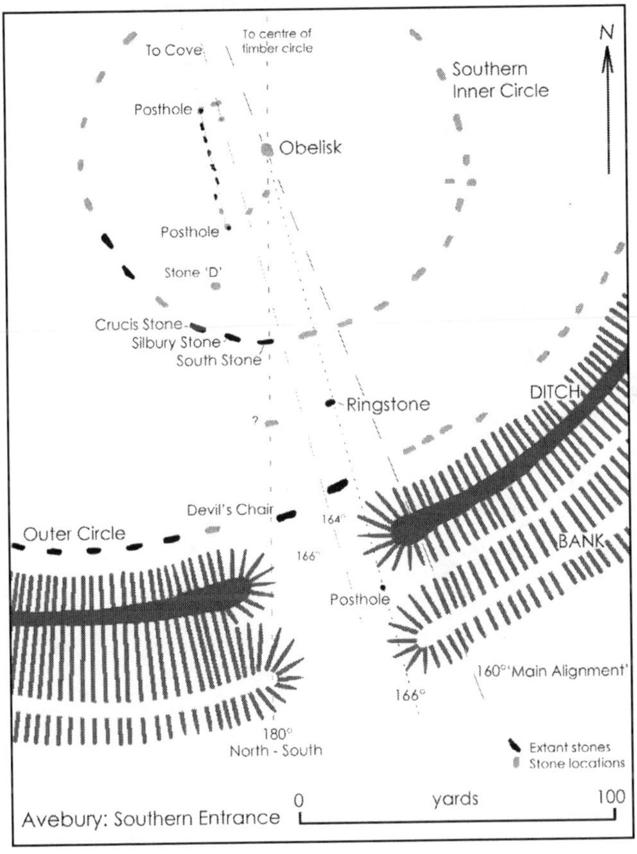

Figure 25b. The southern entrance area and Southern Inner Circle include some anomalous stones and some undated postholes. The postholes may be earlier than the other features; there may have been

others lost in the building of the henge or now under the road. Lines of sight from the Cove pass through many of the stone settings at 160°, 164° and 166°. A possible north-south alignment also passes through the centre of a concentric-circle feature in the northeast quadrant shown in Figure 4.

The first stones on the site of Avebury henge, perhaps the largest, followed by the regularly spaced stones of the Southern Inner Circle, would have made the rising and setting points of alpha and beta Centauri easy to observe. If the first stones were in place by 3300 BCE, which is not impossible, their primary 160° alignment through the Cove and the Obelisk would have pointed unerringly to the rising point of alpha Centauri, then at the eastern foot of Waden Hill. The elevation of the horizon provided by Waden Hill helped overcome the extinction angle, so that on a clear night, the giant star, magnitude -0.3, would have appeared just above the horizon. As shown in Figure 23, to observers at the henge, alpha Centauri would then have appeared to skim over the perfectly positioned and smoothly rounded flank of Waden Hill.

By 3000 BCE, the time of the primary enclosure, the rising of alpha Centauri would have been marked by the summit of Waden Hill, and subsequently, circa 2700 BCE, by a marker in the position of the South Stone. Also at this latter date—probably too early for the construction of the Southern Inner Circle—the highest point obtained by beta Centauri was apparently marked by the position of the Silbury Stone, while the descent of gamma Crucis was aligned to a third stone, called here the Crucis Stone. Whenever they were erected, most probably in the second half of the third millennium BCE, these stones surviving *in situ* in this segment of the inner circle and aligned to distinctive features of the horizon, would have given the henge-builders the ability to better observe the low southern rising and setting of the Crux-Centaurus group of stars, especially their first and last appearances over the course of the year.

As the extinction angle of these first magnitude stars was so very low, between two and three degrees—less if the atmosphere was clear—the natural elevation of the horizon (two and a half degrees over Waden Hill, one degree over Silbury Hill) would have greatly helped the sky-watchers in their observations. In fact, the combination of the lowest possible observable southern altitude, an elevated horizon and the gentle slope of Waden Hill meant that alpha Centauri could have been seen 'precessing' over the markers at a much faster rate than stars elsewhere—at an extraordinary rate of approximately one degree in twenty-five years. The elevated horizon would have also helped to cancel out the effect of refraction; where distortion caused by the atmosphere can make a star appear to move horizontally, sometimes as much as a solar diameter or more, as it approaches the horizon.[4]

From the evidence of locations where lost stones once stood (as shown in the Figures) the henge-builders' observation of the rising points of alpha and beta Centauri may also have been greatly enhanced by use of the stones to the east of the South Stone; also by those at the southern entrance to the henge. In the case of Crux, this would have been at a time prior to the building of the outer and inner circles and the henge. Alternatively, perhaps only wooden markers existed at this early time.

From 2700 to 2100 BCE, the period when the stone settings of Avebury and Silbury were all in place, for the star-watchers beside the Obelisk, the three surviving stones of the Southern Inner Circle (and their missing eastern equivalents) were perfectly sited to observe the entire passage of alpha and beta Centauri and the upper stars of Crux over Waden Hill. It is reasonable to conjecture that the builders would have selected distinctive stones for this purpose. For example, the point of the tallest stone, the South Stone, indicates precisely south from the centre of the circle; this alignment, continued north, passes through the centre of the unexcavated double circle in the northeast quadrant of the henge. The South Stone would thus have served to indicate the culmination or zenith of each star's transit through the southern sky, while due to elevation it would also have functioned as a marker of stellar rising points from the western side of Waden Hill. To cap it all, the builders of the henge would have been well aware that behind the South Stone, just behind this now extremely well marked horizon, lay West Kennet long barrow.

It was the next stone, however, the Silbury Stone, standing before the notch where Waden Hill met the distant horizon at about 190° from north, which marked the place where the builders were to locate Silbury Hill. From the Obelisk, Silbury was to be —and still is—hidden from sight by this stone; but as shown in the photographs, it only needs a step either way for the summit of the mound to come into view. The profile of the Silbury stone seems to suggest that it was selected to either receive setting stars or to allow them to roll down its back—an effect possibly enhanced by refraction.

As shown in Figure 26, it would have been possible, on a clear night, for sky-watchers at the Obelisk to have observed Acrux, the alpha star of Crux, rise from the location of West Kennet long barrow, pass over the lower slope of Waden Hill, then set in the notch marked by the Silbury Stone. They would have seen the passage of Acrux over this portion of the sky from the time of West Kennet long barrow and Windmill Hill to almost 3000 BCE. Archaeoastronomy thus suggests a possible timeframe for the erection of the Obelisk.

The third and final sarsen stone is called here the 'Crucis Stone,' because of the dramatic manner in which gamma Crucis would have set into the notch on its top in the period 2500-2400 BCE—as would have all three upper stars of the constellation of Crux over the course of the preceding millennium. The builders appear to have complemented it with another stone, known as 'Stone D,' set between it and the Obelisk. Now marked by a concrete post, Stone D may have helped refine observation of these stellar setting points. The steady southward descent of the Southern Cross and alpha and beta Centauri over these special stones would have continued for several centuries until they became no longer visible in the sky.

Ancient Symbols of Fertility & Healing

The archaeoastronomer Michael Hoskin, in a thorough study of megalithic sites in Menorca, concluded that many of the island's stone settings, known as *taula,* were oriented to the Crux-Centaurus stars. The builders constructed these *taula* in the first millennium BCE, when the stars appeared low on the southern horizon. By this time, the stars had slowly sunk from view across northern Europe, possibly precipitating cultural crises, Hoskin thought, in regions where the megalith-builders had considered these stars important. The Mediterranean builders may have abandoned an earlier site on Menorca, known as Son Mas, about 1700 BCE, for example, when the same group of stars became prematurely lost from view due to an elevated horizon.[5] This raises the exciting possibility that prehistoric European people could have accorded a common symbolic meaning to these stars—and to their loss—perhaps going back for millennia, all across the continent.

On the basis of a few artefacts (bronze hooves and a statue linked with healing) that were recovered from a *taula,* Hoskin further suggested that they could have been associated with a cult of the Centaur figure of Chiron, in anticipation of the Greek mythic identification of the constellation of Centaurus with this figure, the leader of the Centaurs who had healing powers.[6] The Greeks held that alpha and beta Centauri formed the centaur's front hooves; Crux formed one or both of its hind feet. Whether or not the builders of the *taula*, or the Neolithic people of northern Europe two thousand years earlier, could also have linked the Crux-Centaurus group of stars with a mythical creature, half-man, half-horse, who was associated with healing is, of course, unknown. None the less, Hoskin's research hints at the kind of meanings that the southern stars must once have carried for Neolithic and Bronze Age Europeans.

An alternative symbolic interpretation may be that the distinctively shaped Southern Cross could have been identified with a vesica or vulva, while the stars of alpha and beta Centauri—the 'pointers'—may have been regarded as a phallus. In other words, the Neolithic people of Avebury may have associated these bright stars with fertility rather than with healing. I have already noted the possible association of fertility figures with the Southern Cross: the Bear Mother, Creiddylad, and *Sheila-na-gig*—the Milky Way and the vulva of Crux take the fertility symbolism further. Fertility would have been vital for a people whose mortality rates were only just lower than those of birth. A woman first pregnant at fifteen or sixteen might typically have had three children before dying nine years later. More than half of all these children died, most in the first year.[7] The Neolithic population was more or less stable, or only grew very slowly. When the weather was bad and harvests were poor it sometimes must have felt that there was a need for heavenly symbols of fertility and abundance. Could the Crux-Centaurus stars conceivably have provided such symbols?

At Avebury, the stars of Crux would have outlined and defined the uterine or vulvic shape of Silbury Hill, before phallic alpha and beta Centauri symbolically inseminated it each winter night along the brilliant path of the Milky Way. All the stars stretched across the southern horizon—in this case over the smooth arc of Waden Hill—before setting into the area that would later be Silbury Hill. Traces of local sexual symbolism may be preserved in the River Kennet below. Apparently deriving its name from the Saxon for vulva, 'Cunnit,' the River Kennet and its most powerful spring, the Swallowhead Spring, lay in the area close to the eventual location of the primal mound.[8] Waden Spring also rises at the southern end of Waden Hill between the voluptuous rolling hills. By drawing the attention of sky-watchers at Avebury, Silbury Hill would have highlighted not only the setting of the vesica-shaped constellation of Crux and the phallic Centauri, but also the location of the area's remarkable springs.

If we develop this line of thought further an interesting variety of fertility connotations emerge from these stars, including the 'penetration' of West Kennet long barrow from the east by alpha and beta Centauri, as part of a constellation eventually identified with a centaur. The stars passed low over Waden Hill and the location of the long barrow. Greek myth identified the Centaurs not just with wisdom but also with a voracious and wild sexuality. Figures 10, 23 and 26 help us to imagine alpha and beta Centauri as a phallic pair pursuing the vulva of Crux across the southern sky.

The monument-builders may have seen the stars that pointed to or marked the entranceway to the hidden southern or lower world regions as symbols of the uterus or womb. The stars were the heavenly symbols of Underworld sources of fertility: water, wealth and perhaps of fire. The southern stars equated with whatever power the Neolithic thought lay at the root of the *axis mundi,* in the depths of the Underworld. A local shaman, perhaps utilising the symbols of a prominent water or bear cult, may have undertaken highly ritualised journeys to secure the blessings of the Underworld aided by and at the times and seasons indicated by the stars. As the mandorla of the southern stars descended upon Silbury Hill in the autumn, the Neolithic people may even have perceived this as causing the life-giving springs to flow again.

Alternatively, it is possible that the Crux-Centaurus stars

represented an earlier, Mesolithic, hunter-gatherer age—a time seen by the Neolithic people as one of primordial wisdom and abundance, in which nature satisfied the needs of their ancestors without the effort later required of the farmer. Whether real or imagined, an idealised ethos of the hunter and of a lost Golden Age was likely to have prevailed at the time of the first settlements in Britain. These settlers may have seen the recent past as a time in which virtuous and wise ancestors could perform memorable feats of endurance and strength because of their greater harmony with nature. Such an ethos may even have provided a reason for an initial resistance of the trend to settlement and subsistence farming in some areas of late Mesolithic and Neolithic northern Europe. It was better to remain hunters, even though farming was reliable.

The Irish legends of Fionn mac Cumhail appear to have originated in a pastoral age with some similarity with the British Neolithic. These legends emphasise the hunt: describing men and their hounds ranging freely over open land as the preferred and ideal state of existence. Such ideals, which did not become the preserve of an aristocratic elite until much later, may have prevailed at the end of the primary hunter-gatherer culture. The pastoralists and farmers of the Neolithic may have identified the gradual disappearance of the Crux-Centaurus stars with the loss of all that was great about their heavily mythologised and ancestral past.

Following this third option, in which the Crux-Centaurus stars represented the good, previous, unenclosed and nomadic Mesolithic age, the newly agricultural people could have identified the stars with similar values of purity and virtue to those later attributed to them by Dante (who saw these virtues as being the preserve of the ancestors, specifically old Romans like Cato). If so, could the loss of the southern stars have reinforced a notion that a Golden Age was receding rapidly from their grasp: a time when cattle and horses roamed freely across open land, when the deer and bear were numerous, babies were born with ease and hunts were always successful? Or should interpretations remain with simpler and more primal symbols of fertility?

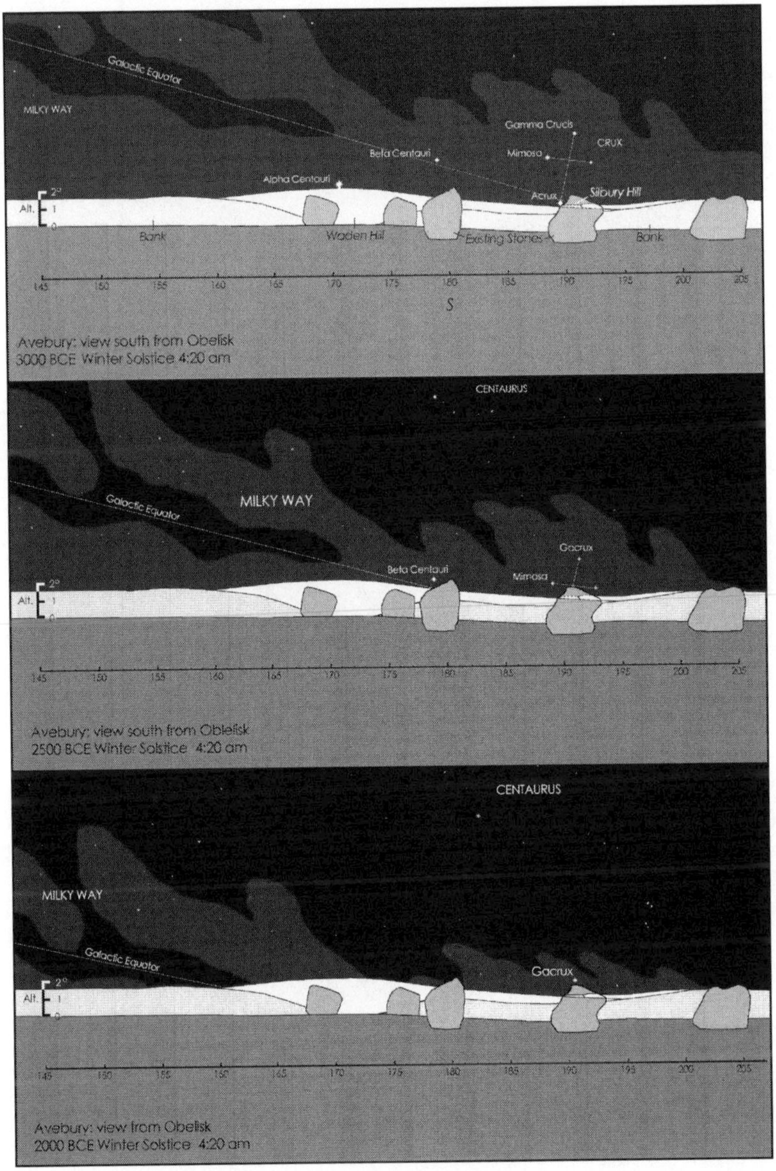

Figure 26. Views south from the Obelisk, midwinter, approx. 4:20 am, showing the progressive setting of the Southern Cross over the Silbury

site. The Milky Way (Galactic Equator) is rising in the east.

Upper section, *3000 BCE: as the Milky Way dropped in the west, alpha Centauri rose over Waden Hill, beta Centauri obtained culmination, and Acrux set into the atmosphere over the notch formed by Waden Hill and the horizon—the future location of the Silbury Stone and Silbury Hill. Alpha Centauri also set here.*

Middle section, *2500 BCE: as the southern portion of the Milky Way sank below the horizon and the upper three stars of Crux set over the location of Silbury Hill, only beta Centauri briefly remained to rise from Waden Hill and set over Silbury. Alpha Centauri has long vanished from sight.*

Lower section, *2000 BCE: as the upper stars of the Southern Cross were lost from sight over Silbury Hill, only Gacrux remained visible, rising from Waden Hill and setting over Silbury before setting over the Silbury Stone and the now complete Silbury Hill.*

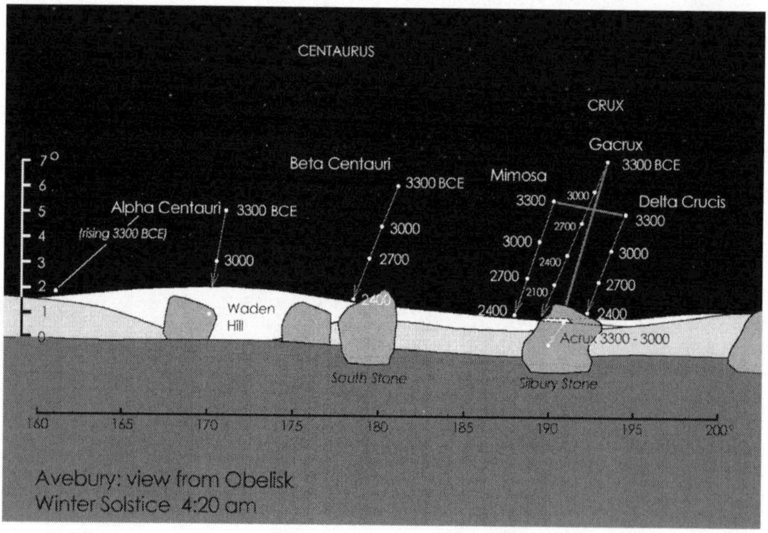

Figure 27. Composite figure showing the descent of the southern stars due to precession, 3300 BCE to 2100 BCE, as seen from the Obelisk of Avebury henge. The stars of Crux appeared to set into Silbury Hill, (or become lost in the extinction angle above it) at times when alpha and beta Centauri were rising on crucial alignments. Stone markers could

have allowed estimation of the time when a star would be permanently lost from view. As early as 2500 BCE, for example, it may already have become clear that the central stars of Crux would be lost within one hundred years, disappearing into the location of Silbury Hill.

The D Feature: Astronomical Precision

The D feature linear setting in the centre of the Southern Inner Circle.

View along the length of the D feature stone row to the southern entrance and Waden Hill.

Figure 28. The stones that mark the southern stars: The two horizontal lines show the extinction angle for the stars of the Crux Centaurus group. The two vertical lines show the narrow line of sight offered by the linear arrangement of stones, the D feature, at an azimuth of166° from the Cove—shown in Figure 18. As Waden Hill virtually eliminated the extinction angle, and additional stones (and possibly posts) framed the line of sight, the alignment was very precise. Although alpha Centauri also rose on this alignment around 3000 BCE, the diagram shows the passage taken by beta Centauri, beta Crucis and delta Crucis through the first half of the millennium, particularly the passage around 2720 BCE—suggesting a date of construction. The builders may have aligned an almost parallel row of the D feature on an azimuth of 164° from the Cove—shown in Figure 25—to these events circa 2800 BCE. Note: the southern stars were precessing over Waden Hill much faster than the standard 1° in 72 years. At the end of the third millennium, after thousands of years of visibility, gamma Crucis would have been the last of the Crux Centaurus stars to rise on this alignment.

In the western half of the Southern Inner Circle is a stone row known as the D feature or D façade: so-called both because of its pattern upon the ground and because it appears to have fronted the area around the Obelisk. This stone row is about one hundred feet long and its alignment of 166° (differing by about 6° from the main orientation of the site) passes through other megaliths including the Cove and the immense southern entrance stone known as the Devil's Chair.[9] I have already noted a 166° alignment from the Obelisk over a (now removed) stone of the Southern Inner Circle, the remains of the Ring Stone and the posthole beside the southern entrance, to the Waden Hill horizon.[10]

The stones of the row that survive are smaller than the stones of the circles, averaging about four feet in height, and have an unusual reddish colour suggesting they were selected from a particular origin, perhaps for a specific purpose. The stone row does not seem to fit well into the overall conception of the predominantly circular monument; it seems to have a more functional purpose. Indeed, archaeologists believe it may well be older than the stone circles, forming one of the original stone settings and acting as a boundary or façade to the activities that went on around the Obelisk. It is fortunate the stone row survives; it provides a level of astronomical detail that has been lost elsewhere due to the deliberate destruction and removal of the stones.

Figure 25 shows the builders aligned the nine stones of the row to the Cove and to the partner of the Ring Stone and the Devil's Chair Stone in the centre of the southern entrance. These megalithic settings are likely to be among the primary features of the monument; indeed, *the 166° alignment through the D feature appears to include as many as a dozen of the eighteen standing stones suspected of being the first permanent stones on the site.* The stone row is therefore a prominent and central feature of the henge, well worth investigating.

It turns out that the 166° alignment would have been extremely useful for observing the rising of alpha Centauri, beta Centauri and all the stars of Crux: alpha, beta, gamma and delta Crucis, during the course of their descent below the southern horizon during the fourth and third millennia BCE. It appears the builders aligned the D feature in a manner that was unusually precise about where the observers should stand and from what height they should observe.[11]

The D feature linear alignment allowed an observer positioned at the northern end of the row to look along the tops of the stones (assuming they have not been severely eroded or restored inaccurately) to observe the horizon at an elevation of two degrees. On a clear night, this would have been above the extinction angle for the stars of the Crux-Centaurus group. Figure 29 draws a lower and an upper horizontal line showing the extinction angle of the stars in question. The lower line shows the point below which no star in the group would have been visible, even alpha Centauri; the upper line shows the point where delta Crucis would have appeared—although on a very clear night its extinction angle may have been lower. The figure thus shows a range of dates in which beta Centauri, beta Crucis and possibly delta Crucis would have been visible over Waden Hill along the line of sight offered by the stone row. Gamma Crucis, the upper star of the Southern Cross—not shown here—would have been visible above them.

This line of sight offers considerable precision. The section of the horizon it defines is framed by the South Stone of the southern inner circle and the west stone of the southern entrance, the massive Devil's Chair. The best date that the Crux-Centaurus stars would have been visible in this small window is toward the end of the 28th century BCE. After this date, the stars would have risen progressively higher up Waden Hill, until by 2500 BCE they were rising out of its western flank. Observers would have seen Gamma Crucis rising on this line of sight about the year 2080 BCE—note the use of decades. Much earlier, observers would have seen alpha Centauri rising on this alignment until about 2930 BCE and alpha Crucis, the lowest star of the Southern Cross, until around 3600 BCE. This is obviously very early indeed, perhaps too early for any permanent markers apart from timber posts; although an almost parallel stone row at 164° from the Cove through other stones of the D feature and the eastern southern entrance stone could have been aligned to these events at this date.

As a demonstration of the detail, in 2720 BCE beta Centauri would have reappeared just before dawn over Waden Hill on the line of sight provided by the D feature. This would have occurred after a summer of invisibility, at the time of year that corresponds to early November. Beta and delta Crucis would have appeared about a week earlier—around the time later associated with the seasonal Celtic festival of Samhain. These stars would then have risen earlier and higher each night until they dominated the southern horizon; even alpha Centauri would have appeared at about 175° from out of the western flank of Waden Hill about a month later in 2720 BCE. By mid to late April, beta Centauri would have risen for the final time on the line of sight just after sunset; the star and its companions would have set by midnight. During the month of May they would have vanished from the sky altogether. The beginning of the month is the time of the Celtic festival of Beltane. Gamma Crucis, the last star visible of the Crux-Centaurus group, due to precession, would have replicated this process in the last quarter of the third millennium: just as alpha Centauri had done at the beginning of the third millennium and alpha Crucis had done in the mid-fourth millennium BCE.

It should be clear from the above that the observations provided by the D feature make it possible to ascribe precise values to years. They also make full use of an extremely rapid precessional movement of stars against the calendar, due to the slope (plus any features there may once have been) of the southern horizon. As shown in Figures 26-28, in the space of less than five-hundred years the Crux-Centaurus stars shifted 18° over Waden Hill. This was two to three times the normal rate of precession; almost one degree in twenty-five years! The Avebury sky-watchers, as part of a lineage of observers who would have passed the precious sky-lore down from generation to generation, could scarcely have missed such a phenomenon and, apparently, they aimed the stone row at its epicentre. The shape of Waden Hill gave a virtually unique means of marking the passage of the brightest and most precessionally affected stars in the sky over the henge's most intensive period of use.

We do not know when the D feature was built, but if its purpose was to watch these winter stars then an early date for its construction is strongly suggested by the above. Gillings and Pollard report that the excavators found prehistoric stake-holes at either end of the stone row. They suggest that the two posts and the stone row could have been in place *before* the Obelisk and the stone circles: the linear setting, they write, "might be regarded as an independent stone row pre-dating the southern inner circle, or a façade fronting the Obelisk."[12] A date of construction in the first quarter of the third millennium BCE would be well within this remit: either before the last appearance of alpha Centauri circa 2930 BCE (a time when the primary henge was likely to have been in place); or, more likely, at a time when the middle stars of the Southern Cross and beta Centauri were rising on this alignment, up to 2700 BCE.

Whatever their exact date, the stones of the D feature, combined with posts, other stones (including the Cove), and the horizon of Waden Hill, were perfectly placed to observe the rising of the Crux-Centaurus group of stars from the mid-fourth through the third millennium BCE.[13]

The Changing Galaxy

Although we no longer have the grandeur of the Obelisk, we are extremely fortunate that the two southern entrance stones, most of the D feature, the Cove and a number of the great stones of the Southern Inner Circle, remain *in situ* at Avebury.[14] My observations have led me to conclude that these stone settings, upon the main axis of the monument, and also among the largest and the earliest stones, were some of the most astronomically critical. The situation elsewhere, especially in the north of the henge, is not so easy to reconstruct, although surviving segments of the Great Outer Circle, including the majestic Swindon Stone, provide some compensation.

A consideration of the whole midwinter night sky at Neolithic Avebury reveals that alpha Centauri, beta Centauri and the stars of Crux were highly important in the southern skies, while and Ursa Major and Cygnus enjoyed similar importance in the north. To the visually oriented monument-builders the passages of these stars defined the *axis mundi* and the Poles in the Upper- and the Underworld. Their importance demonstrates why the builders considered it was worth marking the loss of stars from the position they had held for so long in the south—their slipping from sight below the southern horizon—with such great effort and precision by the stones on the main alignment of Avebury henge and by so gigantic a mound as Silbury Hill.

At issue are the Poles, the *axis mundi* or 'world axis,' and what they meant to the Avebury monument-builders. To this primary axial alignment we must add the Milky Way and Zodiac. As remarked, we can draw a persuasive comparison between early Avebury and similarly 'neolithic' and predominantly shamanistic cultures where the *axis mundi* marks the centre of the world and the road between its many tiered realms. As Avebury became the world centre, its axial alignment and galactic encirclement may have defined the connection and the boundaries between those realms above and those below. The inner circles of the henge may have represented these worlds. In the shamanic traditions of the northern hemisphere, the 'axle' of the heavens ran from the hidden pole, located in the Underworld and the south, through the world centre, to the Northern Pole in the Upperworld. As mentioned, there may have been many worlds, one on top of another. The *axis mundi* provided the road or star-path to the Otherworlds of the spirits, the deceased and the ancestors.

The Egyptian, Maya, Inca and other ancient star-watching cultures saw the Milky Way as a road of the dead, a road of souls, as well as the Tree of Life. Upon death, Maya kings 'entered the road' of the Milky Way in anticipation of rebirth. The two Paddler Gods, Jaguar and Stingray, guided the canoe of souls along the river of the Milky Way. The points where the galaxy crossed the ecliptic were of especial importance, they were the 'portals' to the Otherworlds. Passages in their pyramids aligned to the North Celestial Pole carried the *ka* or *ba*, the 'soul' of the early Egyptian pharaoh to immortality. The Milky Way provided the path through the sky in the same way as the Nile was the path through the Earth. For the Inca and other Andean peoples in the southern hemisphere, the Southern Cross marked a key cosmological location in the great river of the Milky Way. Known as the *chacana*, it represented the Tree of Life and provided the entranceway to the other levels of existence.[15]

In summary, it seems clear that their uniquely privileged view of the Milky Way in the first part of the third millennium BCE would have given the monument-builders a distinctive means through which they could mark out and define their world. As the Milky Way formed a complete circle around the horizon, it defined their sacred centre, their location upon the cosmic axes, and the symbolic boundaries of their relatively newly settled world. Each astronomical element: the Milky Way, the east-west crossroads of the ecliptic and the galaxy, the north-south axis, and ultimately the brilliant stars of Crux and Centaurus, pointing to the root of the *axis mundi*, must have cut large figures in their mythic, astral and presumably polytheistic cosmology. It is these stars that seem to have been emphasised above all others from Windmill Hill and Avebury (and, as will be shown, from the Sanctuary) in the late fourth and third millennia BCE.

As said, an understanding of the meaning of the Crux-Centaurus group of stars to the Neolithic people of Northern Europe will never be possible. But if we put the scant remnants of an ancient British mythology and documented shamanic practice alongside a careful effort to recreate the skies as a whole at this time, a suggestive range of possible symbolic meanings begins to appear. In general, the stars' associations were likely to have encompassed the ancestors, death and the underworld, as well as the divine forces that animate the cycles of life and fertility. The stars mapped out a complex pluralistic world, providing the characters and the backdrop for a divine but natural drama; indeed, as fire, storm, lightning and thunder, they *were* the natural drama. From a shamanistic point of view the stars provide the map of the divine world and represent its many powerful actors and guardians—some human, some animal, some a mixture of both. The stars chart the journey into the animating forces of the cosmos. It is here, through the portal at the centre of the worlds, that contact can be made with the primordial energies of light and fire, the causes of birth, death and healing, and knowledge won of great cycles—some always hidden—of rebirth and return. It may not be possible to change these cycles, but it is the task of the shaman to understand and work with them. With the right spiritual observances in the right places at the right times, the Neolithic people could gain their blessing.

It is now necessary to take a closer look at Silbury Hill, the

Sanctuary, the Avenues and other monuments in Chapters 6, 7 and 8, before returning to a further interpretation of Avebury in Chapter 9.

6

Silbury Hill

No history gives any account of this hill; the tradition only is, that King Sil or Zel, as the countrey folke pronounce, was buried here on horseback, and that the hill was raysed while a posset of milke was seething.

John Aubrey[1]

Silbury Hill from the northwest.

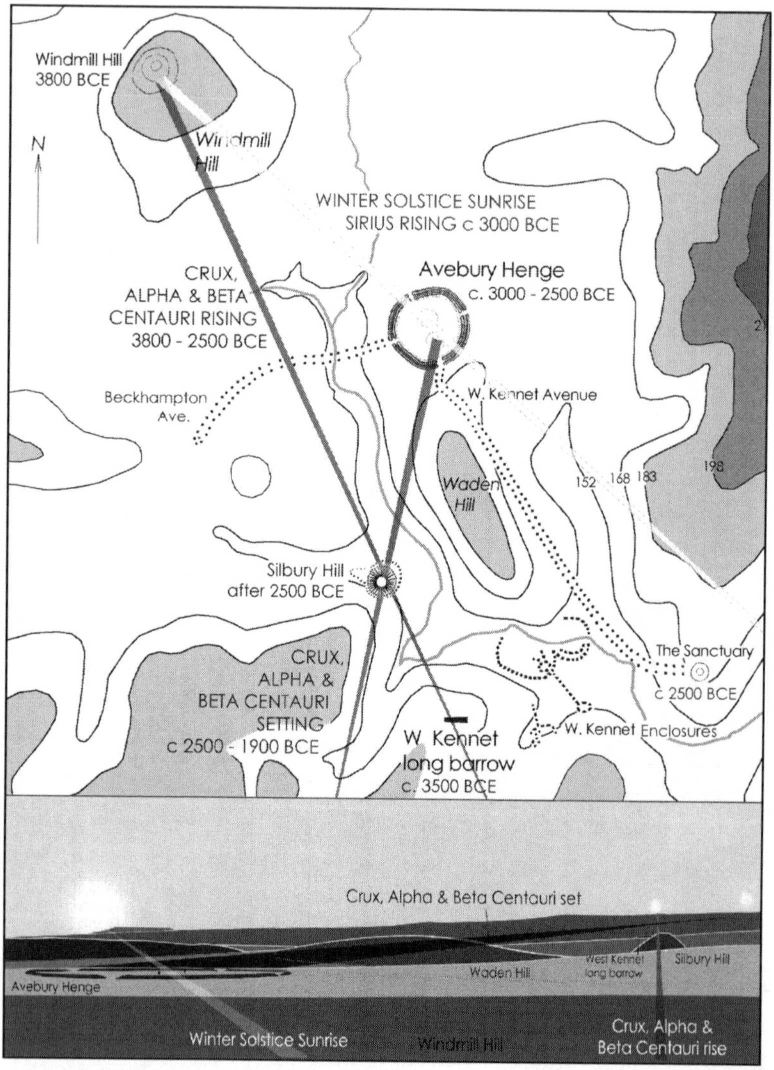

Figure 29. The alignment from Windmill Hill over West Kennet long barrow to the rising of the Crux-Centaurus stars in the fourth millennium BCE intersected the alignment from Avebury henge to the setting of those stars in the third millennium BCE over the location of Silbury Hill.

Mound of the Ancestors

Recent archaeological research has shown that the Late Neolithic people began to build Silbury Hill from about 2450 BCE, over a thousand years after an Early Neolithic tribe built the causewayed enclosure on Windmill Hill.[2] Since this is a very long space of time, it is hard to evaluate the relationship between these two eras, their people and their key monuments. Yet we may assume that the Late Neolithic and Early Bronze Age inhabitants of the Avebury area would have thought of the Windmill Hill people as their ancestors, possibly as heroic figures whose feats were to be admired, venerated and, when possible, imitated. The ditches and banks of Avebury henge repeat the elements found at Windmill Hill, as did those of the Longstones Enclosure, described in the next section. And while the Sanctuary and the West Kennet palisade enclosures echo Avebury's stone architecture in wood, the henge's circles and avenues of sarsens themselves refer to Mesolithic timber enclosures. In other words, these third millennium monument-builders were making constant references to the past. Evidently, it felt right to the Avebury builders to acknowledge and position themselves favourably toward their ancestors. Indeed, it is likely that they built the way they did because their past sanctioned these practices; in return, their monuments sanctioned and honoured the past.

In one sense, Avebury is a geometrically perfect Windmill Hill; its segmented enclosure is more precise. Certainly, its main alignment is to the same southern stars formerly observed on the axis between Windmill Hill and West Kennet long barrow. What may have been the earliest features on the Avebury site—the Cove and the Obelisk, both aligned to the rising point of the southern stars at the base of Waden Hill—apparently remained the most hallowed. Subsequent building reinforced their *a priori* position, the later stone circles serving to enhance the original monumental focus. Further alignments incorporated into the body of the henge respectfully maintained this inaugural emphasis on the southern stars, while enhancing the perennial alignments to the Sun and Moon (as well as adding alignments to Cygnus and Capella, described shortly).

Life for the Neolithic people would have been a constant process of negotiation, reconciling mixed motivations and diverse symbolic associations. Cross-cultural comparisons suggest this society was conservative, ritualistic, formal and 'implicit:' shared values were not made explicit but tacitly understood within a complex context of belief that involved the surrounding natural world and powerful, other-than-human, beings. Strong moral codes, perceived as sanctioned by the divine or cosmic order, would have governed behaviour. Any individual initiative would have required legitimation from the shared and inherent belief system. New projects would have had to accord with a seasonal round of ritual observances and ceremonies that sought favour with divine beings, with the Otherworld and with animal and plant powers. Thus proposals for a new monument would surely have required a great reason—such as a message from the spirit world—to be accepted and built.

What, then, could have motivated the major new departure that was Silbury Hill? This huge conical hill, begun in a location originally out of sight of Avebury henge, placed beside the sacred springs, was entirely new in its conception. Nothing quite like it had been attempted before. The great mound of white chalk and clay, about 130 feet high with a base of about 550 feet and a flat top of about 100 feet, would be the tallest man-made prehistoric mound in Europe. Its top may later have been levelled for Saxon or medieval defensive purposes, suggesting an original summit of perhaps 150 feet.

Work began on Silbury Hill some time after 2500 BCE, probably closer to 2400 BCE. It seems the primary mound only grew slowly as the builders laid successive layers of chalk, clay and turf onto it—some carried from far away.[3] But within a few generations, perhaps a few centuries, its builders took their artificial mound to ambitious heights.[4] As shown in Figure 49, the phase known as Silbury II greatly increased the size of the initial mound. A few generations or even a few hundred years of work now passed before a new generation of builders decided there was a need to increase the size and height of their monument, with a third and final phase of construction. Perhaps they had realised that if they made it tall enough, the white mound could be seen from Avebury henge.

The builders planned their arduous work very carefully, using a complex series of retaining walls and multiple tiers to ensure the mound's long-term stability. They had not attempted anything like this before, yet it definitely referred to the past. Unlike many Neolithic sites, it was not set upon a skyline. It lay between gently swelling hills. It was somewhat like a long barrow, yet its circular shape took a simpler more primal form. Those who encountered it or worked upon it would have needed to look no further for a comparable symbol of fertility than to a swollen breast or pregnant belly. The chalk mound with its winter moat would have found congruency of meaning with those symbols that evoked the primal and fertile power of the feminine. Were these Late Neolithic people consciously evoking the divine feminine? Were they directed to build Silbury Hill by dreams or other intimations that this was what the ancestors or the great powers wanted them to build? We will never know. But one thing is clear: in both its form and location, the Silbury builders were connecting their sacred mound with stars that had been venerated by their ancestors.

World Mountain

There is a very striking correspondence between the location and shape of Silbury Hill and the view from Avebury of the setting place of the three upper stars of the Southern Cross. These stars were making their slow precessional descent at precisely the time of the enormous mound's construction, the latter half of the third millennium BCE. Chapters 4 and 5 have described how the Crux-Centaurus stars provide a crucial and hitherto missing link between Avebury and Silbury Hill. From Avebury, most of these stars rose on the main axis of the henge every winter, passed south over Waden Hill then set into the future location of Silbury Hill. Given their axial significance to the hidden Southern Pole, the Avebury sky-watchers plausibly saw these stars as marking the southern root of the World Tree, the axis of the Earth and of the heavens. Did they intend Silbury Hill to represent the regenerative powers that lay in the Underworld, identifying the powers hidden below the horizon—at the place of vital springs—with the divine feminine? Was there a direct symbolic association between the great earthen mound and the sky vulva or *yoni* formed by the stars of Crux?

Situated in the setting place of the ancestral stars, the great multi-layered mound—with three main phases within, but as many as seven in its final construction—seems to be a totemic and multi-tiered World Mountain, defining the entranceway both to the Upperworld and the Underworld. The builders replicated the location and shape of the final precessional descent of the upper stars of the Southern Cross on the ground by the location and the shape of Silbury Hill when seen from the most phallic stone of Avebury. Because these southern stars—especially alpha Centauri and the vesica-shaped constellation of Crux—had been revered by the Windmill Hill people of the previous millennium who had built the West Kennet long barrow, the mound was also apparently an enigmatic reference to the ancestral past.

The builders also positioned Silbury Hill so that from the summit of Windmill Hill (at that time still in use) the now ancient West Kennet long barrow was visible just beyond it. In fact, the long barrow appears to be issuing from and to the east of the top tier of Silbury. The Crux-Centaurus stars had risen over this barrow at the time when their Mesolithic and early Neolithic ancestors were on Windmill Hill. As shown in Figures 29 and 49, Silbury Hill may therefore refer to both the rising *and* the setting of ancestral stars; the stars that had once rose over the long barrow now set into a mound. The long process of infilling and finally sealing West Kennet long barrow may have coincided with the slow descent and disappearance of the stars. Did the similarly long process of raising Silbury Hill mean that the great mound was intended to replace both the long barrow and the southern stars as a symbolic entranceway to the Lowerworlds, the regenerative 'cave' of the Bear Mother? Many excavations have never found any deposits within Silbury Hill. The almost complete lack of artefacts suggests it was not a monument to either the dead or the living, but to something outside of both time and the human.

As shown in Figure 40, and described in the next chapter, when viewed from the Sanctuary, Silbury Hill also lay on the alignment to the setting stars of Gemini, Taurus and the galactic equator during the last half of the third millennium BCE. The Sanctuary-Silbury alignment would now have marked one of two crucial fixed points in space, indicating the intersection of the plane of the solar system and that of the galaxy. Finally, as shown in Figure 42, Silbury Hill was positioned between the Kennet Avenue and the Western Avenue in a location strikingly similar to that between the horns of the constellation Taurus. It could therefore have been seen as an earthy embodiment of the Gemini crossing-point itself, with all the associations of fertility and healing that this star region possessed for ancient peoples.

King Sil & Wayland's Smithy

Returning to the symbolism of King Sil and his horse mentioned in Chapter 4, let us briefly consider the Neolithic long barrow of Wayland's Smithy, located on the Ridgeway a day's walk to the northeast of Avebury. The Saxon legend attached to the place tells how an otherworldly smith-god, Wayland, would shoe any horse left there overnight with proper payment. Wayland's Smithy lies close to the White Horse at Uffington. This huge and highly stylised equine figure, made from exposing the underlying chalk of the hillside, is now thought be at least three thousand years old, originating in the Bronze Age. The great age of the White Horse suggests the Wayland legend is much earlier than its apparently Saxon source. John North has shown that the builders of this long barrow aligned its megalithic chamber to the winter rising of alpha and beta Crucis, circa 3700 BCE; he reminds us that astronomers once considered these stars, now part of the Southern Cross, as part of the massive constellation of Centaurus.[5] According to ancient Greek and other Mediterranean peoples, alpha and beta Centauri formed the front feet of the Centaur, while Crux formed the hind feet. In ancient Babylon, Centaurus may have been identified with a bison-headed man, a celestial image that is extremely old. In ancient Arabia, the hindquarters of Centaurus were those of a bear.[6] If the identification of a part-animal, part-human being with these stars derives from the Neolithic or Mesolithic eras, these small remnants of local myth and legend may help reveal the manner in which these ancient sites were perceived.

Like the Wayland legend, the enigmatic story of King Sil centers on the horse. This king, buried on horseback, both man and horse in some accounts, of solid gold, is remembered as fused with his horse in a manner akin to the half-man, half-horse character of the centaur. In the ancient Indo-European traditions shared by the monument-builders, the 'power animal,' whether elk, reindeer, bear or horse, accompanied the shaman on his or her journey to the Otherworld. Shamanic lore repeatedly says the shaman 'becomes the horse;' this animal was often seen as the ideal vehicle for passage between the worlds. The half-human half-animal shaman—equine, cervine, lupine or ursine—could travel between the worlds. Some commentators think that because of its virility the stallion eventually became the greatest Indo-European totem of them all, closely linked with fertility, sacrificial and funerary rites.[7] In Britain, the horse was later central to Celtic cults of sovereignty, where the king was identified with a stallion and the goddess of the land with a mare. The Celts also saw the horse as a vehicle for passage between the worlds; for them it often carried the soul into the beyond. And many Northern European traditions describe horses drawing the gold disc or the chariot of the Sun across the sky. This association of horse and Sun, of shaman and king, brings the symbolism of the Silbury myth back full circle.

A half-man, half-animal character similar to that of the centaur and the Bison-man is also found in the myths of the Bear son. This theriomorphic being, like his mother never directly named but sometimes known as the 'Golden King,' makes the journey along the *axis mundi* between the worlds. In the third millennium BCE, the stars of Ursa Major, the Great Bear, rotated around the Northern Pole as the Crux-Centaurus stars rotated around the southern horizon and Cygnus dived into the Underworld of the north. Early shamanic traditions preferred the bear to the horse as the vehicle of passage between the many tiers of the cosmos, probably because the bear had cave connections, climbed trees and had simply been around much longer than the horse.

If the Neolithic people of Southern Britain associated the Crux-Centaurus stars with fertility and renewal the legend of golden King Sil may preserve a specific association with these stars. Did the people of Avebury associate the Crux-Centaurus stars with the horse/centaur or bear, with attendant connections to shamanic rites of renewal and Otherworldly journeying upon the world axis, especially to a southern Underworld? It seems likely that their practices associated with the stars, especially those prominent at midwinter, were allied with burial cults of mythologised ancestors, the renewal of sacred springs and with deep sources of uterine fertility and regeneration.

Mound of the Stars

As the monument-builders closed West Kennet long barrow and raised Silbury Hill, they may have been paying tribute to the spirits of those particular stars—the stars watched by the first ancestors. For an age that relied so heavily upon precedent and legitimated itself through doing so, the hill may have symbolically incorporated a wish for the ancestors and the primal order they represented to return. If the Neolithic farmers felt the age of their hunter-gatherer ancestors was slipping away and with it their original communion with nature, there may have been a mythic sense in which the people who laboured on the hill were saying to their ancestors: "Here, we give back to you what you have given to us. This mound will hold your stars for an age, if needs be, until your time comes round again. The place where you entered the Underworld will give birth to you. Your time will be here again across the land."

The carefully built up multiple layers of Silbury Hill suggest the layers of the cosmos once perceived by the Neolithic people to lie above and below the axial centre of Avebury. The nearby springs, the River Kennet and the Winterbourne stream, flowed and often flooded around the base of the mound in the late winter months. By referring back to the time of ancestors—for whom the ancient Crux-Centaurus stars were so significant—the mound builders were declaring that here was a vital realm whose important powers ought to be acknowledged and propitiated. But until additional evidence, say of milk or blood offerings, or another fragment of the ancient narrative emerges to substantiate that declaration—something more definitive than the legend of golden King Sil, or later hints of Celtic goddesses beside spring and mound—Silbury's precise function will remain unknown.[8]

The astronomy indicates that the builders of Silbury Hill may have been struggling with a growing sense of decline and loss; that they were anticipating the ending of the order of the age as their southern stars sank from view. They may even have seen themselves as completing the long cycle during which their ancestors had constructed the monuments at Avebury. As the inheritors of the past, were they offering a final act of reverence to the ancestral stars as they finally departed into the Underworld by incorporating them into the ever-rising layers of their white chalk mound? Silbury Hill may have been intended to simultaneously 'open' an entranceway for the ancestral stars to enter the earth, and also to maintain a symbolic connection with those now hidden forces connected with the Southern Pole.

If Avebury henge was a mirror of the cosmos, specifically the Milky Way, and if Silbury Hill marked one particular moment in the precessional relationship between the Milky Way and (the ecliptic of) the Sun, then the purpose of Silbury may have been an attempt to fix that relationship once and for all upon the Earth. Did the builders intend Silbury Hill—as the place where the southern stars were setting—to end the decline in the skies, perhaps even initiate the return of these mythically significant stars?

One answer to the question why the builders made Silbury Hill so large and permanent may be that just as their chief ancestral stars had set into it, its builders thought those stars would one day reappear above it—be reborn from it. It was worth sweating so much blood for the great mound, week after week, year after year, digging and hauling, carrying water and chalk blocks, constructing something bigger than anything ever seen because it contained the stars of the ancestral age. This act is comparable, of course, to what was happening at the time in Egypt. Perhaps the builders even intended Silbury Hill to hold or preserve a connection with the mystery the southern stars represented over a complete 'Great Year,' a vast cycle of star-ages, until the far distant time arrived when those stars would return and the golden age of the ancestors would be restored.[9]

If this, or something like it, were the case it would have been a long wait for the mound-builders. Due to precession, they would not have seen the stars of the Southern Cross and alpha and beta Centauri over Silbury Hill for more than fifteen thousand years. Perhaps the permanence of the mound was an implicit acknowledgement of this fact. Perhaps the builders knew that Silbury simply marked the end of their moment, the end of their age in the Great Year of Precession.

The Silbury legend may preserve a reference to Avebury's close association with the Milky Way. Its builders raised the hill, records Aubrey, "while a posset (a pan) of milke was seething." Everywhere around the world, the galaxy is associated with milk. In Greek and Roman mythology, for example, the Milky Way was formed by milk spurting from the breast of the mother goddess, Hera. The springs coming from the earth beside the originally white chalk mound may have been seen as a source of fertility and healing, the vesica in the sky as a quintessence of the energies of the Milky Way. The suggestive legend of golden King Sil seems to offer us a tantalizing fragment of the potent energy originally associated with Silbury Hill, through Avebury's cult of the *axis mundi*, particularly the southern stars.

The great conical mound may well have been a feminine symbol, or a World Mountain, but only stellar alignments explain the position, shape and development of Silbury Hill. The triangle of the upper three stars of Crux would have set each winter night over the mound, finally becoming lost from view to those standing beside the Obelisk in Avebury after 2400 BCE. These stars were vanishing in the location of Silbury at precisely the time the builders were raising the mound. The fourth star completing the vesica of Crux had vanished over four centuries before. Moreover, the three stars and the mound matched each other in shape and scale when viewed from Avebury. The triangle of stars perfectly fitted the outline formed by the mound of Silbury, especially if its builders rounded the summit. The hidden fourth star completed the vesica below the Earth. The ascent of the mound paralleled and coincided with the builders' realisation of the slow descent of the stars. As the stars sank into the lower worlds, so the mound-builders raised the hill to meet and contain them.

7

The Longstones Cove & Other Enclosures

When the Pleiades, daughters of Atlas, are rising, begin your harvest, your ploughing when they are going to set. Forty nights and days they are hidden, when they appear again as the year moves round, first you sharpen your sickle.

Hesiod[1]

Adam, Eve & the Beckhampton Avenue

The Longstones. 'Adam,' in the foreground, formed part of a four-stone Cove. 'Eve,' in the background, was part of the Western or Beckhampton Avenue.

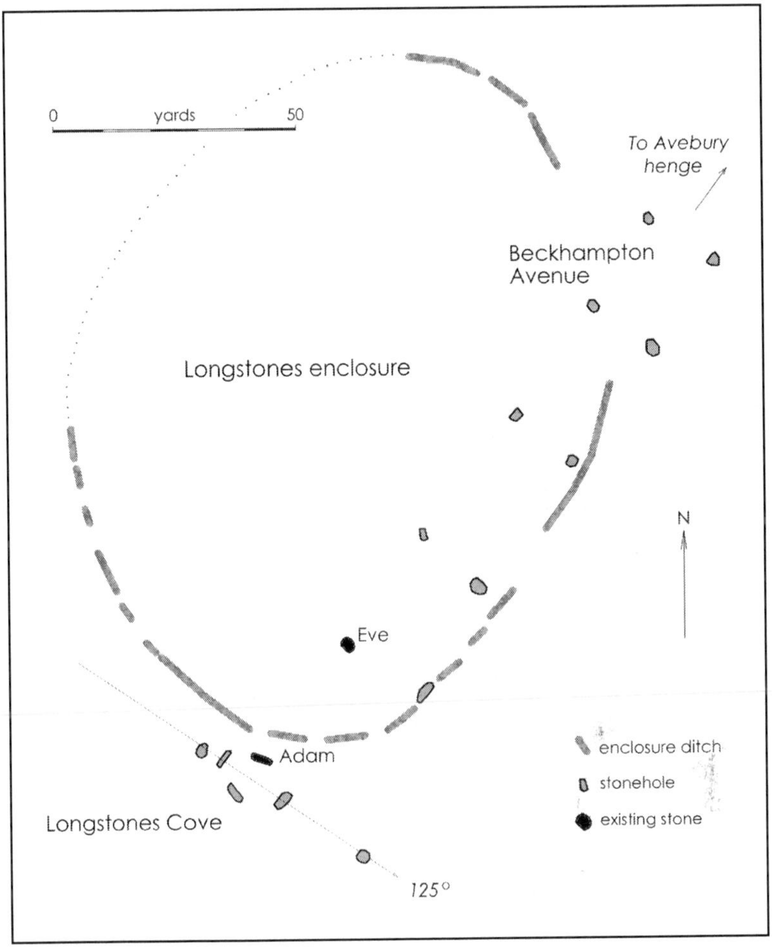

Figure 30. Beckhampton Avenue terminated at Longstones Cove. Both were built between 2500 and 2200 BCE, on the site of an earlier circa 2700 BCE enclosure. All that remains are the 'Adam and Eve' stones.

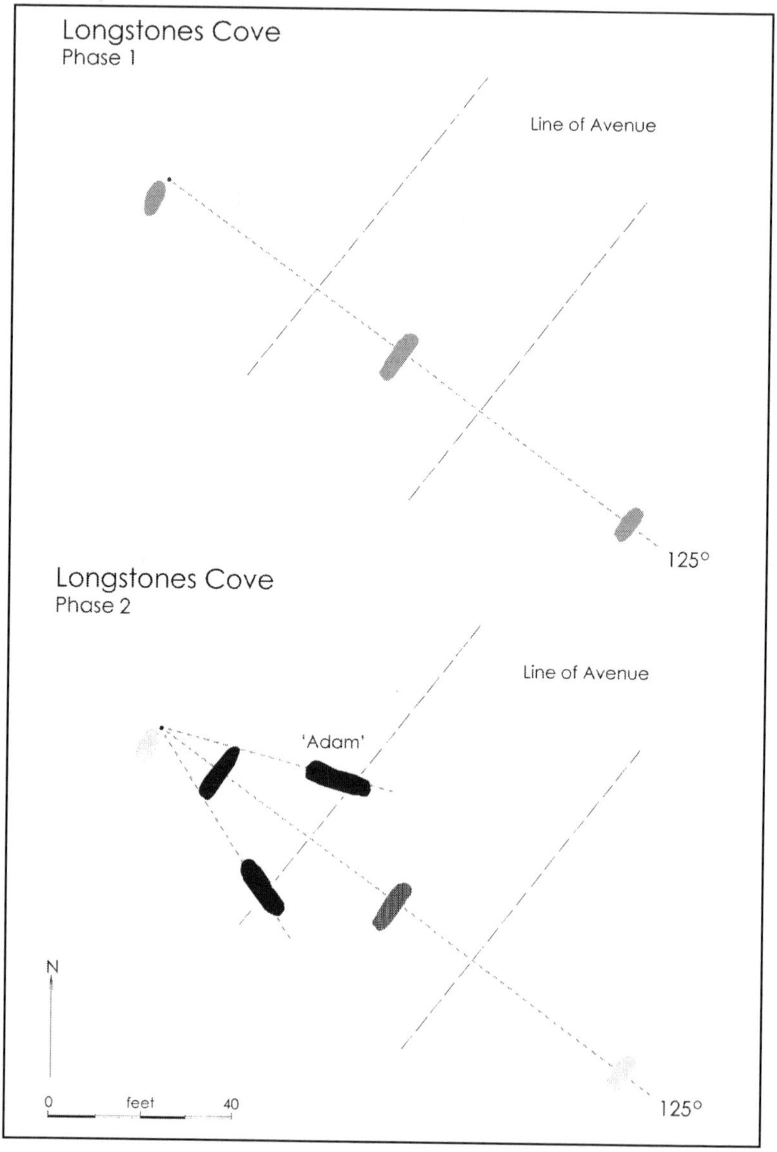

Figure 31. The Longstones Cove (after Gillings 2008). Phase 1. Three large stones lay across the end of the Western Avenue. Phase 2. Remove the two outliers and introduce three new stones to form a cove that incorporates the central stone and the original axis of the first stone row. The internal geometry emphasises a base angle of 36°.

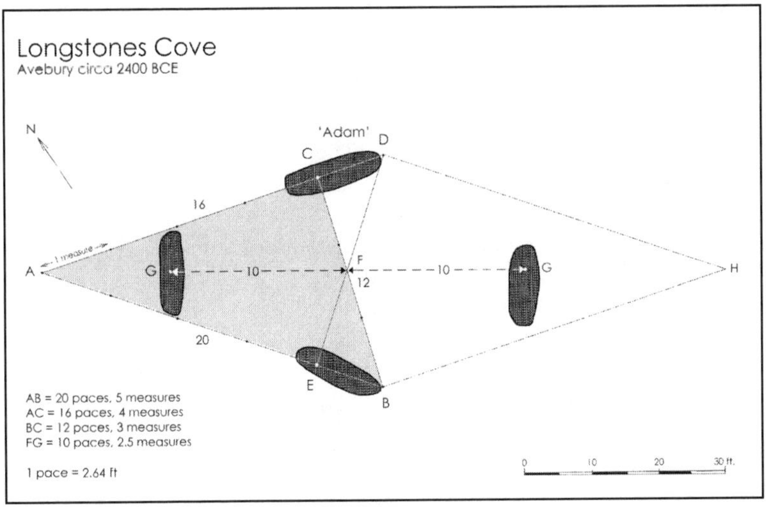

Figure 32. Lay out the original Longstones Cove as follows: with primary point A and axis determined, take 20 paces to point B. Find C at 12 paces from B and 16 paces from A. Lay out the 3-4-5 triangle with a cord evenly knotted at paces, a pole of two paces or a measure of four paces. To complete the figure, draw the second 3-4-5 right-angle triangle ADE and locate Adam and its partner on CD and EB. From centre F, take ten paces to locate the two remaining stones on the primary axis. The progression is either: paces, 20, 16, 12, 10, poles, 10, 8, 6, 5, or measures, 5, 4, 3, 2½. The pace of 2.64 feet suggests a regional variation of the megalithic yard of 2.72 feet. The excavations of the Cove show that the builders took considerable care to lay out its Pythagorean right-angled triangles.

When the antiquary William Stukeley visited Avebury in the 1720s, he described a second avenue of stones extending from the western entrance of the henge. He wrote that a great avenue passed through the 'Adam and Eve' stones or the Longstones, which formed a cove, and continued towards Beckhampton long barrow and possibly even further to Knoll Down. According to Stukeley, this avenue formed the tail of a 'dragon' or 'serpent' that wrapped around Avebury, its head lying at the end of the

West Kennet Avenue, at the Sanctuary. When little evidence for the second avenue or the cove emerged, Stukeley's ideas came under question, but recent excavations have vindicated the accuracy of many of his observations.

'Adam' has turned out to be one stone of a four-stone cove, now called the Longstones Cove, while 'Eve' is a stone from the recently found and almost certainly complete Western or Beckhampton Avenue that apparently terminated at the Cove. The evidence provided by a surprising number of buried stones, but mostly by empty stone sockets, showed that the pairs of stones in the Avenue overlaid a much older enclosure, an irregular oval circle, built hundreds of years earlier, possibly as early as 2800 BCE.[2] The oval circle of earth and stone, over a hundred yards across, known as the Longstones Enclosure, had a short life, possibly only decades; the archaeologists regarded it as a referral to the much earlier causewayed enclosure above on Windmill Hill. None the less, it proved the importance of the neglected western area of Avebury. The builders removed any remains of the enclosure when constructing the Western Avenue a few hundred years later in the third quarter of the third millennium BCE; yet the Avenue still seemed to refer to the former structure. Apart from commenting that there would have been about fifty paired sarsens along its entire length, the archaeologists could say little more about the Western Avenue without further excavation.[3]

As shown in Figure 31, the builders of the Longstones Cove removed two stones and incorporated one stone of a slightly earlier stone row set perpendicular to the end of the Western Avenue. These changes appear to have taken place as the monument-builders developed their ideas about what form the terminus to the Western Avenue should take. The huge stones and box-like shape of the Longstones Cove would have made a sharp contrast to the circles of the Sanctuary, the terminus of the Eastern or West Kennet Avenue.

The builders set up four massive stones to form the final Cove between 2500 and 2100 BCE. Adam, the single surviving stone, provides an indication of their size. Unfortunately, the dating cannot yet be more precise. The four stones, as shown in Figure 32, enclosed a well-defined space. The main axis of the Cove closely followed that of the earlier stone row, on an azimuth of 125°. Adam and its original partner—shown in a Stukeley drawing to have been 'diamond' shaped—radiated outward from a new northwest stone and opened to the retained southeast stone.

Prior to the construction of the Cove, the builders removed the two outliers of the slightly earlier three stone row, set NW-SE. The archaeologists thought the builders might have incorporated them into the new Cove or the Avenue. They left the central stone in place, which thus became the southeast stone of the Cove. The builders carefully located the three new stones so that they opened to and focused attention upon the southeast stone. The overall effect is that the Cove was oriented to the southeast. Obviously highly regarded, the southeast stone, now destroyed, was located on the centre of the line of the Western Avenue.

Armed with this evidence, there are two points to consider before entering into an astronomical discussion: First, the main axis of the Longstones Cove appears to depart from the orientation of the original stone row by about 3°. Second, as shown in Figure 31, there is a suggestion that the builders carefully placed the three new stones of the Cove to make a point of focus in the northwest, beside the location of one of the original outliers.

The main axis of the Longstones Cove at 125° meant it was oriented towards the summit of a low rise 400 yards away to the southeast known as Beckhampton or Folly Hill. The now vanished South Street long barrow, its 'business' end at an orientation of approximately 122°, lay on the eastern side of this rise. Folly Hill presented a symmetrical, slightly domed horizon like that of Waden Hill; its 2° elevation was the minimum needed to overcome the problems of extinction and refraction, making it perfect for viewing Sun, Moon, planets and stars. Noticeably, on the same 125° alignment from the Cove to the summit of Folly Hill, but below the line of sight, was Silbury Hill.

Although the original stone row at 122° had a 3° difference in alignment to that of the Cove, if a 'viewing point' beside the original northwest stone is adopted for both the original stone setting and the Cove their alignments come out the same, around 125°. Figure 31 shows that this viewing point made the stone row closer to perpendicular to the Avenue while providing a line of sight central to the other two stones. When the builders came to set up the three new stones of the Cove they appeared to focus carefully upon this point in their design.[4] The Cove, therefore, seems to have elaborated upon and finalised an orientation initially established by the simpler stone row, while utilising the central stone of the latter as a key feature. The evidence from the socket of the central or southeast stone suggested to the archaeologists that this stone was as large as the other stones, reaching over eleven feet in height, and had a special status as the central 'blocking' stone on the line of the Western Avenue. The drawing made by Stukeley in May 1724 seems to confirm this. Certainty will remain impossible, as although their sockets remain in the ground, apart from Adam and Eve, the stones themselves are long gone and with them, their exact height, shape and character.

The alignment of both the primary stone row and the later Cove suggest a broad window of astronomical observation around midwinter Sunrise (on a level horizon, azimuth 129°). As shown in the proposed reconstruction of Figure 33, an observer returning to the backsight A, over the course of midwinter would have seen the Sun enter the 110-140° window between Adam and its partner, slow down, cross the southeast stone at the centre of the alignment, stop, then reverse direction. This sky-watcher would have seen the exact winter solstice Sun rising between the central stone and Adam's partner, at an azimuth of approximately 133° allowing for elevation. The day-by-day progress of the Sun would have greatly facilitated observation, as it is easier to watch the Sun crossing a fixed point *before* and *after* the solstice than it is to catch the Sun at the exact point of its turn or return, when it is literally 'standing still.'

Figure 33 assumes the central southeast stone would have been visible over the nearer northwest stone. This is a big assumption, as the drawing by Stukeley and excavation of the northwest stone socket suggests this was an extremely large and heavy stone. Yet even if it was a large stone, observations still could have taken place. Sky-watchers could have stood *inside* the Cove—intuitively the right place to be—with their backs to the northwest stone to see the midwinter Sun rise beside the southeast stone over Folly Hill, and also over any markers upon the hill.[5]

The Longstones Cove may also have had a function in tracking the Moon, especially the southernmost rising Moon, the lunar major standstill. From the backsight, within or behind the Cove, the midsummer full Moons would have risen at their lowest, the major standstill, close to the stone opposite Adam. At the minor standstill of its 18.61-year cycle, the midsummer Moon would have risen between Adam and the central stone. The sky-watchers may have considered these low in the sky full moons as 'harvest moons.' Again, watching the rising Moon each night from the back of the Cove, as it progressed one way and then the other across the horizon framed by the stones, would have made it easier to track the lunar cycles than watching a fixed point marking an extreme.

Tracking Sirius

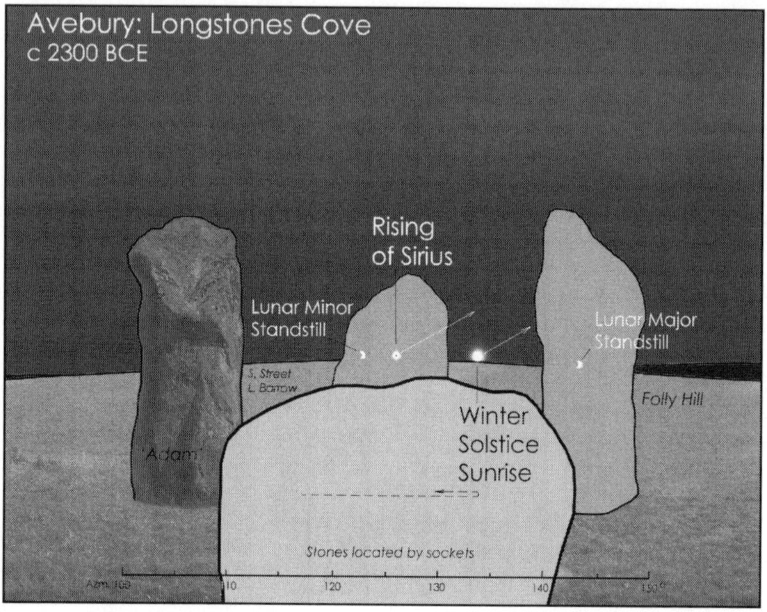

Figure 33. View along the 125° axis of the Longstones Cove to Folly Hill; altitude approx. 2°, from point 'A', late-third millennium BCE. Silbury Hill is below the line of sight on an alignment of 125°. The Sun rose at its lowest in midwinter, around 133°—slowing, stopping and returning through the stones of the Cove. The path of Sirius coincided with that of the midwinter Sun circa 3300 BCE. It then moved progressively eastwards until a thousand years later, the time of the Cove, it was rising at 125°. The heliacal rising (first reappearance before dawn) of Sirius took place over Folly Hill in late July/early August and the star continued to rise there until the New Year. Apart from 'Adam', the reconstruction is based on stone sockets and Stukeley's drawing.

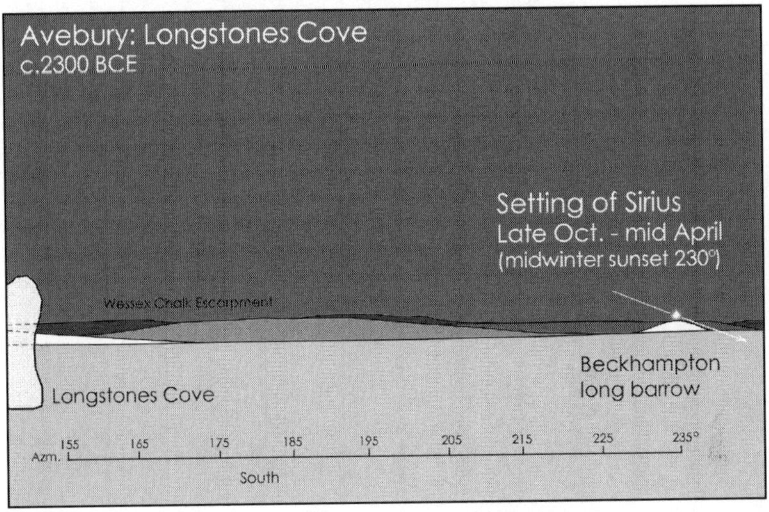

Figure 34. From the Longstones Cove the setting point of Sirius would have been visible over the Longstones or Beckhampton long barrow, built in the mid-fourth millennium BCE. The heliacal setting (last appearance) of Sirius took place over the long barrow in mid April at sunset; the star continued to set there until late October. The path of Sirius coincided with midwinter sunset at 230° about 3300 BCE.

When we examine the critical, central 125° azimuth of the Longstones Cove more closely, however, it is the annual reappearance of Sirius, the brightest star in the sky, which must have been the greatest astronomical attraction for later sky-watchers using this location.

In the latter part of the third millennium BCE, 2500-2200 BCE, Sirius was *last* visible each year rising at sunset on the 400 yard alignment between the Longstones Cove and Folly Hill (azimuth 125°, altitude 2°) shortly after the winter solstice. The star would then have appeared higher and higher in the sky each night after sunset. Perhaps more importantly, Sirius was *first* visible on this alignment, at its significant heliacal or pre-dawn rising, in late July or early August—the beginning of what

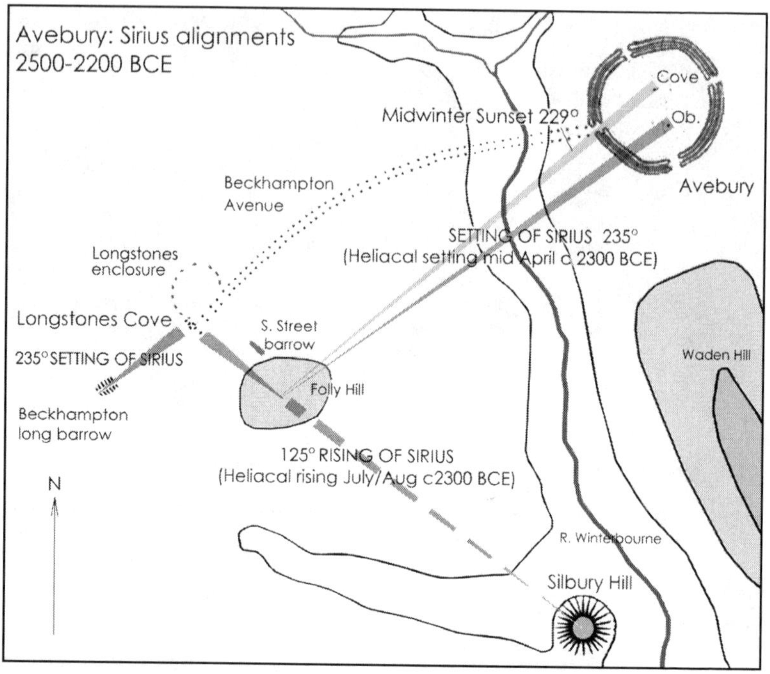

Figure 35. Longstones Cove appears oriented to the summit of Folly Hill along its main axis—an azimuth of 125° that continues below the line of sight to Silbury Hill. Sirius rose on this azimuth after 2300 BCE, from the time of the star's first reappearance in late July until after midwinter. When seen from the Longstones Cove the last appearance (heliacal setting) of Sirius took place over Beckhampton long barrow (and from the Obelisk at Avebury over Folly Hill) in mid April. At this latitude, the star would have vanished into the earth during the time of planting and growing, then reappeared (its heliacal rising) at the grain harvest.

was later called the 'Dog Days' at this latitude—when the star would have presided over high summer, abundant grazing and the beginning of the grain harvest. This star therefore may have functioned in the manner described by Hesiod circa 700 BCE, quoted at the beginning of the chapter; however, instead of the Pleiades it was Sirius that provided the indicator of when it was time to plough or to "sharpen your sickle." The star also rose in the southeast as Cygnus set in the northwest, another stellar event that appears to have greatly interested the sky-watchers at Avebury.

The sky-watchers at the Longstones Cove could have seen the star reappear over Folly Hill, after a period of about 120 days of invisibility, just before dawn at the time of year that later became known as the Celtic harvest festival of Lughnasadh. Sirius would then have risen earlier and earlier each night, until it rose for the final time on the line of sight at dusk about two weeks after the winter solstice, and so on throughout the annual cycle. Judging from the size of the socket of the central southeast stone—the remaining stone from the primary row—Sirius would have risen behind it in the period 2500-2200 BCE. Depending upon the shape of the stone, it would only have required a slight movement, right or left, by observers at the backsight or within the Cove, to observe this event. But it is also interesting to ask how aware these sky-watchers would have been that the star was rising on an alignment to the newly built Silbury Hill.

An observer at point A, to the northwest of the Longstones Cove, would have been standing close to the backsight of the first stone row, that is, its northwest stone. By using the summit of Folly Hill (and any markers there) as a foresight for Sirius, both stone settings would have allowed excellent observance of the star and the regular calendrical cycle it provided. Having proved its value over a few years or decades in establishing the alignment, it seems the builders may have removed the first stone row and replaced it with an arrangement that immensely increased the site's symbolic and ritual significance. They apparently utilised the key central stone in continuing their observation of the dying and rising star upon the southeastern horizon, adding further stones that framed the rising of the star over it. The stone selected to end the Western Avenue may, therefore, have been a 'Sirius Stone,' perhaps also allied to Orion and the striking stellar passage of the Pleiades with Taurus. It seems that although the Longstones as a whole marked the annual passage of the Sun, especially the winter solstice, and the cycles of the Moon—so providing, like most Neolithic sites, a fundamental measure of the important soli-lunar cycles—the later Longstones Cove would have been devoted primarily to the cycle of Sirius. This intense focus upon a singularity, a distinctive star, is also suggested by the enclosed and exclusive nature of the Cove itself. In this respect, the location of the Longstones Cove, at the end of the Western Avenue radically differs from the multiple alignments and radiating character of the Sanctuary at the end of the eastern Kennet Avenue.

But why did the builders go to the trouble of aligning the Longstones Cove to the location of Silbury Hill when they were not on a line of sight? The builders of the Longstones Cove appear to have been principally interested in the rising of Sirius over Folly Hill, only secondarily in the co-incidence of that alignment with Silbury Hill. The significance of Sirius for the Avebury builders may be further underscored by another earlier alignment to the star, between Avebury henge and the summit of Folly Hill. As shown in Figure 35, throughout the winter months, when viewed from the Obelisk in the last half of the third millennium BCE, observers would have seen Sirius *setting* at an azimuth of 235° (altitude negligible) over Folly Hill. Observers at the time would very probably have been aware that Sirius had risen and set on the path of the midwinter Sun in the late-fourth millennium BCE; also that the star remained close to the solar path even in the latter part of the third millennium. Yet the Sun always affected the visibility of the star. By 2300 BCE, for example, Sirius was setting for the last time at dusk, its heliacal setting, at an azimuth of 235° in mid April; an event extremely pronounced over Folly Hill to anyone watching the sky from Avebury henge.

In short, Sirius would have reappeared for the *first* time at dawn in late July/early August on an azimuth of 125°—the azimuth between the Longstones Cove and Folly Hill. The star rose on this 125° alignment for the *last* time not long after the winter solstice. Sirius then appeared higher and higher in the night sky at dusk, before entirely vanishing in April on the other side of the sky, in the southwest, at 235°—the azimuth between the Obelisk and Folly Hill. Sirius' absence lasted a period of about 120 days. Moreover, as shown in Figure 34, there is evidence of further Sirius-watching at the Longstones Cove. As Beckhampton long barrow lies on the same azimuth from the Longstones Cove as Folly Hill from the Obelisk (i.e., 235°), and as the long barrow offered a clear foresight on the horizon, the sky-watchers at the Cove not only had the benefit of seeing the heliacal *rising* of Sirius over Folly Hill, they also would have seen the heliacal *setting* of Sirius over the long barrow. The star vanished in the spring over the already ancient long barrow before reappearing along the axis of the Cove over Folly Hill 120 days later. While this alignment also would have been useful for marking the passage of the midwinter Sun at 231°, the consistent differing of the azimuths by those crucial 4° suggests that at least in the late-third millennium BCE Sirius was again the primary object of view.

The low rise of Beckhampton or Folly Hill thus appears to lie at the centre of an intriguing set of solar and stellar alignments. When viewed from Avebury henge, this hill formed the foresight for the setting of the Sun at the winter solstice and the disappearance of Sirius at the time of planting and the turning out of cattle in the fourth and third millennium BCE. When viewed along the alignment of the Longstones Cove, Folly Hill was the foresight for the rising Sun at midwinter and for the reappearance of Sirius at the time of the harvest in the late third millennium BCE. This latter alignment continued to Silbury Hill below the horizon. It is also possible the Longstones Cove formed a backsight for the observation of the setting of Sirius over Beckhampton long barrow—the later Cove referencing the thousand-year old barrow. Finally, we shall see in the following chapter on the Sanctuary, that the acronychal setting of beta Taurus, the point of one of the horns of Taurus, took place over the area defined by Folly Hill and its associated monuments when cattle were brought in and culled for the winter.

Archaeological excavations found evidence of cultivation, plough marks, and pasturage beneath South Street long barrow, Beckhampton long barrow and the Longstones Cove. Excavators found three ox skulls, but little more, at the still massive Beckhampton long barrow. The implication is that this was an important area for grazing and cultivation long *before* any monuments were built here. The inhabitants seem to have cleared this area, fairly level, relatively well watered, south and below Windmill Hill, at an early time. Perhaps first noticed as astronomically significant from Avebury henge, the heliacal setting of Sirius in April over Folly Hill could have provided observers with a marker for agricultural activities in the fourth millennium BCE. The Longstones Enclosure and then the Cove, in the midst of a long-standing agricultural area, and eventually connected to the henge via the Western Avenue, may conceivably have been built to conduct ritual practices associated with cattle and the harvest, timed in the heavens by the loss and reappearance of Sirius.

As a traditional—even perhaps curiously anachronistic—monument, modelled on an ancient design, the builders may have intended the Longstones Cove firstly to honour the ancestors, those who had farmed the land before; and secondly, to mark the reappearance of Sirius—the planting and harvest star so closely aligned to the path of the midwinter Sun. They may have intended the Cove as a primary location for paying tribute to the fertility of the land. But what of the significance of Sirius, the Hound of the Hunter, Orion, pursuing the Bull across the night sky? The monument-builders may either have seen Sirius and Orion hunting the Bull, Taurus, or capturing and domesticating it, bringing it and its gifts to the people. Whatever the case, the Cove could have provided an important setting for ritual observances at the times of the heliacal rising and setting of Sirius, the times of planting, and the times of the low, summer full Moons of the harvest. Or, as suggested in the next chapter, at times when bright Alnath, at the point of the horn of the constellation Taurus, set over Folly Hill and the Cove in the autumn and the spring—the later Celtic festivals of Beltane and Samhain when the cattle were turned out and brought in.

Finally, this reading of the evidence regards the extension of the alignment of the Cove to the location of Silbury, constructed at the same time, as simply a symbolic acknowledgement. The two sites had different concerns: the Longstones Cove was directly concerned with the ongoing fertility of the land, perhaps with cults of the grain and the bull. Silbury Hill was concerned with maintaining ancestral tradition. Although Silbury Hill and the Longstones Cove refer to each other, the builders may not have seen the Cove as part of the stellar loss otherwise associated with the great mound. Indeed, as Sirius rose slightly higher in the sky with each passing century there may have been a feeling on the part of the people that here, at least, at the Longstones Cove, was significant gain. Although the Crux-Centaurus group of stars were abandoning Avebury, Sirius, the brightest star in the sky, closely connected with another order or cult of fertility, clearly was not. Indeed, the late Neolithic monument-builders may have been focused on obtaining the wealth of the Earth, and were willing to break with tradition to get it.

Upper: Reconstruction of the Longstones Cove and the Western Avenue in the last quarter of the third millennium BCE. Folly Hill lies southeast behind the Cove. Lower: Stukeley's drawing of the Longstones Cove, May 1724, looking in the opposite direction. The lozenge shape of Adam, 'A', and stone 'D' are clearly visible.

Feasts & Games: The West Kennet Palisade Enclosures

View toward Silbury Hill across the location of the West Kennet Palisade Enclosures. The trees on the right mark the River Kennet.

The Late Neolithic, the latter half of the third millennium BCE, was a busy time for the people of Avebury. As well as completing the Great Outer Circle, redesigning the Longstones Cove, finishing the Avenues and building Silbury Hill, they also built several huge timber enclosures at the southeast foot of Waden Hill, beside and straddling the River Kennet. These palisade enclosures were discovered in the mid-twentieth century and investigated recently by an archaeological team led by Alasdair Whittle. Whittle described the enclosures as consisting of continuous rows or palisades, of closely set unshaped timbers. The oak tree trunks were so large, and set so deeply into the ground, that in places the palisades could have reached over twenty feet in height. Each of the two main enclosures were oval, contained about ten acres of level ground and required over a thousand trees, all cut with stone tools. The largest enclosure carefully linked to the smaller and earlier enclosure, also contained three circular arrangements of closely set posts, the largest about 120 feet in diameter. The surveys also found various linear arrangements of posts, some of which radiated southeast to link with further smaller palisade circles.[6]

The radiocarbon dates suggest a broad overlap of use of the several phases of the enclosures between 2500 and 2000 BCE, contemporary with the building of Silbury Hill, the final stages of the Avenues, the Longstones Cove and the Sanctuary.[7] In each phase, the substantial character of the timbers involved meant they could have stood for a century or more. Finds included great quantities of charcoal, bone and antler; the users had deliberately placed them against the posts of the enclosures both at the time of construction and during their subsequent use. The quantity and the nature of the bones suggested to the archaeologists that whole joints of animals, especially those of pigs, had been partially feasted upon and partially deposited, perhaps as "sacrificial offerings."[8] While the enclosures could have been used for habitation, for animal stockades or for defence, the overall conclusion of the archaeologists was that they were used in a ritualised and symbolic manner, although exactly how remains unclear. What is clear is that the palisade enclosures shared features with other monumental sites in the area. They contained inner circles just as Avebury henge contained inner circles; while their lines of posts could be seen as replicating the lines of the stone avenues.

But while the West Kennet palisade enclosures may appear to copy or mirror the monumental structures of the region, they are also quite different. Although there is an equivalence of scale, the enclosures of Windmill Hill were set upon an open hilltop related to distant sites, while the West Kennet enclosures were set in a valley bottom and had a limited horizon related to nearby sites. The enclosures of Windmill Hill were broken by causeways, inhabited, open and inclusive, while the continuous

West Kennet enclosures tightly controlled access and were uninhabited, closed and exclusive. Both featured practices of feasting and deposition of animal parts—mostly cattle on Windmill Hill, mostly pigs at West Kennet—but whereas these practices referred to the sky and pits of earth on Windmill Hill, in the West Kennet enclosures these practices seem to be connected closely with water, the nearby River Kennet.

It appears that the palisade enclosures served a vital role in what Avebury had become in the second half of the third millennium BCE. Avebury had grown on an enormous scale, involving hundreds, perhaps thousands of people on a regular basis. The many visitors coming at particular times of the year for the various formal, practical and social activities would have required a high degree of organisation, supply and even entertainment. The next chapter describes the nearby timber and stone circle known as the Sanctuary, as a point of entry into the area from the Ridgeway. It was a place where visitors could be formally welcomed, rested and oriented before approaching the main ceremonial centre of Avebury itself. It is likely these visitors would have come for a period of time, not just a brief visit, especially if they were committed to hauling stones, cutting timber, scouring chalk, supplying food, making ropes or moving earth. The palisade enclosures lay near the Sanctuary; and where better for visitors and their animals to remain for the duration of their stay than beside the River Kennet, taking advantage of the sheltered valley and the good water supply. Imagine them putting up shelters in the valley, near the water, next to the enclosures, beside the Kennet Avenue and the Sanctuary.

The excavators commented upon the great numbers of pigs, mostly young, that had been used in an extravagant and "wasteful" way at the palisade enclosures. They thought this might have meant not just sacrificial and other formal ritual behaviour but also feasting, fun and games. The pig was the

Late Neolithic animal of choice for feasts. It is possible to imagine large numbers of spectators watching from behind the safety of wooden barriers as hunters showed off their skills with hounds, horses and weapons, especially the longbow. The heavy timbers set deeply into the ground could have contained a cattle stampede: nothing could have broken through or jumped over them. Perhaps the palisades provided pens for the oxen that helped with the hauling of stones, or served as corrals for the small but highly desirable horses coming into use at this time. Perhaps the palisades held all the animals the visitors had brought with them: pigs, sheep, cattle and goats. The palisades may have offered many varieties of useful enclosure where the animals could be driven, conveniently held, watered, fattened, slaughtered and prepared for a particular event. The animals in the enclosures could be counted, admired, bred, conspicuously gifted, used in displays and games, and not be stolen by status-seeking young men or attacked by wild animals. The enclosures could have allowed large groups of spectators to observe, in safety, events taking place within them. The slopes of Waden Hill allowed direct views into them. The assembled animals provided muscle power, food for large numbers of travellers, opportunities for public gift-giving, feasting and sacrificial offering, as well as opportunities for displays of skill, prestige and prosperity.

As mentioned above, and explored further in Chapter 10, Neolithic society was likely to have been a highly formal one, full of elaborate protocols. Based on comparison with similar societies it is likely that the gathering of different groups at special times of the year demanded particular 'meeting and greeting' rituals. These rituals probably included games as well as feasting, and would have been times when both hosts and guests were expected to provide numerous and specific items, services and resources: food, beverages, gifts, prizes, ritual objects, regalia, live animals, musicians, athletes, dancers and so forth. Codes of hospitality observed in traditional societies worldwide inform us that not to fulfil requirements of this sort could have led to a severe breaching of the standards by which tribes and their leaders were judged. A serious breach could result in a loss of hard-won social standing, authority and reputation. Sources from early Irish literature (that contain material from a strong and already ancient oral tradition) reveal a society that seems likely have had some features in common with the society of the Neolithic. At the great Irish courts, warriors competed in displays of skill, horses and cattle were admired, bards entertained, boys played games, feasts took place, hierarchies became visible, and power was measured by the hospitality, wisdom and largesse of the rulers.[9]

As well as providing appropriately structured contexts for ceremonies of meeting and greeting, for feasting, drinking and games, the Neolithic people may have used the palisade enclosures for formal social rituals, quite apart from what went on in the great henge itself. Strong social protocols would have prevailed in the British Neolithic and there would have been a constant round of alliance making, gift exchange and marital arrangements. People carried out their relationships in a highly formal and structured manner according to kinship: family, clan, age, marital and gender status. Matters such as sexual relationships and pregnancies would have been tightly controlled. Marriages typically would have been arranged and conducted according to strict rules of endogamy, in-marrying to relatives, or exogamy, out-marrying to a relatively small number of lineages or related clans. In many equivalent traditional societies, including the Old Irish, marriage carried an exact bride price of so many cattle and pigs according to social rank. The marriage or its negotiations could not happen without a certain number of animals being given and feasted upon in the course of the ceremonies. The people, intra- and intertribal, also had to deal with the recently deceased: making offerings to departed spirits, telling their stories and other acts of remembrance. Even before the great individual round barrows and cairns of the Bronze Age, the death of a great progenitor, leader, heroic horseman, storyteller, innovator or wise elder would have been the cause for a special memorial event, just as it is today.

In the context of the enclosures, it is not hard to imagine the Neolithic people combining many activities of this kind. During games and feasting, public displays of oath-taking and allegiance-making, rounds of augury, story telling and divination, they would have slaughtered animals and given selected parts of suitable animals to the living as well as to the dead. They probably would have seen cattle belonging to one category of spiritual observance, pigs and sheep to another, and wild animals to quite another. They may have seen pigs, like the later Celts, as the totemic beasts of the Underworld, whose wildest manifestations in the form of the great sow or boar must be slain to avoid destruction. They may have seen the River Kennet, flowing directly through the site after the dry summer, as a source of life, as a goddess, or as a River of the Dead. Like the Milky Way in the sky, the river may have represented the road onto which not only the ancestors had departed but so also could the selectively honoured recently deceased. Perhaps the people threw ashes into the revived river after appropriate memorial ceremonies in the enclosures. We know that this type of activity, complete with sacrifice, feasting, games and solemnly depositing items in rivers, was common practice in Homeric Greek society and among the Celtic tribes. Evidence from the comparable Durrington Walls near Stonehenge, suggests the River Avon featured strongly in the ceremonial activities—including the killing of young pigs—that took place there.[10]

Given the present limited evidence, it is hard to build a full picture of what went on in the palisade enclosures. But it seems plausible to think that in the Late Neolithic / Early Bronze Age, extended family, clan or tribal groups arriving in the area with their animals could have encamped beside them in the shelter of the valley. They may have arrived in the autumn when there was abundance, or later when the springs came back to life. The flocks and herds could be held and admired in the enclosures—the numbers and quality of the cattle declaring their owners' wealth and thus their status.[11] Perhaps after spending part of each day adding further layers to the nearby Silbury Mound, the visitors could have returned to the enclosures, drunk from the stream, washed off the sticky chalk, and participated in whatever hospitality and social events were on offer that evening. Such events, while separate from the ceremonies of the great henge, would nonetheless have been governed by their own strict protocols. They fulfilled a vital social role in auspicious surroundings. As I will describe in the next chapter, perhaps visitors also came to the West Kennet palisades to prepare for the major assemblies. At the appropriate time, when the necessary costumes, dances, songs and offerings were ready, when all the necessary preliminaries had been observed, the correct animal sacrifices made, the excited, curious and possibly overawed visitors would have made their way along or beside the stone avenues, to arrive at the great henge and its vast circles of stone.

8

The Sanctuary at the Galactic Crossroads

The Milky Way girdles the zodiac, its great circle meeting it obliquely so that it crosses it at the two tropical signs, Capricorn and Cancer. Natural philosophers called these the "portals of the sun" because the solstices lie athwart the sun's path on either side, checking further progress... Souls are believed to pass through these portals when going from the sky to the earth and returning from the earth to the sky. ...Cancer is called the portal of men, because through it descent is made to the infernal regions; ... Capricorn is called the portal of gods, because through it souls return to their rightful abode of immortality, to be reckoned among the gods.

Macrobius[1]

The Sanctuary

A view of the Sanctuary today: uninspiring concrete posts lie close to a very busy road. The West Kennet palisade enclosures once lay in the

valley bottom between the Sanctuary and Silbury Hill. Inset: Silbury Hill between Cherhill and Knoll Down.

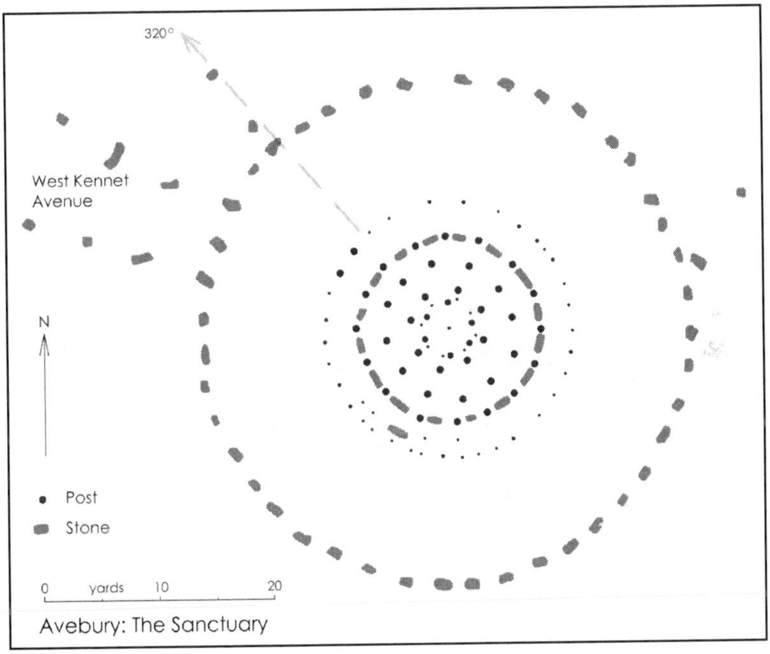

Figure 36. Plan of the Sanctuary: concentric circles of posts and stones. As the builders developed this site, next to the Mesolithic Ridgeway, in the early-third millennium BCE, they often renewed the timber circles, adding around 2400 BCE, two concentric circles of stones. The Sanctuary formed an appropriate terminus for the West Kennet Avenue.

The Sanctuary site may have first come to the attention of the prehistoric people of the area because it lay beside the Ridgeway, the ancient track over the great curve of Overton Hill onto the Marlborough Downs. The Ridgeway ran due north from the Sanctuary up to and through the sarsen fields on Fyfield Down, the most likely source of the Sanctuary's stones. The way would have held post-Ice Age memories of migrations, of animals and people. But as well as connecting the Sanctuary

Reconstruction of the Sanctuary circa 2400 BCE. View from the end of the West Kennet Avenue looking southeast.

with sites further north and east that were sources of good quality flints, an extension of this ancient track also led south to the causewayed enclosure of Knap Hill, across the Vale of Pewsey, towards Salisbury Plain. It is widely held that sarsen stones from the Avebury region were taken by this route to Stonehenge, about twenty miles to the south. This route presumably crossed the River Kennet where it does today, marking an important territorial and spiritual boundary. A few thousand years later another important boundary, the Wansdyke—Woden's dike—intersected the Ridgeway two miles south of the Sanctuary. Today the Sanctuary sits beside the crossing of the Ridgeway and the A4, once the main road west from London and a Roman road. It is best to approach the Sanctuary by foot from the river.

Figure 37. Partial restoration of the view due south from the Sanctuary, mid-third millennium BCE. The upper stars of the Southern Cross are setting over the Ridgeway, which ran due south to Knap Hill over the horizon. The original posts are likely to have been thicker and more numerous than those shown.

Long barrows are conspicuous in the nearby landscape, notably at East and West Kennet. To the south and west are several hills once favoured as Mesolithic campsites. As mentioned, the causewayed enclosure Knap Hill is located due south only a few miles away—a pleasant hour's walk along the Ridgeway. In the west, Cherhill Down and Knoll Down form a stretch of horizon intersected by the rising cone of Silbury Hill, while Tan Hill (St Anne's Hill), Milk Hill and Furze Hill rim the chalk escarpment to the south. To the east lies the head of the Upper Kennet valley. To the west along the valley, near the future site of Silbury Hill and beside the river Kennet, once stood the West Kennet palisade enclosures. These huge rings of closely set oak presumably shared the same woodworking techniques as those at the Sanctuary. Finally, the area just to the north of the Sanctuary, on Overton Hill, reveals traces of a Mesolithic camp site—possibly a causewayed enclosure.

When first investigated in the 1930s, the density and size of its concentric circles of posts led to the proposal that the Sanctuary was originally a roofed structure; but this is no longer favoured. Recent interpretations see it as several concentric circles of massive timber uprights, with plenty of wooden lintels, arrangements of smaller posts and two circles of human-height sarsen stones. Trees at ceremonial sites suggest a whole host of meanings, ultimately related to the ancient and universal tradition of the Tree of Life, the World Tree—the *axis mundi*.

There can be no doubt of the woodworking skills of Neolithic society. Many contemporary sites, such as Stanton Drew, Woodhenge and 'Seahenge,' provide tantalizing evidence that the Neolithic peoples of Britain developed a wide variety of complex wooden forms which could have been sculpted, carved with animal or human figures, coloured, adorned with leather, stone, bone, skulls, antler, shell and other materials. Sophisticated timber circles with lintels and astronomically oriented entrances appear on the Continent in the fifth millennium BCE (the end of its Mesolithic and the beginning of its Neolithic period, which began significantly earlier than in Britain).[2] The Goseck palisade circle in Germany dates to as early as 4900 BCE, and includes alignments to the solstitial extremes. The problem is wood decomposes so rapidly in this damp climate that almost nothing remains from the era. But if woodworking techniques such as the open mortise and tenon joints that were transferred to stone by the builders of Stonehenge are anything to go by, then the monument builders certainly had the techniques and the skill to exploit the aesthetic and monumental possibilities presented to them by the versatile medium of wood. Nor do we have to conceive of anything primitive: the Sanctuary's oak uprights, eighteen inches to over two feet in diameter and twenty feet or more in height, could have been stripped of their bark, trimmed smooth with stone axes, adzes and chisels and given joints able to support carefully shaped wooden lintels. These oak posts could have resisted the elements for up to a century or more. The speculative reconstruction at the beginning of the chapter shows that if the builders had added decorative features such as ox skulls, *bucrania,* to the posts of the Sanctuary, they could have achieved a wide range of visually striking designs.

Its first excavators concluded that the Sanctuary was a lively site. Large numbers of workday deposits occur in the area; flints were worked on site and nearby. The first posts may have been set up at an early date. Archaeologists have nothing firm, but think a primary circle of wooden posts at the Sanctuary may belong to 3000 BCE. Its 1930 excavators concluded that construction and use of the Sanctuary probably reached a peak just after the mid-third millennium BCE. As the builders developed this monument in the mid-third millennium, they put up posts, then removed and replaced them on a regular basis. One posthole appears to have had its timber post replaced at least four times.[3] The builders may have been experimenting, trying out forms until they got it right. The larger postholes may have carried two posts, supporting a wooden lintel, which either stood as independent features or carried a continuous ring of lintels. If several of the circles had carried carefully carved lintels, what might otherwise have appeared as a meaningless forest of posts would immediately have become a comprehensive set of concentric circles. On average, the builders arranged the posts about eight feet apart, which, with a diameter of two feet, meant they could have spanned the six-foot gap with wooden lintels of a corresponding diameter. At heights of 15 to 18 feet, these dimensions are close to those of Stonehenge.

Concrete posts on the site now mark out the structure at the time of the mid-third millennium BCE. Two circles of closely set stones, one sixteen yards in diameter the other forty-five yards in diameter, complemented five concentric circles of posts.[4] The enclosing stones of the inner circle were set so tightly between the posts that in places little room remained between them for access. Viewing would have been very restricted. Yet the 1930s excavation of the Sanctuary may well have resulted in some inaccuracies.[5] For example, what is visible today may give little clear indication of the size or even the position of some of the posts and stones at a given time.

Once the builders of the Sanctuary had the circles of wood and stone in place, visibility through the structure would have been limited. Any activities at its deepest centre, limited to just a few by reasons of space (as at Stonehenge), would have been invisible to those remaining outside. But the lines of sight through the structure to the horizon would have been very precise. In other words, this was quite a different arrangement to that of Avebury henge, which could contain many people, where there were many foresights over an artificial horizon, and where the most likely backsights were at multiple centres. Yet from the third quarter of the third millennium BCE, a stone avenue connected these two very different monuments. The two sites were already seen as being in a close relationship, both to each other, as well as to the Longstones Cove at the terminus of the second, Western or Beckhampton Avenue.

Whether backsights were located inside or outside the central structure, the intricate posts and standing stones of the Sanctuary would certainly have facilitated precise observation of the heavens around the local horizon. Through the entrance to the Sanctuary, the observer can see the trees on the summit of Folly Hill or Beckhampton Hill, over the end of Waden Hill, between 292° and 294°—but only just, an elevated view or one slightly south would have been better. But most intriguingly of all, its builders positioned the Sanctuary so that Windmill Hill lay at the bottom of a conspicuous notch in the northeast horizon formed by the junction of Waden Hill and Overton Hill. These builders located the Sanctuary very carefully to obtain these views. Were the circle just a few feet lower, Folly Hill and Windmill Hill would have been invisible. From here, it is also possible to see the stones of the West Kennet Avenue for a good portion of its length, especially those stones set upon the ridge just before Avebury henge, directly below Windmill Hill. This line of sight is of a length to be of considerable astronomical value.

We have seen that from Windmill Hill, the Sanctuary lies on the orientation of midwinter sunrise (above the future site of Avebury and below Martinsell Hill on the horizon), but the Sun would have been several diameters in the sky by the time it was over the Sanctuary. Although this kind of general observation would have been adequate for many of the purposes of the people of the time, observers standing three or four degrees lower—an altitude provided from locations along the West Kennet Avenue in the dry valley below—would have seen the midwinter Sun rising precisely over the Sanctuary. Several writers have suggested solar and lunar alignments from and through the Sanctuary. In his evocative recreation of the Neolithic era, *Hengeworld,* Mike Pitts, mentions the link of this site with midsummer sunrise.[6] In addition, there is a suggestion of an alignment to Sirius in the latter part of the third millennium BCE because of an azimuth of 124° derived from the cross-axial arrangement of the Sanctuary. John North thought good use also could have been made of the combination of West Kennet Avenue and the Sanctuary as lunar markers. The extreme northern moonsets lie on azimuths of 320° and extreme southern moonrises close to 140°; this is the orientation between the Sanctuary and the restored section of the avenue near Avebury henge. Such alignments may have value. However, they are not ones most obviously marked at the Sanctuary.

As shown in Figure 36, the builders of the mid-third millennium BCE took particular care to connect the West Kennet or Eastern Avenue to the outer stone circle of the Sanctuary. They narrowed the avenue and joined it to the circle with what were probably the three largest stones. The strange monument on Overton Hill now represented an architecturally strong and definite terminus to the avenue, which in turn provided the main entrance to and exit from the circle.

While it appears that the stones of the Sanctuary were of a similar size, around five feet in height, some of its posts were clearly very large. The postholes suggest a uniform size for many of the posts. Their regular spacing and considerable height combined with the regular stones must have given the circle an extremely impressive formal appearance. The site was much visited, but what went on in the centre of the circle was private. It represented something important. The regular posts bearing lintels may conceivably have provided the inspiration or prototype for the carved stone lintels of Stonehenge; indeed, Woodhenge near Stonehenge is similar in scale and conception and contemporary in time with the Sanctuary. The late Neolithic monument-builders may have honed their skills at Woodhenge before they went on to construct some of the final stages of Stonehenge, where posts and lintels were made of stone; the transition from wood to stone is a very interesting one and the Sanctuary provides a classic and significant, although not firmly dated example. Since the use of wooden lintels in timber circles on the Continent can be dated to as early as the fifth millennium BCE, a timber post and lintel circle could have been at the

Sanctuary at a time either contemporary with or even *before* the other monuments in the area—making the Sanctuary a very significant monument indeed.[7]

In outline, the archaeological evidence shows that the Sanctuary was an extremely dynamic site. Its builders changed the posts there frequently from about 2500 BCE, seemingly to maintain its complex structure. It look like the relatively small but carefully located stones enhanced and made permanent a striking symmetrical, and apparently astronomical, order first defined by the posts. The last phase of the Sanctuary occurred at approximately the same date as the West Kennet palisade enclosures sited in the valley below; but the circle on Overton Hill is of a far more architecturally precise order. It also seems clear that the West Kennet Avenue was built to connect the Sanctuary to the henge at Avebury in the same way as the Western Avenue was built to connect the henge to the Longstones Cove.

The Sanctuary may have been the place where generations of Avebury monument-builders developed and demonstrated their skills. It may possibly have been an orientation site, approached by visitors to the huge and complex ritual landscape when entering via the Lower Kennet valley or the Ridgeway. Visitors who travelled north to Avebury from Salisbury Plain along the Ridgeway—perhaps to obtain sarsen or other stone—would have passed through a striking portal into the area provided by the already ancient sites of Knap Hill and Adam's Grave. Such companies could possibly have been received at the Sanctuary and the main features of the area pointed out by baton-bearing and increasingly-high in status local 'engineers,' 'astronomers' or other site officials. Visitors may have prepared themselves at or near the Sanctuary, utilising the Palisade Enclosures, before approaching the henge via its astounding, almost two-mile long processional way. They may have walked (or rode) outside the occasionally huge stones of the Kennet Avenue, at the astronomically most auspicious time. Its builders may also have used the Sanctuary to teach engineering, construction skills, astronomy and star lore to a selected few. As at Windmill Hill, the prehistoric scatter found on site showed it had been in active daily use, in striking contrast to the ritual cleanliness of Avebury.

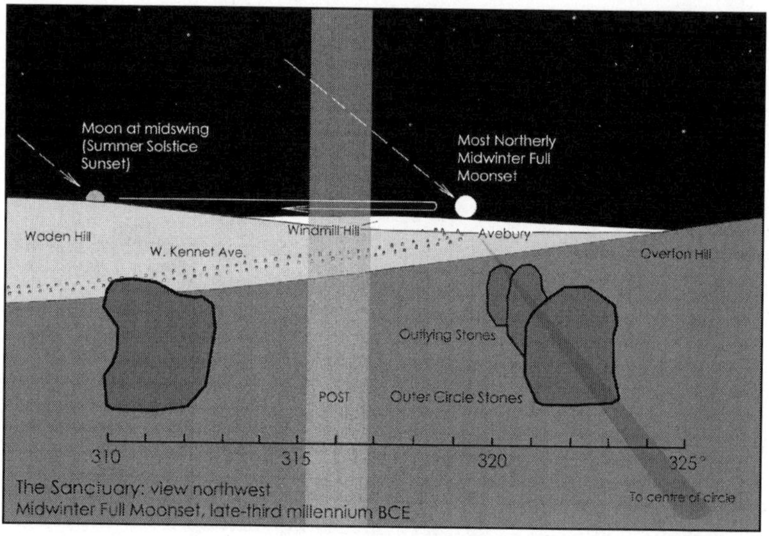

Figure 38. Two stones outside the Sanctuary point to the Northern Major Standstill over Windmill Hill (near the centre of Avebury) at an azimuth of 320°. The Moon has moved about a degree away from this extreme over the past five thousand years, setting over Windmill Hill from the Sanctuary at approximately 319°. It last reached this extreme in 2006 and will do so again in 2025 CE. The Moon orbits the Earth every 27.33 days, waxing and waning rapidly, making about thirteen orbits of the Earth during each annual cycle of the Sun. The lunar orbit is inclined at 5.2° to the orbit of the Earth around the Sun—the ecliptic—crossing it about every thirteen days, causing eclipses. From the ground, the extreme rising and setting points of the Moon appear to fluctuate. Every 18.61 years, the full Moon appears in the north at its highest point in midwinter, remaining in the sky for the longest time, and six months later it appears at its lowest point in the south, rising above the horizon for the shortest time in midsummer. Midway

between these extremes, the Moon oscillates least, providing least illumination at night. Although this 18-19 year phenomenon is most impressive at the higher latitudes (where the Moon may never set at all or only skim over the horizon) it was known to the Greeks and Romans. Alexander Thom called the extremes of the cycle the 'Major' and 'Minor' 'Lunar Standstills.'

West Kennet Avenue

View north to Avebury henge along the West Kennet Avenue, late-third millennium BCE. Many of the stones shown in this reconstruction are still in place.

View south along the West Kennet Avenue from the summit of the rise before Avebury.

Throughout the Neolithic era it seems likely that people came to the Upper Kennet valley from far and wide, travelling along already ancient trackways, to congregate at the great 'temple' of Avebury. Avebury's status must have benefited from its location on a confluence of many different ancient paths. Numerous visitors, bearing offerings, their tools, trade and exchange items, must have walked along these tracks, probably in the autumn after the harvest, in search of the blessings that this strange and powerful place had to offer. Some of the travellers may have come to obtain the great sarsen stones, or more likely, to seek good quality flint from the Avebury area or other good stone that had found its way there. They may have brought with them raw antler, ochres, shell, jet and amber; highly polished and prized axes from East Anglia, Cornwall, Sussex, Cumbria, Wales and the Continent; worked goods, including hides, carved bone, harpoons, needles, tusks, maceheads, beads, jewellery and ceramics. Their herds of cattle, their high-status bulls and hunting dogs, sheep, goats and pigs would most likely have accompanied them. By whichever route they came, it seems likely they would have come first to the Sanctuary.

If these Neolithic travellers had journeyed up the ancient Ridgeway from the south, they would have crossed the Vale of Pewsey and passed between the highly impressive causewayed enclosure on Knap Hill and the immense barrow now known as Adam's Grave—the one a ring, the other a nipple of earth—on their respective hills. There were few places quite like this in the Wessex landscape, and they must have walked this part of the way respectfully. They would have proceeded due north, until, on descending a stretch of the Ridgeway, the great long barrow at East Kennet (now covered in trees) would have appeared to their left, on a line of sight to Windmill Hill, the ancestral gathering-place of the people of the area. The widest end of the long barrow was oriented toward them, while its great length—the longest in the country—pointed to the ancestral hill behind.[8] Shortly after this, they would have crossed the River Kennet into the Avebury *temenos*, the sacred domain proper, and climbed the hill to the Sanctuary. If they had travelled from the north or east along the Ridgeway, the passage through the sarsen fields of Fyfield Down—the main source of Avebury's stones—would also have directed them to the Sanctuary.

Once they had arrived, the visitors would have set down whatever they had brought with them and organised their animals and temporary shelters. This was probably near or in the palisade enclosures on the valley floor by the River Kennet and its springs. At some point, according to their status, they must have been appropriately welcomed and inducted into the protocols of the great landscape temple. These ritual processes of meeting and greeting would surely have been very complex, especially when large numbers were involved; probably the palisade enclosures would also have assisted in this process. At the appropriate time, the visitors may have gathered at or beside the Sanctuary, noting that the circles of wood and stone hid the centre of the structure before them. There was mystery here, as there was in the whole ceremonial landscape, a mystery to which they did not necessarily have access. But the way ahead for them along the stone avenue leading from the Sanctuary, would have been clear enough. We can imagine that only at the right moment—when they had observed all the correct formalities, exchanged the necessary gifts, put on the appropriate regalia, made or readied their offerings, looked for auguries and consumed the appropriate food and beverages—would visitors have set off along the way marked by the Kennet Avenue to approach the great henge.

They would have dropped from Overton Hill, and passed by the river—with both the palisade enclosures and (the future site of) Silbury Hill to their left—and proceeded along or beside the avenue of paired stones. From this direction, West Kennet Avenue always appears to progress onwards, up to the skyline. It is possible that its builders never completed the pairs of stones at the lowest points in the dry valley and woodland broke this part of the avenue.[9] The avenue turns several times, making imposing sweeps across the hillside and valley, before reaching the crest of the rise, giving the first view of Windmill Hill standing above Avebury henge. This is not dissimilar to the visual impact of Stonehenge, whose first visitors also approached it via an avenue leading from below. Even then, the avenue oriented the Avebury visitors to the line between the Sanctuary and Windmill Hill before making one final tangential turn toward the Southern Entrance between increasingly large and more carefully paired stones. The outer bank still concealed the secret heart of Avebury; but with the final turn, the visitors would have seen, perhaps for the first time, the interior of the great henge. There, pairs of immense stones, with two entrance stones far greater than those in the Avenue, would have led all eyes to the tallest stone of all, the 'Obelisk,' at the centre of the Southern Inner Circle.

These travellers had been manipulated, it is true; like the approach to Stonehenge, the stone marked route had guided the visitor in a manner certain to impress them. But since the reality of Neolithic Avebury must always have been one of a site in progress, which the visitors might have come to assist, any formal behaviour was likely to have undermined by the casual. There would have been chatter, jokes, attention to simple human needs, children and dogs running underfoot, and the attendant noise and tending of grazing animals. Avebury must have been a place that wove together profound mythic resonances and symbolic meanings in a manner that implicitly or matter-of-factly embodied their deepest sense of the sacred.

Like numerous other megalithic sites springing up across Britain and Europe at this time, Avebury, the Sanctuary and the Avenues, were monuments to the divine powers that Neolithic peoples encountered in their daily experience of life. Their rich cognitive, oral, mythic, but still low technological life involved a constant struggle to decipher how the Sun, Moon and stars mapped or measured out the great natural cycles of life, fertility and death. Yet, however inaccessible its deeper mysteries might have been to many visitors, the encounter with the immense circle studded with gigantic 'living' stones would have awed everyone, not least the children. Neolithic Avebury was surely a place where all the forces and nuances of life came together. Here people came to haul stones, scour the banks, share skills, tell stories, meet, feast, obtain goods, exchange ideas, as well as to costume themselves, sing, dance and make ceremony. Here they must have experienced a deep sense of shared intent, within the secure protection of the great powers of Earth, the ancestors, and the Sun, Moon and stars.

The Sanctuary & Capella

From the Sanctuary, the stones of West Kennet Avenue are visible before they enter Avebury henge, just below the line of sight. Windmill Hill is on the horizon.

What is most striking about the view northwest from the Sanctuary is the visual alignment to Avebury and Windmill Hill.[10] Looking out from the Sanctuary, towards the bottom of the notch between Waden and Overton Hill, we can glimpse both the fourth millennium enclosure on Windmill Hill and the third millennium Avebury henge. As shown in Figure 39, the summit of Windmill Hill occupies an azimuth of 316-18°, while Avebury henge reaches from 317° to 324°. 320/1° is about the centre of the henge. This vital alignment referenced bright stars that were then setting at similar azimuths between 314° and 324°.

Both the distinctive constellation of Cygnus and the first-magnitude orange star of Capella set on the alignment to

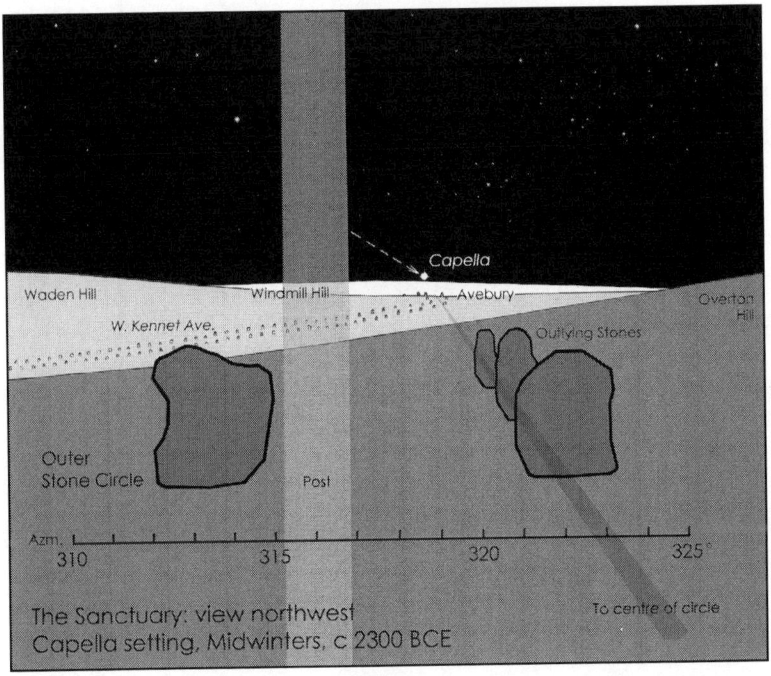

Figure 39. A telescopic view of Windmill Hill from the Sanctuary, with Capella setting in the third-quarter of the third millennium BCE, 3am, midwinter. The Milky Way has levelled and is beginning to dip below the horizon; the constellation of Cygnus is rising in the northeast; Crux is reaching its southern culmination. Capella is approaching the Windmill Hill notch between Waden Hill and Overton Hill. At this time Capella was setting at an azimuth of approximately 320°; by 2150 BCE the star was setting over the centre of Avebury henge at 322°. While the shape of the stones shown is entirely conjectural, they are located correctly, and appear aligned to 320°. The foreground posts suggest possible timber structures.

Windmill Hill, directly over Avebury henge, during midwinters from the fourth millennium throughout the third millennium BCE, the time of greatest activity at the Sanctuary. In 2600 BCE, just after winter sunsets and at an azimuth of 317°, Cygnus, the Northern Cross, appeared to plunge vertically into the centre of

Windmill Hill, along with the Milky Way. This large birdlike constellation of Cygnus, which Celtic tradition later described as a goose, has the bright star Albireo at its head with its brighter alpha star Deneb at its tail. Eight hours later, shortly before dawn, Capella would have appeared to set over Windmill Hill at 317°. Capella in the constellation Auriga is the sixth brightest star in the sky. By about 2300 BCE, this star was setting over the end stones of the West Kennet Avenue, in an area defined by Avebury henge at 319-320°.[11]

The excavators found two sockets for independent stones just beyond the outer circle of the Sanctuary. These stones, along with one of the outer circle, lie on an azimuth of 319-320°.[12] The builders very possibly set up these as marker stones to point to the notch on the northwestern horizon containing Windmill Hill and Avebury. Recreated in Figure 36, the most likely date for the erection of the two stones coincides with the passage of Capella, circa 2300 BCE. However, (as shown in Figure 38) this alignment would also have been useful for the observation of the northernmost setting point obtained by the Moon in its 18.61-year cycle, and for the observation of the Milky Way.

As each winter night progressed, sky-watchers at the Sanctuary around 2500 BCE would have seen the northern and western segments of the Milky Way appear to swivel around Windmill Hill as it lowered itself onto the horizon. Most of the constellation Cygnus set into Windmill Hill shortly after dusk; its alpha star Deneb setting slightly later. As described above, the Milky Way was now lower in the southern sky than it had been a thousand years before, it no longer formed so high or bright a circle around the winter horizon. But the Milky Way still levelled upon the horizon in the small hours of the morning in the mid-third millennium BCE, at the same time as Cygnus reappeared in the northeast, Capella approached and set into the summit of Windmill Hill. This would have been a majestic sky spectacle.

Did Neolithic people light fires in the enclosures on the summit of Windmill Hill during the winter months of the mid-third millennium BCE, so enabling them to mark events such as the setting of Capella when seen from the location of the Sanctuary? The setting of Capella heralded not only the return of Cygnus from the lower world below the horizon, but also the reappearance of the much-favoured southern stars; therefore the Sanctuary-builders may have perceived Capella's descent into Windmill Hill as a reminder of their ancestors, who had dwelt there from the early-fourth millennium BCE.

The high northern passage of Capella across the night sky, and its descent toward the northwest, would also have provided a useful time-keeping device for sky-watchers at the Sanctuary. Capella later came to be known as the 'Shepherd's Star' for its value in keeping the watches of the night. Neolithic sky-watchers could have used the star to gauge time: to estimate, for example, how long it would be before the stars on the other side of the Galactic Equator—the central plane of the galaxy—would appear again in the southeastern sky. For as Capella set into Windmill Hill in the third millennium BCE, the stars of the Southern Cross would have stood upright precisely due south and beta Centaurus would have risen on the southern horizon.[13] And as Capella set, Cygnus—that had set at twilight over Windmill Hill—reappeared over Fyfield Down. Thus, the north-eastern and northwestern horizons of the Sanctuary emphasised the rotation of the stars around the Northern Pole and inexorably pointed, like an arrow, to the southern stars of Crux and Centaurus.[14]

The following chapter describes this synchronised dance of stars from Avebury, which occurred from approximately 3000 to 2100 BCE. This was the era when the stone and timber circle of the Sanctuary was in use. From here observers throughout the winter months could have seen Cygnus emerge in the twilight pointing downward to Windmill Hill and to Avebury, on an azimuth of 317°+. Later in the night, as Capella and the Milky Way sank toward the horizon in the west, the stars of Cygnus, particularly Deneb, reappeared in the northeast on the other side of Overton Hill. As they did so, the Southern Cross and beta Centauri imposed themselves upon the southern horizon and the Galactic Equator became fully extended in a 360° circle above the horizon. As the Milky Way began to rise in the east, and Cygnus, the Northern Cross, climbed higher into the north-eastern sky, the Southern Cross reached its culmination due south over Furze Hill. See Figure 37. Later in the night, the stars of Crux set toward East Kennet long barrow. Time and space does not allow a full description of these alignments, but it cannot have been an accident that the great curve of Overton Hill, due north of the Sanctuary and intersected by the ancient Ridgeway, provided this focus upon the Polar axis and the subterranean passage of Cygnus.

During the Sanctuary's most intense period of use from 2600 to 2100 BCE, the setting of Capella moved progressively northwards, due to precession, until it reached Windmill Hill and the part of the landscape closely defined by Avebury henge. In 2600 BCE Capella was setting over the summit of Windmill Hill at 317°—allowing just over 1° extinction angle for the first-magnitude star—an alignment that coincided with the western part of Avebury henge, whose outer bank lay just below view. By 2300 BCE and 320°, Capella was setting over the area marked by the most prominent stones of the West Kennet Avenue and the centre of the henge, as shown in Figure 39. By 2100 BCE and 322°, the sky-watchers would have seen Capella setting over the whole of Avebury henge, even on the many nights when its extinction angle was greater than 1°. These are not, nor do they have to be, precise alignments, but there can be no doubt of their striking character.

In summary, the prominent notch between Waden Hill and Overton Hill, in which lay Windmill Hill, Avebury henge and the northern terminus of the West Kennet Avenue, provided a highly symbolic window for certain astronomical events when viewed from the Sanctuary. The first-magnitude star Capella moved across this window in the third millennium BCE, but it also allowed viewings of lunar extremes, the passage of prominent constellations and of the equator of the Milky Way. Two outlying stones set squarely on a line running from the centre of the Sanctuary strongly reinforce the impression the builders were looking purposefully in this direction.

The Sanctuary & Silbury Hill

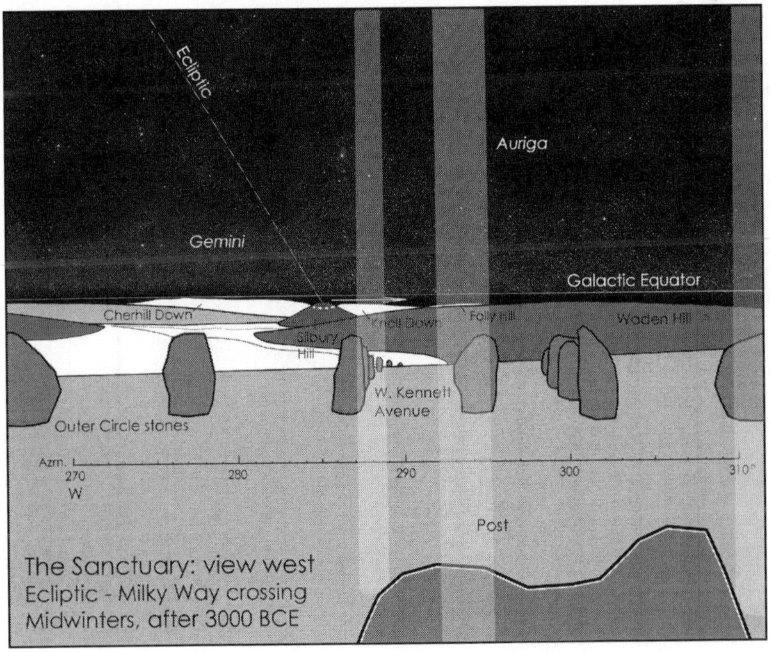

Figure 40a. This recreated view west from the centre of the Sanctuary, omits several concentric rings of wooden posts. The Sanctuary was in use from at least 3000 BCE, at which time a notch in the horizon, formed by the junction of Cherhill and Knoll Down (shown by the dotted line), occupied the place of Silbury Hill. The view shows the crossing-point of the ecliptic and the almost level Milky Way, setting

in the notch in mid April. This stellar crossing-point moved progressively northwards over the course of the third millennium. By 2200 BCE, it was over the centre of the junction of the West Kennet Avenue and the Outer Circle of stones—an alignment to Folly Hill (and the setting of Alnath). The next figure describes the time of year when the setting Sun was upon it.

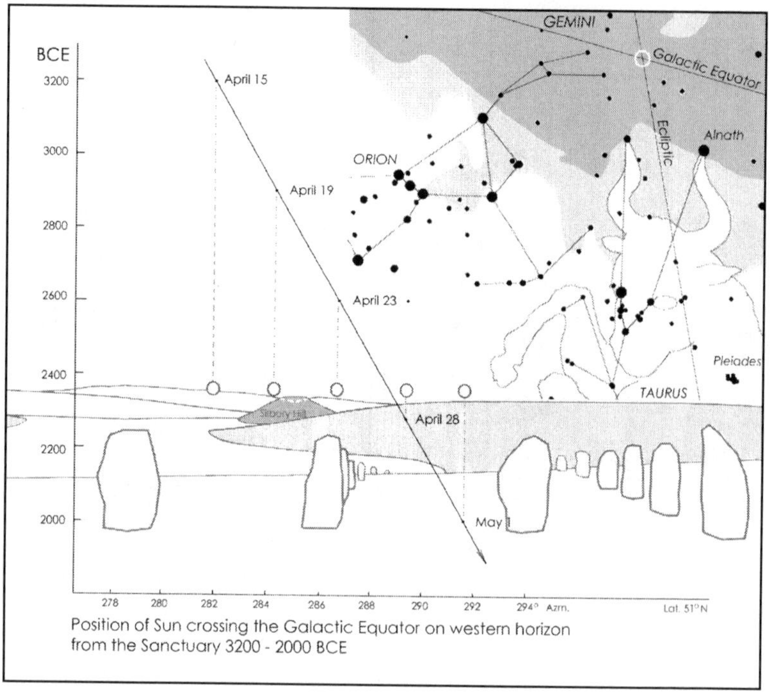

Figure 40b. Graph showing the relationship between time (BCE), the horizonal setting points (degrees from North), and the season (time of year), as the Sun sets on the Gemini crossing-point of the ecliptic and the Milky Way when viewed from the Sanctuary site 3200-2000 BCE. The Sun was setting on the crossing-point in the late spring, 20-21st April, in the notch on Cherhill Down between 2800 and 2700 BCE (as the Galactic Equator levelled around the horizon); by 2000 BCE this event had shifted to Waden Hill over the entrance to the Sanctuary, in a season corresponding to 1st May. Although the builders did not begin Silbury until the 2400s BCE, it would have continued to be a marker

of this event (i.e. sunset on the crossing point) after this date. The Sun, stars and planets would have been visible through the posts and stones of the Sanctuary, now oriented towards and above Silbury, prior to their settings over the stones of the West Kennet Avenue. A well-marked event horizon of this sort was capable of generating very detailed knowledge of the relative movements of the stars and seasons.

The view directly west from the Sanctuary is compelling. It was to become even more so in the second half of the third millennium BCE when Silbury Hill rose into the sky. But long before the building of Silbury, the meeting of Cherhill Down and Knoll Down already formed a convenient and significant notch in the horizon from the Sanctuary. The conical mass of Silbury Hill—the 'mother mound' itself—was to rise and fill this distinctive notch in the western horizon in the last quarter of the millennium.

For the privileged Neolithic observer standing at the centre of the Sanctuary, the southernmost stone of the entranceway—at the junction of the West Kennet Avenue and the outer circle—stood on this alignment to Silbury and Knoll Down, at approximately 285°. The summit of Folly Hill lay between 292° and 294°, near the centre of the entranceway, while Waden Hill formed the remainder of the horizon. Sufficient stone sockets survive to determine the course of the avenue, shown here in reconstruction in Figure 40a. Its builders obviously considered the meeting of avenue and circle as very important. The Sun would have set over the entranceway, on the Silbury-notch alignment, at the times of year seasonally corresponding during late April and mid August in the last quarter of the third millennium BCE.

An observer at the Sanctuary in that period would have seen the bright yellow star *beta Taurus*, Alnath, the distinctive point on the uppermost horn of Taurus, approach and set into the centre of the entranceway over Folly Hill on the horizon. The orientation of the centre stone of the Sanctuary entrance is approximately 290° but with such short distances involved, these stones had substantial width. The azimuth of Alnath setting was 292° circa 2300 BCE, 294° circa 2100 BCE. Alnath is the brightest star nearest the crossing of the ecliptic and the Milky Way in Gemini. The crossing followed the setting of the star on the same azimuth over Folly Hill at the latter date. Folly Hill, just visible above the end of Waden Hill, is near the terminus of the Western or Beckhampton Avenue, the Longstones Cove. It is also near the South Street long barrow and the massive Beckhampton long barrow. We will see the possible implications of this in a moment.

As shown in Figure 40a, what is interesting is that from around 2800 BCE, as the Sun set in the notch between Knoll Down and Cherhill Down, it set in Gemini, the crossing-point of the ecliptic with the Milky Way, at the time when the Milky Way levelled around the horizon. This event, taking place in mid-late April, subsequently moved northwards, until by 2200 BCE, it was taking place over the centre of the junction of the West Kennet Avenue and the Sanctuary, on the alignment to Folly Hill, at the time of year which seasonally corresponded to early May.

In summary (as shown in Figure 40b), circa 3200 BCE from the Sanctuary, the Sun set on the Gemini crossing-point in mid April over Cherhill Down. By 2800-2700 BCE, it set on the crossing-point in the notch of the Downs around the 20-21st April. By 2000 BCE, this event, close to 1st May, was over the entrance stones of the Sanctuary and Folly Hill. These alignments fit the dates when the Sanctuary was in use. They reveal how observers at the Sanctuary could have seen the changing relationship between the stars and the season of the Sun. In this case, however, it seems that instead of employing just a single star or star group to track precessional change, it was one of the fixed crossroads of the ecliptic and the Milky Way that provided the sky-watchers with the key reference point. This is one of the two crossing-points described in the 'Dream of Scipio,' the late classical text quoted at the beginning of the chapter.

A Conspicuous & Convenient Notch

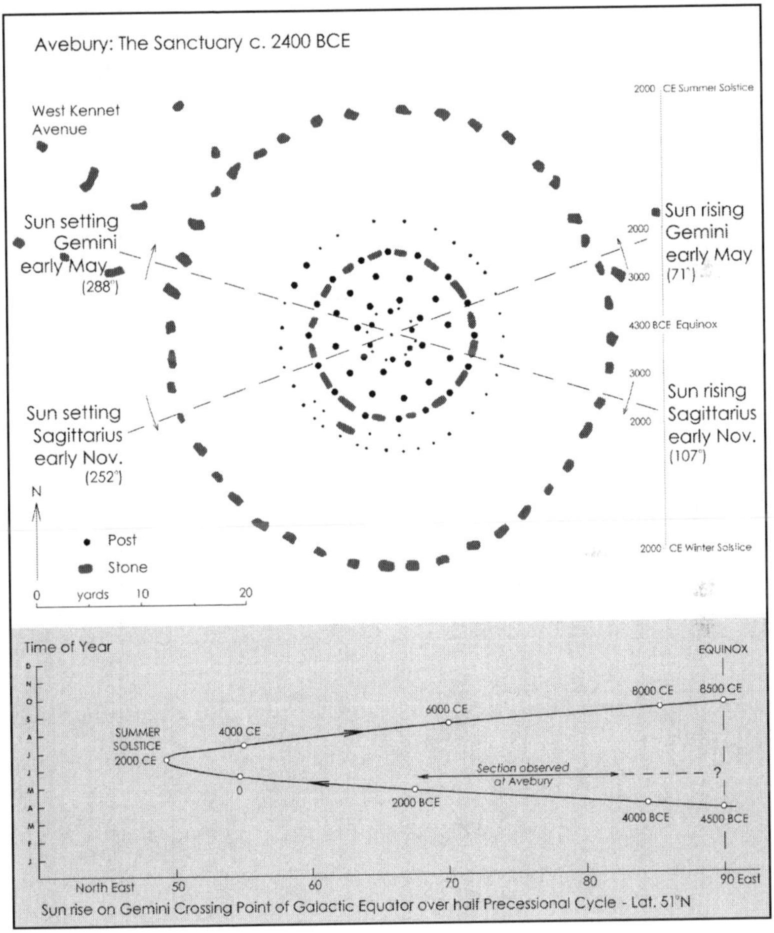

Figure 41. In the mid-fifth millennium, 4500 BCE, the Sun rose on the two crossing-points of the ecliptic and the Galactic Equator in Sagittarius and Gemini due east at the equinoxes. Over time, due to precession, the crossing-points moved away from east and the Sun rose upon them progressively later in the year—by the late-third millennium BCE, in late October and late April. The arrows in the

upper diagram and the marked section of the curve in the lower diagram show the amount of horizonal movement visible from the Sanctuary, 3000-2000 BCE. The pairs of stones just outside the circle of the Sanctuary may show the builder's greater interest in the rising and setting Sun on the Gemini crossing-point, as there are no corresponding stones oriented to the Sagittarius crossing-point. In 2800 BCE (when the Pleiades rose due east and set due west), the Milky Way levelled upon the horizon as the Gemini crossing-point set and the Sagittarius crossing-point rose. The lower diagram shows how, today 2000 CE, the Sun rises a quarter of a cycle later upon the Gemini crossing-point at the summer solstice, while (not shown) the Sagittarius crossing-point is upon the winter solstice. The crossing-points will now start to return towards the equinoxes, obtained circa 8500 CE; until by 15000 CE, their positions will have reversed—Gemini midwinter, Sagittarius midsummer. See Figure 56.

The sky-watchers obviously located the Sanctuary to take full advantage of the horizon. The northern horizon, described by the great sweep of Overton Hill, and the features on the escarpment in the south, defined the ancient Ridgeway as well as the Polar axis of the stars. The western horizon, marked by a wealth of sites including West Kennet long barrow, Cherhill Down, Silbury Hill, Knoll Down, Folly Hill, Waden Hill, Windmill Hill and Avebury itself, provided them with an excellent means of viewing the setting Sun, Moon, planets and stars. The Poles, the constellations and the fixed stars, especially those that first appeared briefly upon the horizon after sunset and those that set last before sunrise, became the constants against which the Sanctuary sky-watchers could watch and anticipate the cycles of the Sun, the Moon and the wandering planets.

Due to precession (as shown in Figures 40 and 41) from 2800 to 2200 BCE, the crossing-point at 3° Gemini moved about 5° further northwards and the Sun was upon it about eight days

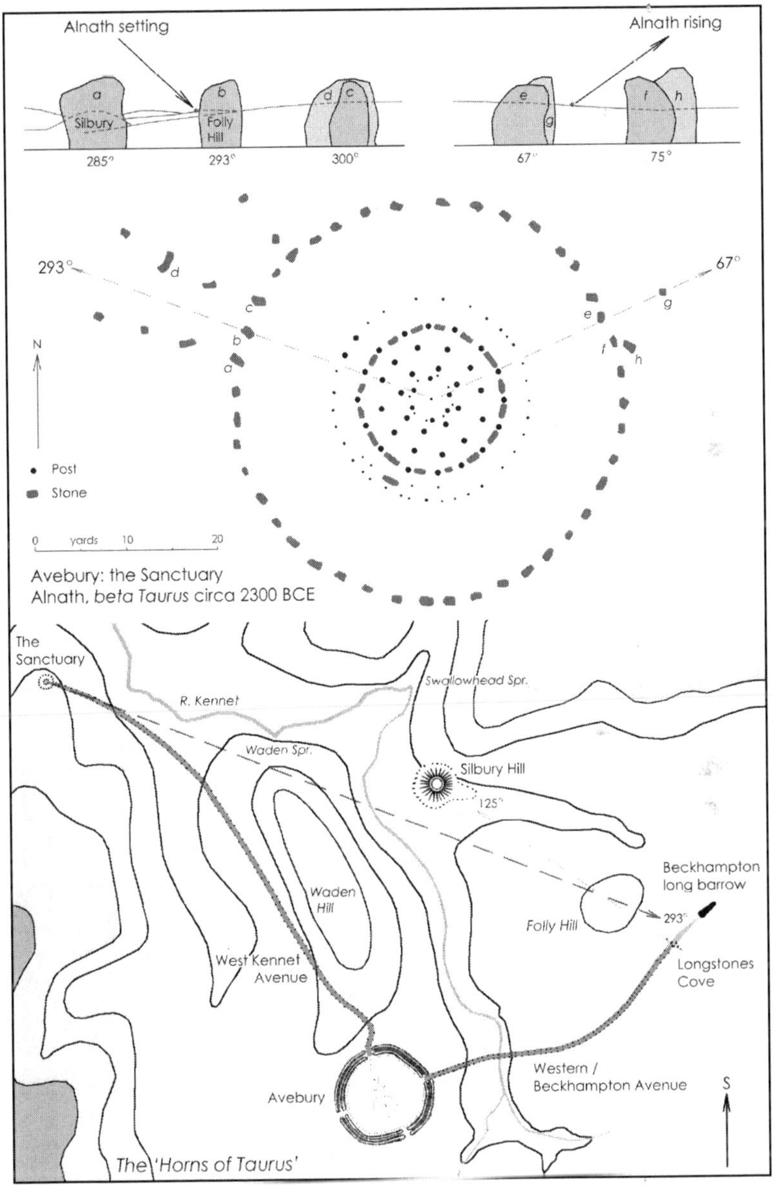

Figure 42. *Top: Although these views from the centre of the Sanctuary can only guess at the shape of the stones, they show the rising and setting of Alnath, circa 2300 BCE. Alnath is the point of a horn of Taurus and the brightest star nearest to the galactic anticentre.*

Middle: The heliacal rising of Alnath took place just before and on the same azimuth as the Sun, 67°, over the stones in the northeastern part of the circle in late April i.e. the ancient fire festival of Beltane. The last (acronychal) setting of Alnath took place over the entranceway to the circle, at 293°, in late October, the ancient fire festival of Samhain. Bottom: the azimuth of 293° links the Sanctuary to the Longstones Cove via the just visible summit of Folly Hill, the setting point of Alnath. In this context, the Avebury monuments can be interpreted as representing the horned head of a bull—Avebury is the head and the two Avenues the horns. Silbury Hill lies between the horns like the ecliptic and galaxy crossing-point between the horns of Taurus.

later in the year. The builders could have tracked this movement from the Sanctuary, using timber markers and, eventually, permanent stones against the horizonal foresights.[15] The Gemini crossing-point coincided with the levelling of the Milky Way as it *set* upon the horizon in the west. The Sagittarius crossing-point coincided with the level Milky Way as it *rose* in the east. What is interesting is that the builders of the Sanctuary erected outlying stones on both the rising and setting Gemini crossing-points, while no stones mark the corresponding events in Sagittarius.

From the Sanctuary, Silbury Hill is also on this alignment, but it appears to have been built too late to be an accurate horizonal marker of the key Gemini setting event. Figure 40a shows that around 2820 BCE, when the Galactic Equator levelled with the horizon, the Sun upon the crossing-point in Gemini set exactly on the 285° azimuth from the Sanctuary to the notch between Cherhill and Knoll Down—the place where Silbury Hill was to rise about 400 years later. But as the setting Sun, Moon, stars and planets crossed the Milky Way in the western sky after 2400 BCE, when viewed through the tall posts and stones of the Sanctuary, they still would have appeared over or setting towards Silbury Hill. If this conspicuous and convenient notch marked the event circa 2800 BCE and Silbury marked it in the final quarter of the millennium, then the Sanctuary was in continuous use for a very long time.

On the eastern side of the horizon, the Sun *rose* on the crossing point in Gemini, preceded before dawn by Alnath. In 3000 BCE, the Sun was rising on the Gemini crossroads at an azimuth of 76° at a time of year corresponding to mid April. By 2000 BCE, the Sun was rising on the crossroads at an azimuth of 67°, well over a week later in late April. This was later the time of the Celtic cross-quarter festival of Beltane, now our Mayday. Perhaps more significantly in 2300 BCE, the rising Sun at the time of the Beltane fire festival was heralded by the heliacal rising of the star Alnath on the 67° alignment. At the Sanctuary, these eastern azimuths are marked by an excellent viewing horizon, and by two outlying stones, shown in Figure 41, one of which lies at 67° from the centre of the circle. These two anomalous stones in the east may therefore be equivalent to those connecting the Sanctuary to the Avenue in the west, where, over the centre of the entranceway at 293°, the Sun *set* on the Gemini crossing-point, marked by its closest star Alnath, at its acronychal setting date in late October—the later fire festival of Samhain. There is more on Alnath in the next section.

From the Sanctuary, the valley of the River Kennet (which runs east to an immense, but undated, mound now in the grounds of Marlborough College) at approximately 84°, would have marked the rising of the Sun on the crossroads around 4000 BCE. But, remarkably, due to the movement of the Poles, both events, the rising of the Sun upon the Sagittarius crossing and upon the Gemini crossing, would have taken place *due east* (90°) at the equinoxes circa 4500 BCE, while their settings would have taken place due west (270°). This date may be far too soon for any construction at the Sanctuary, but not, perhaps, for the presence of early sky-watchers and the beginnings of local tradition.

The Crossroads of the Stars

Inevitably, the sky-watchers at the Sanctuary would have noted the complete ring of the Milky Way upon the horizon in the early third millennium BCE. This was the front-page news of the time. They also would have noted the two points where the path of the Sun, Moon and planets on the ecliptic intersected the galaxy. These two points, indicated by the stars of Sagittarius, Ophiuchus and Scorpius on one side of the horizon and by the stars of Gemini, the arm of Orion and the horns of Taurus on the other, offer a never changing marker of the order of the heavens. Only the times of the year when the Sun is upon them will change in the 'Great Year' of the stars.

It is time to consider these two crossing-points—which will remain in their respective constellations as long as the Earth occupies its current place within the solar system and the Sun within the galaxy—in the light of the quotation from Macrobius at the beginning of the chapter.

Although Macrobius begins, "the Milky Way girdles the zodiac, its great circle meeting it obliquely so that it crosses it at the two tropical signs, Capricorn and Cancer..." this is clearly an error. The great circle of the Milky Way crosses the Zodiac in Sagittarius and Gemini. The Neo-Platonic Macrobius is actually referring to the Sun, which in his day, the fourth-fifth Century CE, was rising in Capricorn at the winter solstice, and in Cancer at the summer solstice. He continues: "Natural philosophers called these (crossing points) the "portals of the sun" because the solstices lie athwart the sun's path on either side, checking further progress." In this context, Macrobius seems to be saying that the two crossing points of the Ecliptic and the Milky Way are necessarily defined by the limits of the solstitial extremes, the precessional movement of the Milky Way never goes outside of the Sun's path, that is, the solstices check further progress. But admittedly, it is unclear; he could be saying something else.

What is clear, however, is that these two "portals of the sun" are the two crossing points of the ecliptic and the Milky Way, one in Sagittarius and one in Gemini. Macrobius (or his translator) is confusing several difficult subjects: the time of year the Sun is upon the crossing points, the solstitial extremes and the crossing points themselves.

With these clarifications, the final and most important part of the quotation should be read:

Souls are believed to pass through these portals when going from the sky to the earth and returning from the earth to the sky. Gemini is called the portal of men, because through it descent is made to the earth; Sagittarius is called the portal of gods, because through it souls return to their rightful abode of immortality, to be reckoned among the gods.

Macrobius is quoting an ancient belief, older than Homer; important to Egyptian, Vedic and Maya astronomers, described in more detail in Appendix 2. And, if the alignments at the Sanctuary are anything to go by, the two galactic crossing-points—the two 'portals' of Macrobius—where the ecliptic, the Sun and planets, always cross the galactic equator in Sagittarius and in Gemini, were of great interest to the Neolithic sky-watchers. These two points, fixed 180° diametrically across the sky from each other, could have provided the basis for an early primary division of the galaxy, the ecliptic and the celestial sphere—a role later entirely assumed by the twelve-fold Zodiac. The crossing points of the two greatest star paths around the heavens—the Ecliptic/Zodiac and the Milky Way—complemented by the north-south axis of the Poles, may have formed the earliest primary division of the heavens.

As shown in Figures 40 and 56, the time of year in which the path of the Sun, the ecliptic, is over the two crossing-points slowly changes over the course of the Great Year. As one precessional cycle of about 26,000 years is necessary for everything to return to the same place, the wheel of the year turns like a compass point to the galaxy. In 4500 BCE, the horizonal dial was aligned east-west with the spring equinox Sun over the centre of the galaxy and the autumn equinox Sun over the galactic anticentre. Today, the winter solstice Sun points inexorably—or at least for a few decades—to the galactic centre and the summer solstice Sun points away from it.[16] Such alignments provide simple, but all-inclusive markers for people coming to terms with the times, periodicities and powers of the greater cosmos.

As we have seen above, at the time of Macrobius in the early fifth century CE, the winter solstice Sun rose in Capricorn and the summer solstice Sun rose in Cancer. At the time of the Sanctuary, the winter solstice Sun rose in the constellation of Aquarius and the summer solstice Sun rose in that of Leo. The Sun rose in that era upon the two crossing-points in late April and October. During the centuries the Sanctuary was in use, observers could have tracked differences in the time of year relative to the movement of the Sun over the two crossroads of the galaxy by the multitude of markers provided by the tall posts, lintels and notches. Such observations would potentially have provided the Neolithic sky-watchers with a handle on the order of precession. Although the Sanctuary sky-watchers may have missed the event of 4500 BCE when the two crossing-points both stood exactly east-west, they could not have missed the great event of their time: the levelling of the Milky Way upon the horizon. The sky-watchers must have felt the divine powers were showing them the great cosmic dividers, markers of all time and space. Two sets of otherwise anomalous outlying stones at the Sanctuary appear to have marked the critical rising and setting points of the Gemini/Taurus crossroads in this era.

The Horns of Taurus

The star *beta Taurus*, Alnath or El Nath, is universally seen as the point of a horn; that is, it marks one of the points of the horns of the Bull, Taurus. Its Arabic name means 'one who butts.' The star, the second brightest in Taurus with a magnitude of 1.65, is visible down to about 2.5° above the horizon. The two horns of Taurus straddle the ecliptic, pointing to the galactic crossroads and galactic anticentre in Gemini. Indeed, Alnath is the brightest star nearest to them. The horns always precede the setting of the Gemini crossing-point in the west, in this case, over the entranceway of the Sanctuary. The horns appear to draw the crossing-point down to the horizon, embracing Silbury Hill; but in the late-third millennium, the crossing-point actually set and rose on the same azimuth as Alnath over the all-important centre of the entranceway to the Sanctuary and the Kennet Avenue.

In Vedic tradition, Alnath represents the fire god Agni; the Gemini ecliptic-galactic crossing is considered the source of the *soma* of the Gods, while the starry region as a whole is the home of the creator god, Brahma.

In the astronomy of the Sanctuary, the horns of Taurus appear very prominent indeed.

Alnath was the heliacal rising star in late April, early May—the ancient fire festival of Beltane—when it rose just before and upon the same azimuth as the Sun. Figure 42 shows that there appears to be an alignment from the Sanctuary to this event at an azimuth of 67°. An observer at the Sanctuary, the end of the Kennet Avenue, in the late-third millennium BCE, must also have been aware of the proximity of the setting point of Alnath over Folly Hill and the hidden Longstones Cove, at the end of the western, the Beckhampton Avenue. They could have observed the star last setting there (at 293°) in late October—this was later the fire festival of Samhain, marking the other end of the year.

The question waiting to be asked is whether the builders saw Alnath as a marker of the end of the Western Avenue, in the same manner as the star marked the point of the horn of Taurus.

In other words, did the monument-builders conceive the two avenues as two horns, *bucrania,* emanating from the head of Avebury? If so, then the builders may have thought of the Sanctuary as the second point of the horn, laying the star patterns on the ground in the form of the avenues. They may have linked the two sites by their stellar alignments. From this perspective, Silbury Hill, as shown in Figure 42, was located between the points of the two horns, in a position that actually corresponds to the galactic-ecliptic crossroads. The Longstones Cove lay in the appropriate direction for Alnath, but the nearby Beckhampton long barrow—where three ox skulls were found—was believed by Stukeley and others to be the final terminus of the Western Avenue. Nor does the alignment of the Longstones Cove to Sirius at 125° and not to the Sanctuary, spoil the picture, as Sirius' heliacal risings and settings appear also to have been linked with cycles of fertility associated with the bull. Finally, Beltane and Samhain traditionally mark the times of the year when cattle were put out to pasture in the spring and brought in for slaughter in the fall. The Celtic custom at Beltane was to drive cattle between two fires. Could a Neolithic custom have been to drive cattle between stones that formed the seasonal pattern of the stars upon the ground?

The stars may have given the Sanctuary star-watchers a further indication of the celestial order. At the beginning of the third millennium BCE, the Pleiades rose and set upon the east-west equinoctial axis. The Pleiades, or the Seven Sisters, are a distinctive cluster of stars that lie in the back of the Bull, the constellation Taurus. Circa 2800 BCE, the Pleiades rose heliacally *due east* in early May and then set heliacally *due west* in late February at the latitude of the Sanctuary. Thus to the sky-watchers, because the heliacal rising of the Pleiades east-west accompanied the rising of the Gemini crossing-point, this would have helped to emphasize the crossing-points further, a complementary celestial axis to that of the Poles. Thus the horizon about the Sanctuary—the great curve of Overton Hill obtaining due north upon the ancient Ridgeway, the path continuing due south through the Furze Hill notch in the Wessex Chalk Escarpment to Knap Hill—lent itself again and again to reminders that all lay between and turned around the Poles—the *axis mundi*.

The subtle relationship of the Sanctuary to Silbury Hill may therefore have given the Avebury sky-watchers the opportunity to create their most sophisticated and perhaps their most labour-intensive 'embodiment' of celestial awareness: a marker of the two crossing-points of the galaxy with the ecliptic.

In sum, in this period, as the Milky Way rotated around the sky and became visible upon the entire horizon just before setting in the west, a viewer at the Sanctuary would have seen the ecliptic cross over it in the area defined by Silbury Hill. The Sun would have been upon this crossing-point in Gemini in late April/May, its presence at dawn heralded by the fiery star Alnath—an event perhaps associated with a cult of the bull. Around 2800 BCE, long before Silbury Hill, a significant notch marked the horizon at the relevant azimuth of 285°. When Silbury was built, filling the notch within a century or two after 2450 BCE, observers would have seen the *setting* Sun, Moon, stars and planets positioned on the Galactic Equator through the elevated structure of the Sanctuary and the stones of the entranceway at a few degrees over the Hill. Alnath, the point of a horn of Taurus, the acronychal setting star, set on this alignment circa 2300 BCE. Further outlying stones on the other side of the Sanctuary, at an azimuth between 67° and 75°, may have marked both the *rising* Sun, Moon and planets on the cross-roads in Sagittarius and the heliacal rising of Alnath at this time. As the relationship between the date, the event and the horizonal markers subtly changed, as the stars moved slowly forward against the seasonal motion of the Sun, the emphasis on these alignments suggests the sky-watchers were thinking and acting in terms based upon the cycle of precession.[17] There were obviously many factors for building Silbury Hill; this alignment from the Sanctuary must be considered among them.

In closing this chapter, I must ask whether the Neolithic sky-watchers in Britain were really so closely attuned to the stars. Although I grant more astronomical skill than currently assumed, astronomers in Mesopotamia, India and Egypt appear to have been tracking the stars at this time, people elsewhere were likely to have been doing the same. Indeed, Vedic astronomers, with whom the Neolithic monument-builders share hereditary and linguistic roots, attributed huge significance to the east-west heliacal rising of the Pleiades in 2800 BCE, an event, at their latitude, which also coincided with the equinoxes. The equinoxes coincided with the crossing-points for the Neolithic people of Europe in 4500 BCE.

While early British or Indian sky-watchers did not understand or model the cause of astronomical events like these in a 'scientific' cosmography, there can be no doubt they keenly anticipated and closely watched the movement of all the celestial bodies. They told and retold what they saw in mythic form, and closely examined any sign in the heavens for its spiritual meaning. The aim of the Neolithic monument-builders was not to rationally or mathematically explain these cosmic events, but to incorporate them into their monuments, so maintaining the necessary adherence to the divine order. These pious people needed no other form of notation than the monuments to mark the passage of time. The monuments were proof, not of their intellectual skills or transcendent longing, but of their integration with life and with the stars.

9

Return to Avebury

The stars will alter their accustomed course, roots and branches shall change their places.

Geoffrey of Monmouth: 'Merlin'[1]

View south from the bank beside the northern entrance of the henge toward Waden Hill. The remains of the Cove occupy the middle ground.

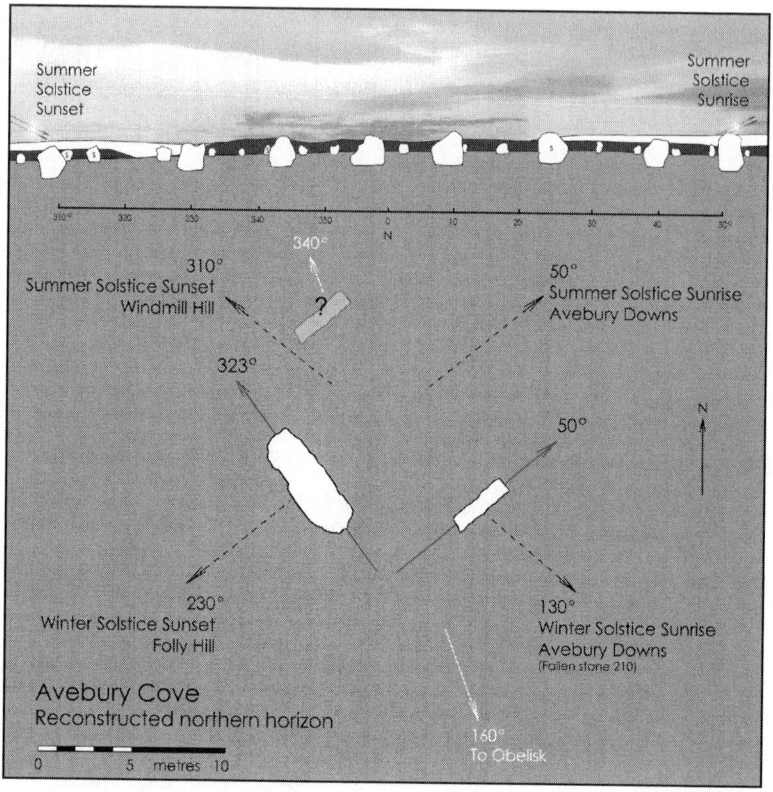

Figure 43. Upper: Conjectural reconstruction of stones north from Avebury Cove, mid-third millennium BCE. Note how the northern bank of the henge is evenly situated between the hills that mark the rising and setting of the midsummer Sun. Figure 46 shows the very different view south. Lower: A good line of sight to Folly Hill at midwinter Sunset complements the opening of the Cove to midsummer Sunrise. Extant stones appear on a midsummer Sunset line to Windmill Hill and midwinter Sunrise to Avebury Down. S = extant stone. (Cove after Gillings et al, 2008.)

Avebury Cove

Avebury Cove today has a stone missing. Unlike most Neolithic coves, the tremendous stones at Avebury were not tightly set. It is likely that one further stone stood opposite the tall, slender southeast stone to form an open rectangular arrangement facing northeast. There were other stones inside the Northern Inner Circle but they do not appear to have been part of the Cove.[2] The huge stones of the Cove and the Obelisk may have been objects of veneration on the site before they were set up. Both in scale and in alignment, Avebury Cove is comparable to the inner settings of Stonehenge, while it is possible there was a further stone on the ground inside the Cove, like the Altar stone at Stonehenge.[3]

The orientation of the longer axis of the colossal 100-ton back stone, grooved by grinding actions, is approximately 143 – 323°. The longer axis of the other remaining stone is not quite a right angle to this, approximately 50 – 230°.[4] The 'opening' of the Cove to the average result of 51 – 52° strongly suggests that the builders intentionally oriented the Cove to align to midsummer sunrise at 50+°, taking the elevation of the horizon into account. This is also midwinter full moonrise (the Moon will swing ten degrees either side of this every 18/19 years). These measurements are identical to those of the main axis of Stonehenge. A pit at 52° from the centre of the Cove suggests a stone of the Northern Inner Circle once stood on this alignment and once, like the Heelstone at Stonehenge, would have the summer solstice Sun sitting on its head. There is another large stone socket on this alignment in the Great Outer Circle. The stone standing in splendid isolation in this section of the circle would have marked the rising of Deneb and Sadr at 22-23°, but Cygnus as a whole rose into the sky in the portion of the sky facing the Cove.

In the previous chapter, I described the importance of the stars of Capella and Cygnus as observed from the Sanctuary. The monument-builders must have also observed these bright northern stars at Avebury henge, where any location between the Obelisk and the Cove would have provided them with an excellent northern viewing horizon. The constellations of Cygnus, Lyra, Cassiopeia, Auriga, their brightest stars Vega and Capella, would have been conspicuous in the northern sky. Sky-watchers at Avebury would probably have seen Cygnus as a long-necked bird: swan, goose or loon and noted the passage of Arcturus, the brightest star in the northern hemisphere, the Corona Borealis, and above all the circumpolar stars closest to the North Celestial Pole (then *alpha Draconis*). While the figures here can only offer approximate reconstructions, they show the complex situation in the heavens at a glance.

Now, there is an azimuth of 312° between the northern half of Avebury henge and Windmill Hill; this differs from that of 317° between the Sanctuary and Windmill Hill, but in fact, both locations looked to the *same* events in the sky, merely at a different time. As shown in Figures 39 and 45, circa 2900 BCE, Capella was visible setting into Windmill Hill[5] when observed from the Cove at Avebury on an azimuth of 312°. Three centuries later, from the Sanctuary, Capella was visible setting into Windmill Hill at 317°.

This conspicuous alignment from Avebury Cove to the broad summit of Windmill Hill (centre 312°) is also close to the path of midsummer sunset, 310°. Circa 3200 BCE, Capella was setting at this azimuth over Windmill Hill, which may suggest a date for the first stone settings at the henge. This orange-yellow star, the third brightest in the northern hemisphere, was setting over the centre of the hill by 2800 BCE. As shown in Figure 45, primary stones seem to have distinctly marked this horizon. The name Capella is a diminutive of the Latin *Capra*, female goat. In Roman mythology, the horn of this goat became the Cornucopia, or 'horn of plenty,' portending great honours and wealth. In Britain, Capella was later known as the Shepherd's Star, marking out the watches of the night, while in Vedic and Hindu mythology it marked the heart of the creator god Brahma, whose other stars included those of Gemini and some of nearby Orion.

Figure 44 shows how after 3000 BCE, anyone standing in or near the Cove would have seen Cygnus throughout midwinter descending over Windmill Hill at dusk, close to the Summer Solstice Sunset alignment. At the same time, on the other side of the sky along the path provided by the Milky Way they would have seen Sirius rising, close to the Winter Solstice Sunrise alignment. As Cygnus turned around the North Celestial Pole, its diving path levelled out, and the body of the constellation set into the northern horizon. As the Milky Way fell westwards, observers at the Cove would have seen Deneb—*alpha Cygni* or the swan's 'tail-feathers'—setting toward the main 340° axis of the monument.

At this time, therefore, the midwinter setting passage of Cygnus took place over the Northern Entrance of the henge. Just above it shone Vega, *alpha Lyrae,* the second brightest star in the northern hemisphere. This stellar event took place over the well-preserved and noticeably high section of the bank of the henge that lies closest to the stones of the Northern Inner Circle. Unlike Capella, Sirius and the stars in the southern sky, the setting point of Deneb, the first-magnitude, blue-white super-giant in the tail of Cygnus, changed little over the third millennium BCE. As one arm of the cross of Cygnus points towards and so emphasises the turning of the stars around the North Celestial Pole, we now call this constellation the Northern Cross. Cygnus no longer points as closely to the Northern Pole today as it did in 3000 BCE.

Over the following hours, Cygnus 'flew' below the northern bank of the henge. By midnight Deneb lay due north at an altitude of minus 2.5°, that is, *below* the horizon, only its wingtip remained visible, pointing to the Northern Pole.[6] Ursa Major climbed high in the sky to lie directly above it on the other side of the Pole. But as the Southern Cross rose higher in the south, it would have become possible to tell from its wing that the hidden body of Cygnus had begun to rise. Two hours after midnight, observers at the Cove would have seen the body of Cygnus begin to rise horizontally over the stones and northern bank of the henge (and the hills beyond if they were visible). As shown in Figure 46, Deneb rose at an azimuth of 20° (plus the extinction angle of 2-3°) and Albireo, *beta Cygni*, the head, eye or beak of the swan, at 38°+. As Cygnus rose, apparently pulled up by the descent of Ursa Major across the Pole, an observer beside the Obelisk in the south would have seen the stars of Crux and beta Centauri rising on the equivalent azimuth. Finally, with both poles strongly marked, there came the dramatic flourish.

During the third hour after midnight, as Cygnus, almost horizontal, rose clear of the atmosphere and Ursa Major began to sink, sky-watchers at the Cove would have seen the descent of Capella into Windmill Hill. *As Capella, setting over Windmill Hill, levelled with Cygnus rising over the Avebury Downs, the stars of the Southern Cross stood vertically upon the southern horizon, while the continuous, level ring of the Milky Way unified the starry spectacle.* This magnificent sight, seen from the axis between the Obelisk and the Cove in the first quarter of the third millennium BCE and described in Chapter 4, is shown in Figures 46, 48 and the Frontispiece.

Like the Crux-Centaurus stars, the passage of Cygnus was a winter event. At the end of the fourth millennium BCE, observers at the Cove would have first seen Cygnus rising in the northeast before dawn from mid-November on. By midwinter, its reappearance was well before dawn, but it was fast becoming lost from sight in the northwest. Cygnus would have vanished from the northwest and risen for the last time in early April.

This distinctive stellar dance recalls the ancient myth of the Earth Diver, found throughout the northern hemisphere. In this myth, a bird dives into the primordial ocean that covers the whole world and brings back soil to form the first land.[7] The myth is a cosmogony, a myth of creation, which also establishes a centre and a route, an axis and a path between the worlds. The

Earth Diver myth has an ancient Indo-European origin that links it with the swan as the vehicle of the creator god Brahma and with the bear, a parallel creature of departure, revival and regeneration.

"Water birds," write Miranda and Stephen Aldhouse-Green, "are recorded ethnographically as acting as messengers between the otherworld and the earth; as guides to the 'burial beyond the water'; and as guardians to the entrance to the chthonic regions."[8] Ancient and tribal people in the northern hemisphere linked the migratory cycle of waterfowl with the hibernation cycle of the bear to form the principal markers in the seasons of the year. "In the light of this shared oracular power," comments Paul Shepard, "their intertwined presence in the stars is not surprising."[9] We cannot know the story attached to the constellation by the Avebury sky-watchers. But they could not have failed to notice the synchronous passage of the southern stars nor that Ursa Major and Cygnus formed a complementary pair around the Northern Pole, with the Bear attaining the summit of the Pole as the Bird descended into the Lowerworld. The Cove appears keyed to these events.[10]

In summary, for third millennium BCE sky-watchers at Avebury Cove—quite apart from the important solar and lunar functions of the Northern Inner Circle—the northern bank formed a significant artificial horizon, ranging from Windmill Hill in the northwest to the Marlborough Downs in the northeast. Throughout the winter months, the stars that formed the body of Cygnus took a dramatic underworld passage, passing *under* the northern horizon of Avebury henge, like a diving bird, close to the path of the midsummer Sun. As Cygnus and its brightest stars Deneb, Sadr and Albireo, emerged in the northeast, and as Capella set in the northwest, the stars of the Southern Cross attained their greatest culmination due south, directly over the southern entrance of the henge.[11] At the same time as the setting and rising of Cygnus and the rising and setting of the Crux-Centaurus stars mirrored each other north and south—their two crosses pointing squarely to their respective poles—the Milky Way became parallel with the horizon. Capella acted as the timekeeper of this event, while

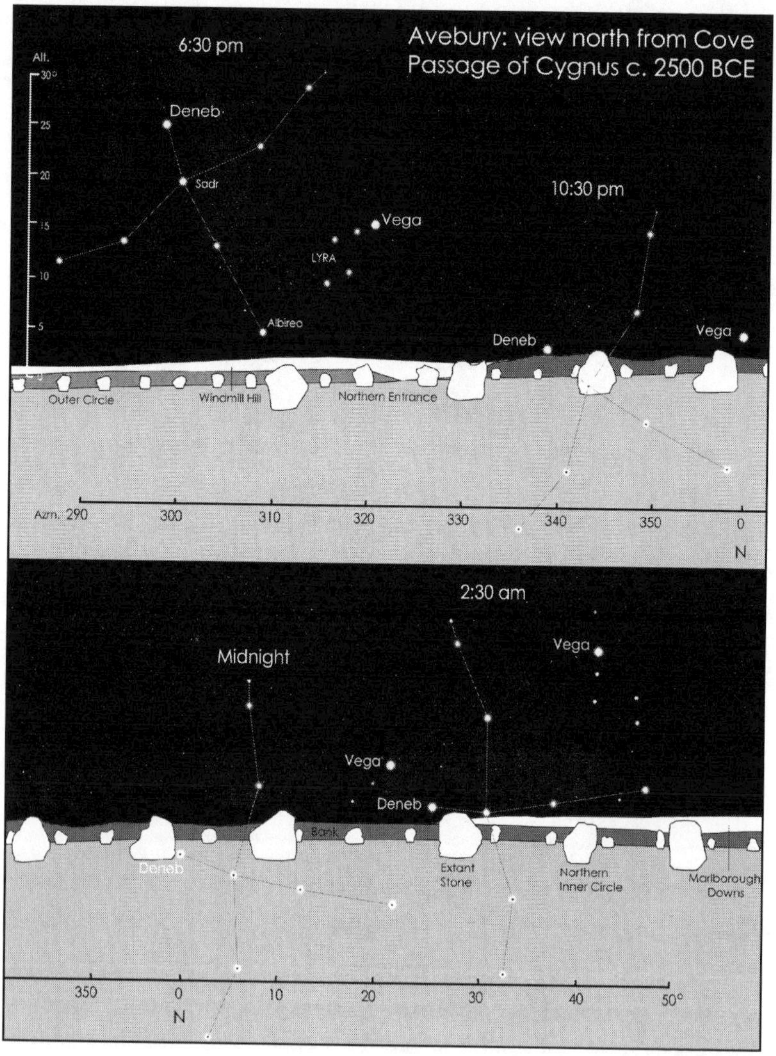

Figure 44. Views of the midwinter passage of Cygnus (the Swan and Northern Cross) in the third millennium BCE. Cygnus would have first appeared at twilight over Windmill Hill. Its brightest star Deneb

set in a trajectory toward the main alignment of Avebury (between the Obelisk and the Cove) at 340°. After Deneb set, only the upper arm of the constellation remained visible above the north bank of the henge, the pointer to the Northern Pole. Cygnus reappeared between the second and third hour after midnight. Deneb (and Sadr) reappeared over a still-remaining stone of the Northern Inner Circle and the Marlborough Downs, Albireo over a lost stone on the 38° alignment of the Cove.

Ursa Major—the counterweight of Cygnus—was perhaps held to be its driving force. These celestial events, closely marked by the primary axis of Avebury, the Cove and the Obelisk, the northern and southern entrances and the outer bank of the great henge, took place in the centuries on either side of 2800 BCE, coinciding exactly with the established date for the construction of the main monument.[12]

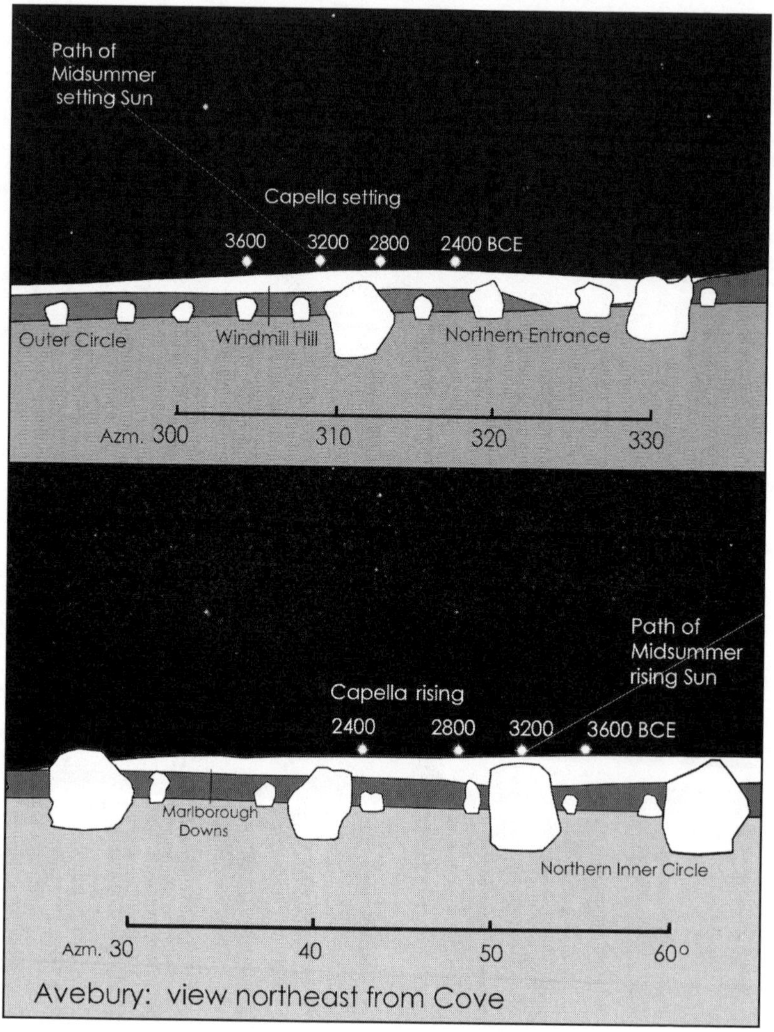

Figure 45. Upper: throughout the time Avebury was in use, 3200 to 2300 BCE, Capella progressively set northwards along the crest of Windmill Hill—the 2° elevation helping eliminate the extinction angle. By 3200 BCE, Capella was setting on the same path as the midsummer Sun: that is, over Windmill Hill when seen from the Cove. In early winter Capella the 'shepherd's star,' was setting at dawn after being visible all night. Lower: Capella reappeared in the night sky shortly after the Summer Solstice at dusk. By the winters of the fourth

and third millennium BCE, it remained visible all night. If the Cove had been in place from 3300 BCE, its open aspect to the northeast, would have allowed observation of the northward movement of Capella over the entire period of time Avebury was in use.

Stars of Precession

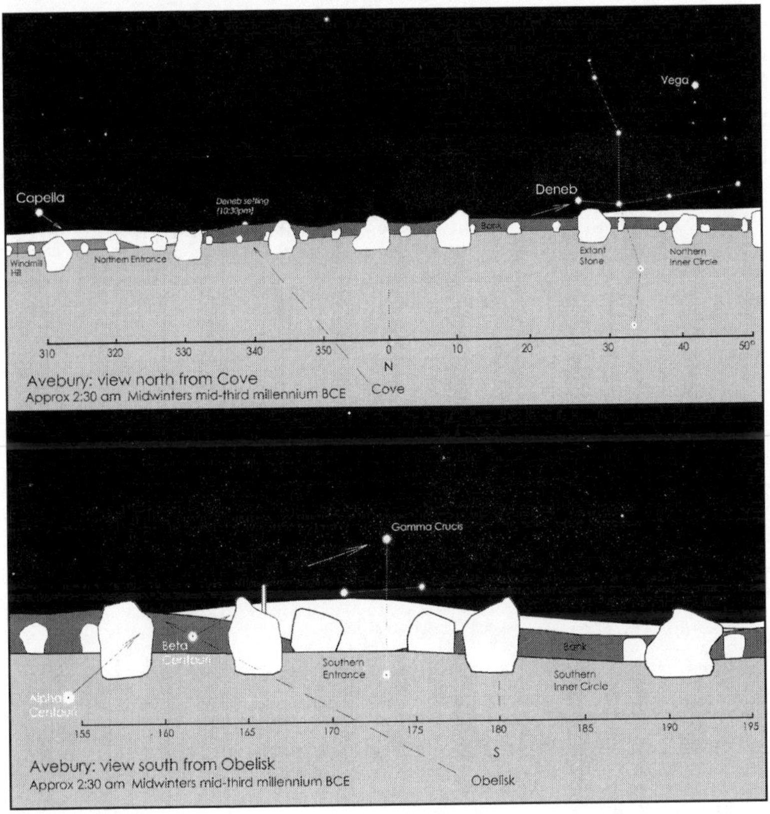

Figure 46. Combined views north and south from the central axis of Avebury, winter months, between the second and third hours of the morning, circa 2500 BCE. As the Milky Way fell in the west and rose in the east to form a complete circle, Cygnus (that had earlier set over Windmill Hill) reappeared in the northeast. As Deneb rose over the Marlborough Downs, Capella set into Windmill Hill. As the two stars approached the same altitude, the Southern Cross stood upright over

Waden Hill; followed by beta then alpha Centauri on the 160° main axis of the henge.

In very much the same way as the sky-watchers at the Sanctuary were referring to Cygnus and Capella over Windmill Hill so, several centuries (even a millennium) earlier, observers at Avebury Cove appear to have been making direct references to the ancestral site of Windmill Hill in their observation of Cygnus and Capella, while both sites linked the movements of Cygnus and Capella with the appearance of the Crux-Centaurus stars in the south. As alpha Centauri would still have been visible from the Sanctuary long after it was lost to sight at Avebury, the Sanctuary became one of the last locations in the area where the precessional movements of the southern sky could be observed. Thus at every stage of monument building, including Silbury Hill, the builders were essentially looking at the same phenomena in the sky.

At Avebury Cove by 3300 BCE and for a few centuries thereafter, alpha Centauri had risen over the Obelisk as Capella set into Windmill Hill. Earlier in the night, Deneb, the alpha star of Cygnus, had also pointed to Windmill Hill, the first home of the ancestors. For sky-watchers at the Obelisk, Deneb would have set over the Cove as Cygnus made its way down into the 'subterranean' world—lost from view beneath the northern bank of Avebury henge.[13]

In outline, and what may be the key figure of the book, Figure 46 shows Deneb and Cygnus reappearing each winter night near the azimuth of the most northerly rising Moon. Albireo on Cygnus' head also approaches the path of the midsummer Sun. These stars are rising just as Capella sets. Counter-pointing these stars in the northern sky is the brilliance of the Crux-Centaurus group of stars as they rise to spectacular prominence on the southern horizon. These stellar events were especially important because they marked the cosmic axis formed by the Poles as well as the distinctive passage of the Milky Way throughout the entire era of early Avebury, centred on 2820 BCE. At that time, the Milky Way would have encircled the horizon, forming a brilliant ring of stars above the chalk-white bank of the henge. The insistent referencing to these key stellar alignments right through to the time when all Avebury's primary stone settings were in place shows how the monument-builders were directing maximum attention, and presumably the greatest veneration, to these stars.

The additional permanence and precision of Avebury must surely have helped its users to realise that key stars were changing their places. Among these stars, Capella could have been especially useful as a marker of precessional movement. Around 3200 BCE, this distinctive star was rising on the same azimuth as the summer solstice rising Sun—the solar alignment of the Cove—setting over Windmill Hill by early November on the same azimuth as the summer solstice setting Sun. Within centuries, sky-watchers at Avebury, using their first permanent markers, would have noticed that the motion of Capella in the northern sky was equivalent to the motion of Sirius in the south—both star-paths coinciding with the path of the solar extremes. Sirius travelled the path of the winter Sun, and Capella the path of the summer Sun. Like so many stellar events above Avebury, the phenomenon was best seen at midwinter, when long nights allowed the viewing of both stars' rising and setting. But by 2500 BCE, these respective star paths had moved significantly away from the solstices, in the case of Capella, almost 8° over the summit of Windmill Hill.

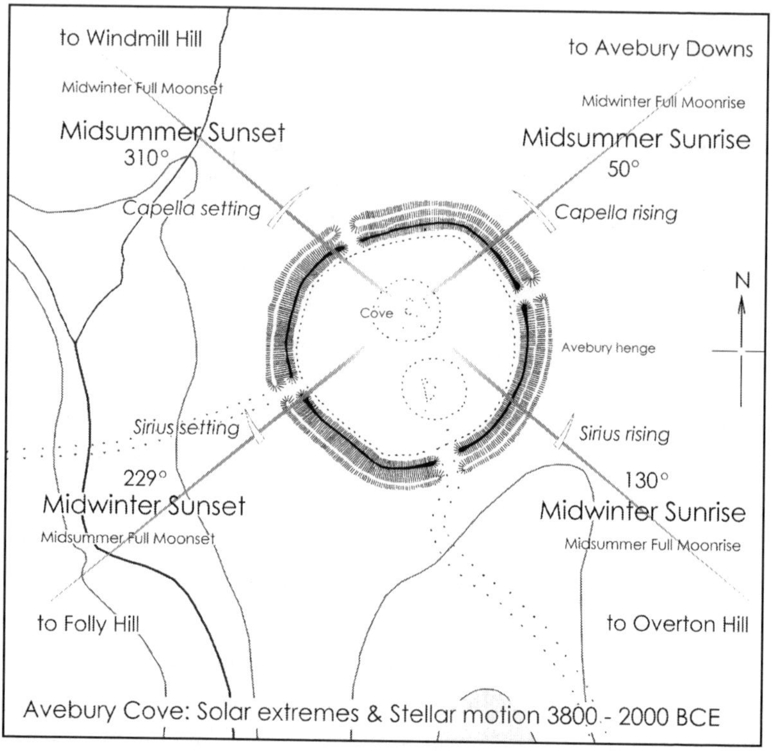

Figure 47. Lines of sight from the Cove on potential winter and summer solstitial (and lunar) alignments. The wedges show the precessional movement of the rising and setting points of Capella and Sirius along the horizon from 3800 to 2000 BCE (the point of each wedge). Each solstice alignment to the horizon included at least two stones.

Figure 47 shows how the constant solstitial extremes relate to prominent landmarks when viewed from the Cove at Avebury. It also shows the precessional motion of Capella and Sirius in this era in relation to these solstitial alignments. There are good alignments to the summit of Windmill Hill for midsummer Sunset and to Folly Hill for midwinter Sunset. There seem to be plenty of stones with the potential to form lines of sight to the horizon on these alignments. The large stone now recumbent beside the eastern lane would have made an excellent winter solstice Sunrise marker, on a scale equivalent to the Heelstone at Stonehenge.

In 2900 BCE, when at least the primary henge and the first stone settings were in place, the close co-incidence of Capella and Sirius with the solstitial points, as well as the lunar extremes, would have remained highly noticeable. Assuming continuous oral traditions, the builders could have used stone markers of the solar year alongside the lunar counts of the Inner Circles to assess the relative motion of these stars. By 2500 BCE, the movements upon the horizon of these stars, over 1° in one hundred years (rather more for Capella than Sirius), meant their heliacal rising and setting dates changing by well over a day per century. Through the use of such fine alignments—sometimes three stones to a horizon a mile or more distant—combined with diligent preservation of the star-lore of the first monument-builders, these changes could have been evident to the new Avebury sky-watchers.[14]

A Place in the Cosmos

Their great megalithic monuments enabled the Neolithic people who used Avebury to ensure that their lives were in accord with the mysterious principles and powers that formed their world. Their monuments recreated the cosmos and helped them make sense of their lives within it. The construction process, its ritual use and the profound knowledge the site provided, helped to ensure that human actions were in accordance with the rules of the spirit world, or 'Divine Law.' By building fires at the right time, by erecting stones, by making appropriate offerings to the determining powers of life, by venerating lunar, solar and stellar passages, the monument-builders anticipated and tried to keep on the right side of the natural, cosmic law. They hunted, bred and slaughtered their animals when the omens were good; they planted, harvested and pastured in the right seasons; they organised sexual and marital relations according to celestial rhythms; and overall, they would have tried to conduct themselves in a manner that honoured and placated the sometimes beneficent, sometimes malevolent forces of the world. In this manner, they would have hoped that serious transgressions of the natural order could be avoided, and prosperity and well-being be assured. The great megalithic monuments as expressions of Divine Law, served as constant reminders to the people that their success, not to mention their very survival, depended upon their veneration and intelligent regard for it.

As centuries of construction and refinement continued, alert Avebury sky-watchers, keen to read or divine the signs of the universe, could have become aware of the subtle motion of the stars against the annual oscillation of the Sun. As Capella moved away from the well-marked summer solstice alignment, and Sirius moved away from the equally well-marked winter solstice alignment—their heliacal rising and setting times subtly altering against the cycle of the Sun—the early sky-watchers could have formed their first tentative insights into the great cycle of the stars. Perhaps as the two ecliptic-galactic crossroads changed their seasonal positions, the Poles subtly shifted, and above all, the southern stars fell from the sky, sky-watchers at Avebury and the Sanctuary had the opportunity to develop astronomical knowledge inside the context of their highly mythic cosmology. How did the closely watched cycles of Sun and Moon, along their ecliptic path of fire and light, fit into the changing pattern of the stars, the moving Milky Way?

Could their careful observation of the skies at Avebury have provided the Neolithic monument-builders with the information to evaluate precession, that is, to start putting numbers to it? Later astronomers were only able to do this when they had formed the appropriate notational systems. The Babylonians, for example, developed an early sexagesimal counting system based upon barley grains. They were clearly counting off the Sun against the stars, and could track long cycles, but apparently had no knowledge of precession.[15] Although the Avebury sky-watchers did not have any such counts, my argument is that their stone circles would have given them the ability to see subtle changes in the relationship between the Sun, Moon and stars, allowing them to gain a proportional or comparative sense of the order of the changes and measures involved.

Long veneration and observation of the passage of the two stellar crosses, Crux and Cygnus, the movement of Capella and Sirius, and interest too in the time when the Sun was upon the two crossroads of the ecliptic and the galaxy, had the potential to provide the Avebury star-watchers with their first real understanding of the relationship between the cycles of Sun and Moon and the stars of the celestial sphere. The movements of Capella and Sirius were comparatively easy to see against the solstitial extremes; permanent megalithic monuments supplied the means to compare and contrast this change.

Figures 48 suggest a provisional 'cosmography' of this era based upon such precessionally affected phenomena. Even if the incorporation of the cycles of the Sun, Moon and stars into their monuments was simply imitative, precise but never scientific, it still would have represented a tremendous achievement: one that the Neolithic people must have perceived as securing congruency between earth and heaven. Their ability to track even small changes in the heavens was a sign of their spiritual good sense. Incorporating what they saw in the sky into their monuments gave new momentum to their mythic narratives, and brought political stability, natural law, regulation and order into their lives.

Many commentators have quite rightly said that it would be a mistake to think of Avebury or the other great megalithic sites as observatories in the sense that we use the word today. As the late John North remarked, the Neolithic people, did not build their monuments to *observe* the heavens, or to advance astronomical knowledge in a scientific manner. They built them so that the order of life on Earth remained in harmony with the greater order of the cosmos. These builders proceeded reverently and intuitively, sincerely emulating to the best of their ability (which obviously fluctuated over time) the patterns they saw both in the world and in the sky. At their best, both the monuments and the practices that took place within them represented everything that was meaningful in the world of the builders. At their worst, the monuments may have fostered excessive sacrificial acts of propitiation, perhaps prompted by an over-zealous or ambitious few. Whatever the case, the monument-builders would have held and transmitted their knowledge and beliefs in oral and mythic form.

An Astral Drama

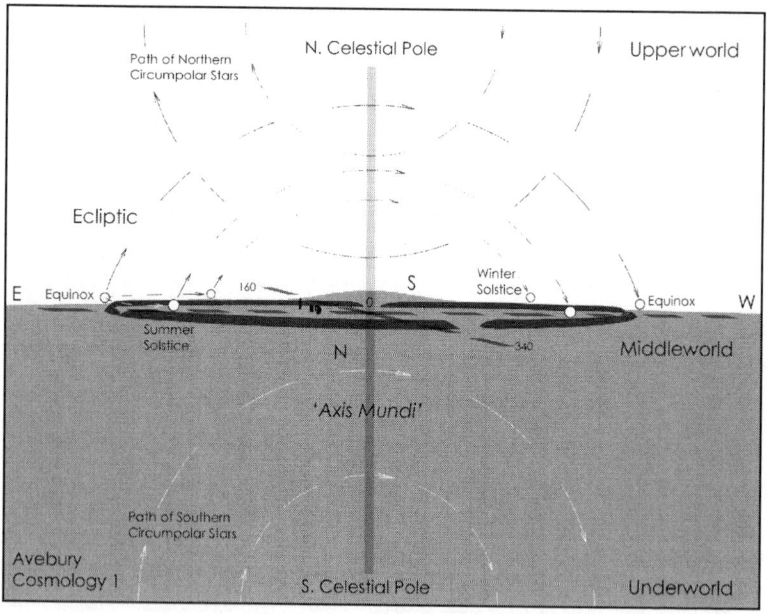

Figure 48a. Avebury Cosmology 1. From the point of view of observer 0 at the centre of Avebury henge: (i) the rising Sun oscillates north-south annually over the bank of the henge; (ii) the Moon and planets

follow its path, the ecliptic, all turning from east to west; (iii) the circumpolar stars of the north rotate around the North Celestial Pole, while the stars of the South Celestial Pole remain unseen. This suggests three worlds: an Upper-, Middle- and Underworld, with the axis mundi *passing through their centre. Stars that rise and set in the north or set then rise in the south will have played a special role. The 'main' 160-340° alignment of the primary stone settings is shown, as is Waden Hill to the south.*

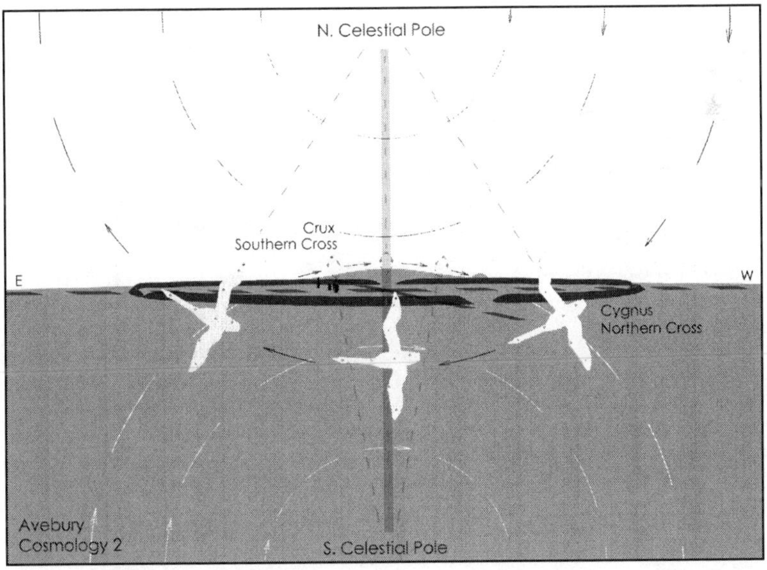

Figure 48b. Avebury Cosmology 2. Over the course of a winter night 3300-2500 BCE, the Northern and Southern Cross, the pointers to the Poles, both in the Milky Way, corresponded along the main alignment of the henge. Alpha and beta Centauri rose with Crux over Waden Hill as Cygnus made its 'Underworld passage' below the northern bank of the henge. These horizonal movements would have emphasised not only the axial symmetry of the North and South Celestial Poles, the axis mundi, *but also the mirroring by the monument of the circle of the Milky Way. As Cygnus made its deepest descent at midnight, Ursa Major, the Great Bear, approached the top of the North Pole.*

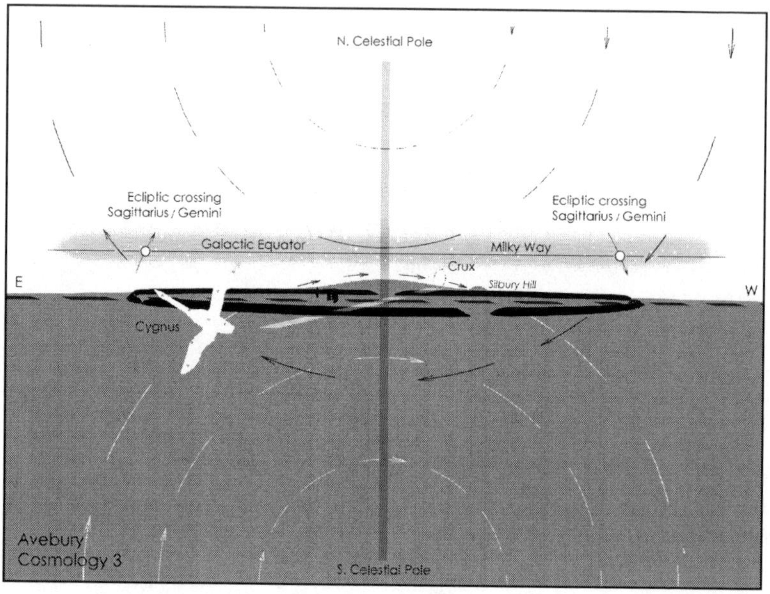

Figure 48c. Avebury Cosmology 3. Each night around 3000 BCE, as Cygnus reappeared in the northeast and Crux began to set toward the south, the Milky Way rose in the east to lie horizontally over the entire bank of the henge. With the ecliptic crossing the Galactic Equator east-west and the stellar movements north-south focusing upon the poles (and axis mundi*), the symbolism of the monument as centre of earth and the heavens was completed by the horizonal ring of the galaxy.*

If we knew the stories that the Avebury builders wove around their key stars, our evidence suggests that these would have related the underworld passage of Cygnus—the diving bird of the north—to the dramatic passage of the southern stars. This particular narrative would have foregrounded the site's connection to the great axis that runs between the Poles and given particular meaning to the monument's striking encirclement by the Milky Way.

The evidence from the Avebury sites suggests that the nocturnal movements of Cygnus in the north and the Crux-Centaurus stars visible in the south at that time upheld and

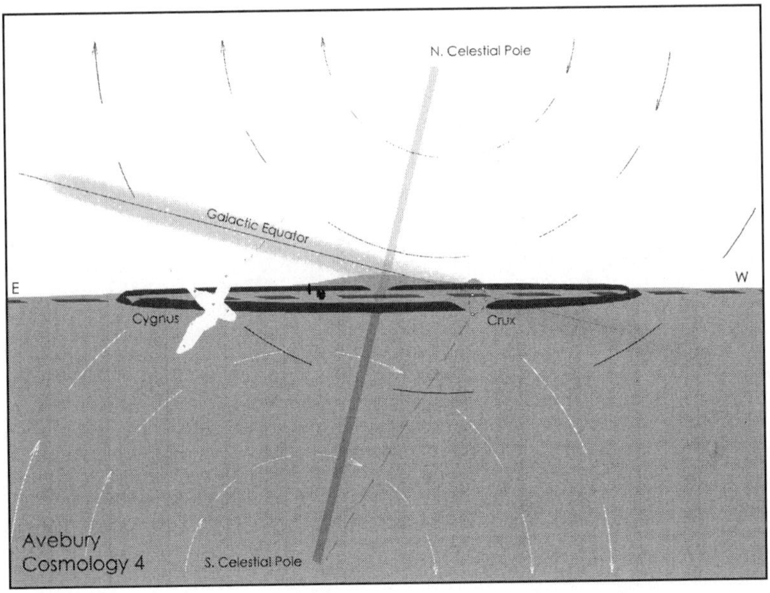

Figure 48d. Avebury Cosmology 4. Due to precession over the course of the third millennium BCE, the stars of the south were slowly lost from sight into Waden Hill and the location of Silbury Hill. By the end of the millennium, the Milky Way no longer lay horizontally around the chalk bank of the henge, the Southern Cross had sunk under Waden Hill, and even the stars of the celestial Poles had changed their positions in the sky. As the celestial axis of the rotating Earth slowly circled around the ecliptic axis of the Earth around the Sun, Avebury lost its alignment to the galaxy and the axis mundi.

defined the polar axis, the *axis mundi* around which the Sun, Moon and entire heavens turned. Next, Sirius, Orion, Gemini, the Pleiades, Capella and Taurus—perennially significant figures centred who marked the Gemini crossroads—defined another primary axis across the sky, whose other end was centred upon the second crossroads of the ecliptic and the galaxy: the stars of Scorpius, Ophiuchus and Sagittarius. Crucially, in the fourth and third millennia BCE, the Milky Way united these four axial-star groups in one symmetrical celestial display. As the galaxy ringed the horizon of the world, the Pointers to the Poles stood upright, north-south, across the sky. To the sky-watchers, this grand visual event—plus those of the Sun and Moon and the passage of the stellar bears, Ursa Major and Minor upon the Polar axis—must have suggested epic tales of primal and animistic forces who upheld and journeyed within the cosmic order.

Like all prehistoric peoples, it seems that the Avebury star-watchers experienced the time of the winter solstice as one of the greatest spiritual and shamanic potency. This was the time of death and rebirth, as shown by the behaviour of Sun, plants and animals. Now the she-bear went into her den to emerge a few months later with new cubs. Many birds migrated, and large waterfowl flew in from the north to over-winter. The plants became latent before leafing once more in the spring. Midwinter was also the time the Southern Cross rose and set, the time that Cygnus dived below the northern horizon to be reborn in a single night, the Sun set into Folly Hill from the Cove, and the galaxy levelled around the axial crosses formed by the cycles of the Sun and Moon. Midwinter was the time perhaps when the great central axis, the *axis mundi* between the Upper and Lower Worlds was seen as most accessible; the shamans could travel freely accompanied by great celestial beings upon the paths of the Milky Way and the ecliptic.

Figure 50 shows a tripartite astral cosmology made up of an Upper-, Middle- and an Underworld. As the stars of Cygnus belong to the Upperworld of the northern circumpolar stars but at the time were sometimes travelling beneath the horizon, the Neolithic people may have seen them as mediating between the different worlds. A shaman (perhaps aided by psychotropic substances) may have travelled with them for the few hours the stars were in the Underworld. Cygnus charted the path of descent into the Lowerworlds and then the safe return. Traditional stories, dances and songs could have recreated such a journey, which in big monuments must have had a performative aspect. People would surely have expected to see things happen at certain times, especially the many children. We can imagine dancers, singers, drummers and elders acting alongside diviners and other specialists in the settings provided by the monuments.

Similarly, as the Crux-Centaurus stars were part of the Underworld realm of the hidden southern circumpolar stars and only briefly appeared above the horizon in the Middleworld of humans, the star-watchers may have seen them too as liminal stars that offered another 'gateway' to the central spindle of the *axis mundi*. Figures 48 show how both these stars of stars embedded in the Milky Way may have offered routes to the *axis mundi*. Highly venerated by ancient peoples, the stars may have mediated the difficult journey between the worlds, especially the journey to the Lowerworld, possibly conceived as the midwinter cave of the uterine Bear Mother, to ensure rebirth or healing. No doubt, there was an equally difficult journey to the Upperworld: to what eventually became the great halls of the ancestors, Bear King and heroes, to receive the mead, honey or nectar found only in the upper branches of the World Tree.

As shown in Figures 48 and 50, the cosmic axis—the *axis mundi*—lay between the celestial Poles, its stars rising on the main alignment of the henge. On midwinter nights, as the Southern Cross stood due south over Waden Hill, as Cygnus, the swan or Northern Cross, rose in the north, as the Great Bear crowned the Northern Pole, and as the Milky Way encircled the horizon with the two crossroads east and west, it may have seemed to the builders of Avebury that they had opened a road to the divine powers. Through the portals offered by the celestial crosses, the great white ring of Avebury became the *omphalos* or navel of the world, anchoring the centre of the *axis mundi*, linking the Earth to the potentially rejuvenative powers of the Upper and Lowerworlds.

Venerating Avebury: the Stellar Crosses

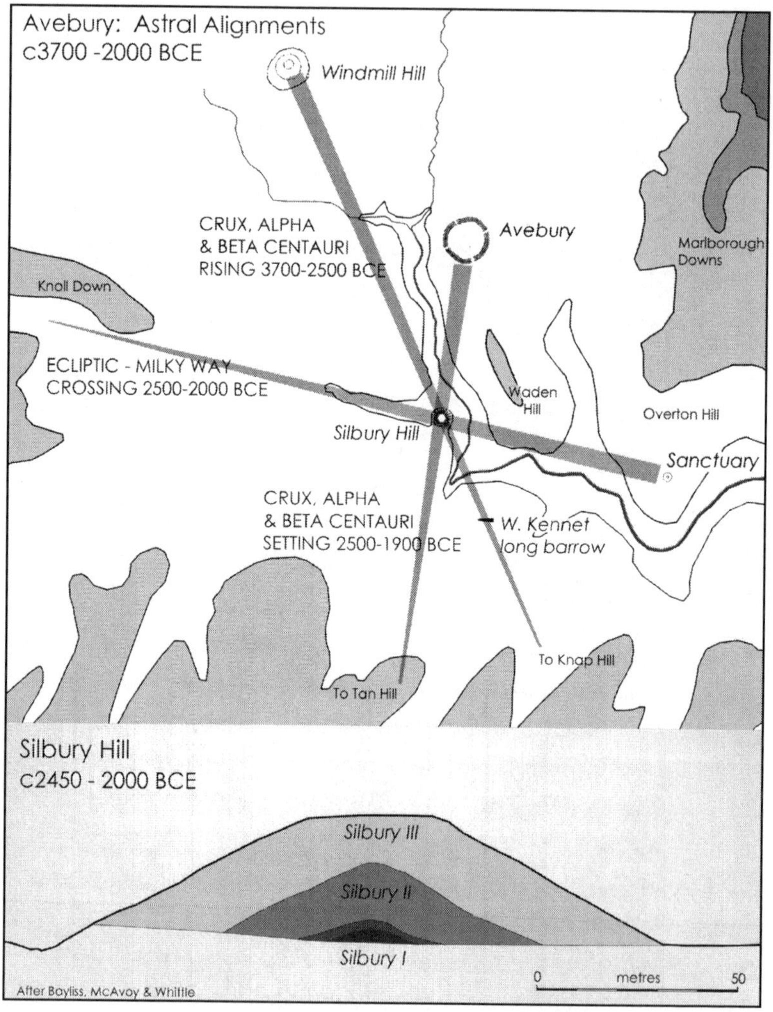

Figure 49. The alignment from 4th Millennium BCE Windmill Hill over West Kennet long barrow to the rising position of the Crux-Centaurus stars intersected with the alignment from 3rd Millennium BCE Avebury henge over the base of Waden Hill to the setting position of the same stars over the location of Silbury Hill. After thousands of years of visibility, these stars were now making the briefest possible passage through the southern sky. The location of Silbury was also

intersected by an alignment from the Sanctuary to the ecliptic/galactic crossing point in Gemini in the latter part of this period. As the monument-builders finally closed West Kennet long barrow and the ancient southern stars were lost to view from Avebury, their efforts became concentrated upon raising the huge mound of Silbury.

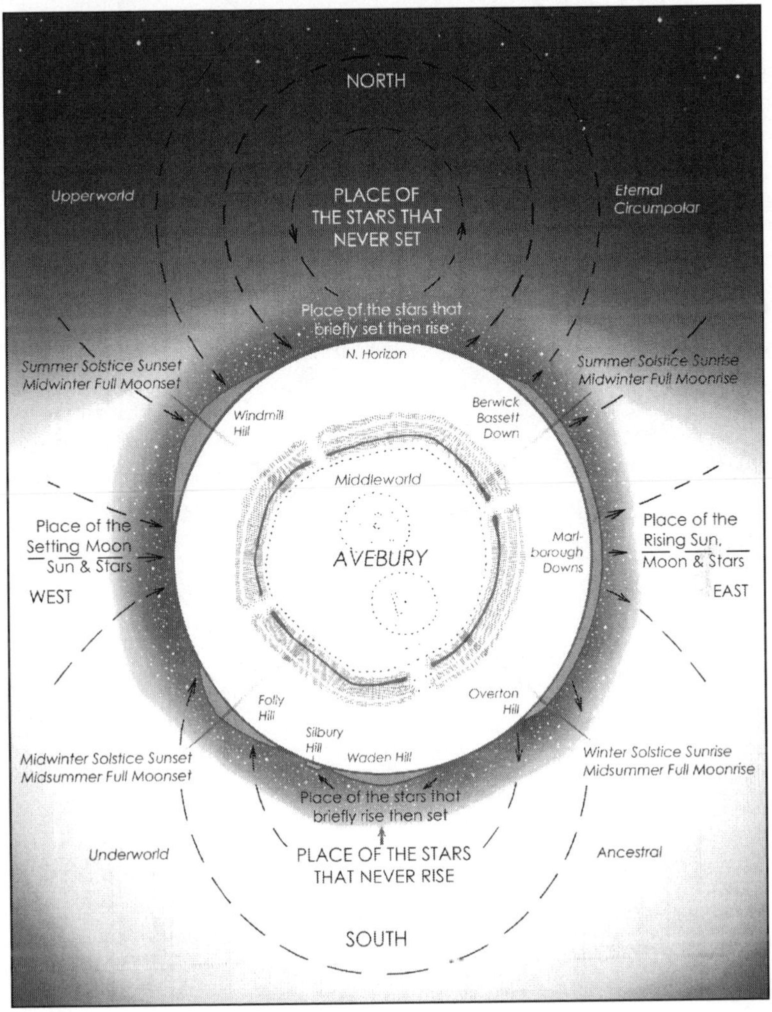

Figure 50. An Avebury Cosmography: A Neolithic sky-watcher at the centre of Avebury had the benefit of the stones and the artificial horizon of the henge against which to observe the Sun, Moon, Milky

Way and the lowest rising and setting stars in the south and north. They would have seen the stars, like the Sun, Moon and planets, rise in the east and move to the west, some northern stars not set at all, some northern stars appear at twilight then set and rise, and some southern stars rise only briefly before setting. The inference is that a hidden Southern Pole matches the Northern Pole and an 'axle' runs between them. The stars suggest three cosmological zones: a northern Upperworld, a central Middleworld and a southern Underworld. As the setting and rising stars of the north and the rising and setting stars of the south pass through several realms, they provide the means of connection, or journeying, between them.

The four causeways of Avebury henge divide the great circle of the ditch and bank into four segments, a four-fold cross. Both the symbol of the cross and the cross in circle appear in prehistoric rock carvings and paintings from around the world. In Mesoamerica, sometimes encircled, the cross is the symbol of the highly venerated morning and evening star, Venus. Further north it is often the symbol of the Pole Star. It is the central symbol of Christian altars, encircled in the case of the Celtic cross. In ancient Egypt, the cross was the symbol of life, the *ankh*—a circle formed the upper arm. In terms of space, the cross represents the centre, the axial directions and, when encircled, the boundaries (horizon) of the world. In terms of time, it suggests intersections and synchronicities. In terms of power, it suggests solidity, containment, convergence, focus, alignment and order.

We may therefore see the cross as the symbol *par excellence*, not of the wandering Palaeolithic or Mesolithic nomad—whose centre is everywhere, whose time is now, whose boundaries remain undefined—but of the Neolithic settler, pastoralist and farmer. For the settler, their territory becomes the centre of their world, their boundaries necessarily become circumscribed and they struggle with the calendar to maintain order and balance with everything within those boundaries. Within settlement, humans must conform in new way to the regulations of cosmic law in order to protect themselves and their way of life. It is precisely the restraint imposed by settlement that defines the great transition between the Mesolithic and the Neolithic—between the nomad and the farmer. The megalithic monuments represent both the final flourish of an ancient way of life and the transition to a new.[16]

We can read the great cross of Avebury, its ditch and bank broken by four causeways, in the context of the many crosses in the sky: the stellar crosses, the annual cross of the solstitial extremes, the cross suggested by the four phases of the Moon, and the cross formed by the intersection of the ecliptic and the galaxy. But when we closely examine and compare the movements of the Northern and the Southern Cross over Neolithic Avebury, we can see the sky-watchers may have held that the cross in the north prefigured and so assured the ascendancy of its partner across the Milky Way, at the other end of the *axis mundi* in the south. The Milky Way connected them around the horizon as it aligned to the Poles. The Northern Cross—perhaps in the guise of a bird diving beneath the primordial waters, perhaps dying and being reborn, perhaps bearing the foundations of new life—ensured the rising of the fiery cross in the south.

The Neolithic people surely also linked Cygnus, the Northern Cross, with Ursa Major, the Great Bear, as the two major constellations—virtually everywhere representing hibernation and migration—circled either side of the North Celestial Pole.[17] The Bear ascended the Pole as the Bird swooped down below the horizon, and then descended the Pole as the Bird rose up. The Southern Cross, once it had risen, may have implied there were further immense riches in an Underworld realm that lay remote and invisible beneath the southern horizon. The goal of the shaman, to make the successful descent into the wealth, healing and fecundity of the Lowerworlds, may have found support in the rising of Crux and the resurrection of Cygnus. To the sky-watchers in this rich astral realm, quite apart from the associations with fertility, the realm of the dead and the ancestors, the animals powers and the spirit-world, the themes of divine and moral law—the cosmic order of the heavens—must have stood out above all else. It was Cosmic or Divine Law that connected the many celestial with all terrestrial beings in their eternal dance.

In ancient Egypt, the principle of cosmic order or Divine Law was called *ma'at,* and was frequently represented as a goddess of truth and justice, often depicted as a small figure with a feather upheld in one hand of the Pharaoh. Ma'at found her equivalent in later Celtic tradition; where the Irish *fír flathemon,* 'the word of truth' or 'the justice of the ruler,' was always obtained from a beautiful woman or a feminine-identified source. This native goddess, representing the moral and mystical qualities of the true ruler, was usually found beside a spring, a stone or a mound.[18] The elected rulers of the Celts had to uphold the supreme principle of *fír flathemon,* described in the text known as the *Audacht Morain,* as "truth, justice, impartiality, mercy, beneficence, hospitality, generosity and stability," in the same manner as those in the office of the Egyptian Pharaoh had to uphold the divine law of Ma'at.[19] Both these traditions insist it was female, otherworldly and divine representatives who conferred sovereignty upon and so inaugurated the kings and pharaohs. There is no evidence of kingship at this early stage at Avebury and only some of a divine feminine, yet these highly important concepts of the ancient world indubitably would have been anticipated in central southern Britain in the third millennium BCE. Where better to look for these principles or the demonstration of such order than in the heavens? In the same way as Isis, for example, a divine feminine principle of tremendous popularity in ancient Egypt, became associated with Sirius, it was only natural that the monument-builders of Britain also would have found divine principles of cosmic order—including symbols of the divine masculine and feminine—in the stars.

If the Southern Cross, seen rising over Waden Hill through the southern entrance of Avebury henge in the first half of the third millennium BCE, was a symbol of the divine feminine—the uterine source, the vulva of the goddess, the midwinter bear cave—it could also equally well have represented the powerful central source or foundation point against which all the great cosmic axes of time and space intersected and turned. Here was a source of cosmic order, of divinely appointed law.

Sex, Gender & the Avebury Stones

From at least the time of Stukeley, visitors to Avebury have made the association between women and the Cove, men and the Obelisk. The Great Outer Circle of stones and the white chalk embankment of the henge may represent the 'union' of a Northern Inner Circle identified as feminine because of the uterine nature of the Cove and a Southern Inner Circle identified as masculine because of the phallic nature of the Obelisk. For this reason, some, like Stukeley, have called the Southern Inner Circle the 'Sun Circle,' and the Northern Inner Circle the 'Moon Circle.' My astronomical analysis, however, suggests that while the enclosure of all its Inner Circles by the henge as the Milky Way underscores their cosmic character, it seems they functioned primarily as lunar calendars, aligned to and calibrated by the solar year. If both Inner Circles are lunar in number and have strong solar alignments, it is impossible to make a strict Cove-feminine-Moon-north, Obelisk-masculine-Sun-south, identification. Possibly the Neolithic people saw all the Inner Circles as lunar, while their actual stones and alignments embodied solar qualities. Perhaps their Sun was feminine, their Moon masculine as elsewhere in Northern

Europe—the permutations are endless.

Although we will never be certain, the sexual symbolism of the monument is still worthy of examination. Did the monument-builders, for example, identify the two avenues with the ecliptic and/or with the Milky Way? Did they see the stone avenues as the paths of the Sun, Moon and stars? Could they have seen the Sanctuary's circles at the terminus of the West Kennet Avenue as feminine and the square Longstones Cove at the terminus of the Beckhampton Avenue as masculine? If each avenue and /or terminus corresponded to a different gender, did this also apply to the ecliptic, the Milky Way and their crossing-points? It is worth keeping in mind that numerous traditions associate the Milky Way with milk from the breast of a goddess and sometimes, but less often, with semen.[20] It would not be stretching a point too far to imagine that Neolithic people would also have seen the galaxy in this manner.

Commentaries on Avebury have long observed that the shapes of the stones themselves suggest a fundamental male-female symbolism. We have already seen the many four-cornered, lozenge shaped stones mimic the Southern Cross and the reasons for connecting this with female fecundity. A deliberate pairing of lozenge or diamond-shaped stones and more columnar, phallic stones is particularly marked in the Kennet Avenue; several good examples remain today. Juxtaposition of such symbols have engaged the interest of early people since at least the time of those who painted the Ice Age caves and made the highly portable 'Venus' figurines.[21]

The name of the 'Adam and Eve' stones at the terminus of the Beckhampton Avenue may preserve a remnant of an original male-female symbolism. As Stukeley's drawings show that the original huge stones of the Longstones Cove were quite distinct from the small, almost delicate stone circles of the Sanctuary, it is tempting to read the Sanctuary as feminine and the Longstones Cove as masculine. In Chapter 8, we saw how the stars of Gemini-Taurus, especially Alnath, setting over the western horizon—thus over the area of the Longstones Cove when seen from the Sanctuary—seemed to confirm the identification of that Cove with Taurus, and all its symbolic association with male virility. Yet, the pattern of the apparently masculine Longstones Cove, aligned to the Sun and Sirius, was also set out in what could be seen as an almost perfect imitation of the Southern Cross (the lowest star at that time lost below the horizon), while at least two of its stones were lozenge shaped. Taken all together, the megalithic mix always seems to point the viewer back to sexual polarity.

Even if a gendered narrative of this sort is notoriously hard to define, it is still likely that the builders attempted to incorporate an ambitious level of fertility symbolism into their henge. The Neolithic people would not have conceived of fertility just in simple sexual terms. They would have conceived it as the union and balance of all terrestrial and cosmic forces for their abundance and the benefit of life. Many ancient and tribal societies believe in a fundamental reciprocity between human life and the cosmos—what is given has to be returned. They often make a cosmic male-female distinction, for example, the well-known 'Grandfather Sky' and 'Grandmother Earth' of the Native Americans. However, this is not always straightforward; both male and female powers can dwell in cracks in hillsides, in rivers, rain, stones, creatures, lightning, the hearth and the heavens. Whatever the case, in such societies there is always a direct link between human potency and that of the 'Great Surround,' for example, between human vitality and the animal powers.

The Avebury monument builders seem to be reaching toward seeing the cosmos as a balanced dance of male and female powers around a central *axis mundi* or World Tree. A feminine portal may have lain at its root, while great powers, perhaps seen as serpent, bird or bear—ringed by Sun, Moon and Milky

Way—ascended and descended its central column. Sources of particular power lay among the stars; but sites like the Longstones Cove also show that the Neolithic people may have seen male and female powers as seasonally interchangeable, or simultaneously present. They may conceivably have seen stone settings such as a Cove as symbols both of fertility and of union, of generative source and the ecstatic power of procreation.

The Roots of the Land: The Two Dragons

The Avebury sky-watchers had seen the order of the sky changing and their role, as ever, was to understand this and incorporate it into their fabric of their monuments. They may have undertaken further building work to ensure that their monuments continued to mirror the changing order of the heavens. For a few hundred years after 2500 BCE, Avebury swarmed with activity. Silbury Hill was under construction; the builders completed the West Kennet and the Beckhampton Avenues, the Sanctuary, the Longstones Cove, as well as the inner circles of the henge. This huge, and, as it turned out, final flourish of activity, may have been an attempt to embody an ultimate mystery, to maintain the cosmic balance, as it were, between Earth and Sky. Thinking of the patterns of their landscape in terms of the balance of dragons or serpents may have provided the Neolithic sky-watchers with the symbolic means to conceive and think about the cosmos.

The Norman font of St. James Church Avebury depicts a unique image whose strange symbolism suggests an ancient source. It shows a central human figure holding a bishop's crosier with twin dragons arranged symmetrically at its feet. The point of the crosier is upon the head of one of the dragons. The dragons are winged and have forelegs—they are technically described as wyverns—their tails are long and convoluted, and foliate forms

The Norman font of St James Church Avebury: a central, Christian figure vanquishes two dragons, wyverns, emblem of Saxon Wessex.

sprout from their heads. The wyvern is an ancient emblem of Wessex. It appeared on the standards of the Anglo-Saxon kings who had entered Britain since the Sixth Century CE, including that of Harold, the last Saxon king before the Norman conquest of 1066 CE. It is tempting to speculate that the font records an effort by an early Christian bishop or saint to vanquish local beliefs that saw Avebury in terms of two dragons. Was this a piece of Norman propaganda aimed to stamp out Saxon resistance? Or does it have an archaic origin?

Dragons as keepers of the cosmic axis are present in many cosmologies. The circumpolar stars of the Upperworld include the constellation of Draco, the Dragon, the keeper of the Northern Ecliptic Pole around which the Northern Celestial Pole continuously churns and grinds its way. See Figure 52. In the cosmos of the Maya, the Vision Serpent lies coiled about the summit of the World Tree. In the Australian Aboriginal tradition, the Rainbow Serpent dwells in both the sky and the Earth. A primal serpent churns the World Axis throughout the entire Indo-European tradition. When the *axis mundi* is presented as the Tree of Life, there is nearly always a serpent wrapped around it.

Sometimes, more often in art, there are two serpents. In Sumeria, for example, the sculptural motif of two serpents around a central column appears as early as 2000 BCE. The Vedic tradition, which may prove to be the oldest record yet, says the gods cut the body of the serpent *Naga Vasuki* in two, after wrapping his body around the primal mountain to churn the ocean of creation.[22] Finally, although examples could be multiplied, in the Scandinavian tradition, the dragon *Níðhöggr* gnaws on the root of the World Tree, while *Jörmungandr* the World Serpent envelopes the world. At the time of *Ragnarök*, the end of the world, *Jörmungandr* will break the balance between Earth, Sky and Sea. The Saxons who lived near Avebury and enjoyed a far better state of its completeness, would undoubtedly have associated traditions of this sort with its stones.

A remnant of a very ancient narrative may help us understand more of this dragon symbolism on the Avebury font. The earliest legend, recorded c.1100 CE, is from the Welsh *Mabinogion*:

'The second plague in your land,' said Llevelys 'is a dragon. Another dragon of a foreign race is fighting with it... measure the length and breadth of the island, and where you find the exact centre have a pit dug... You must trap the dragons and then bury them within the strongest place you know of in the island. As long as they are within that place no plague will come to Britain.' Llud had the length and breadth of the island measured and found its centre... There he saw the dragons fighting... [He trapped them] and put them in the most secure place he could find.

The second legend was recorded slightly later, in Nennius and Geoffrey of Monmouth.

Vortigern summoned his magicians and they all gave him the

same advice: that he should build himself an immensely strong tower, into which he could retreat in safety. He surveyed a great number of places and in the end he came to Mount Erith [Dinas Emrys]. There he assembled stonemasons from different parts of the country and ordered them to build a tower for him…but however much they built one day the earth swallowed it up the next… 'My King,' said Merlin, 'summon your workmen. Order them to dig in the earth, and underneath you will find a pool.' While Vortigern was still sitting on the bank of the pool which had been drained of its water, there emerged two dragons, one white, one red. As soon as they were near enough to each other, they fought bitterly.[23]

These two stories have in common threats from outsiders and in the kingdom disarray. As it is the order of the cosmos itself that has turned against the two kings, they must find the answer to their problems in a cosmological solution. The answer in both cases is the finding of two warring dragons who are undermining the strongest place in the land, a place defined as an *omphalos* or centre. In the first instance, Llud's brother, Llevelys, tells him to settle his problems by making offerings to the two conflicting dragons (near Oxford). In the second instance, the magician Merlin tells Vortigern that he must resolve the conflict between the two dragons, one red and one white, who fight below his tower. These legends were by then being interpreted in terms of conflict between Welsh Celts and Anglo-Saxons, but the mythic themes of red and white dragons securing the stability of the land run much deeper in the topic known as the 'Matter of Britain' than as a simple conflict between two rival peoples.

From the standpoint of the great henge, the builders may have identified the Kennet and Beckhampton Avenues as the projecting arms either of the galaxy or of the ecliptic, or as both. They may have seen the Avenues as the snaking body of a dragon, with the stones as the teeth or the bones of the World

Serpent itself—the living Earth spirit. If the two ecliptic crossing-points of the Milky Way were also associated with the terminals of the Avenues—east at the Sanctuary and west at the Longstones Cove—then they may have played out a symbolism very much in the manner envisaged by William Stukeley thousands of years later, as the head and tail of an enormous dragon or serpent. Alternatively, in keeping with many other ancient cosmological traditions, the Neolithic people of Avebury may have seen the ecliptic or the Milky Way as *Ouroboros*, the Cosmic Serpent turning to devour its own tail, or an eclipse as a great serpent consuming the Sun or Moon.

Of course, we cannot be certain, but such themes suggest that the ancient sky-watchers could have seen the polar axis—the *axis mundi*, the multi-layered axis of Avebury pointed to by the Northern and Southern Cross—in terms of Underworld and Upperworld Dragons holding the universe between them. Each guarded their end of the cosmic tree around which all revolved; each would have been seen as necessary to secure the perpetual balance of the whole.

Now, the two Celtic legends are emphatic that the two dragons should not come into conflict, or fall out of balance.[24] Stability must be maintained, and the legends make it clear that humans can intervene in support of this. The red and white dragons are fundamental not only to the order of the cosmos but also to the order of the island of Britain. There is never any suggestion of removing the dragons, or of killing them. It is important firstly, to ensure that they are not in conflict, and secondly, that they are in the right place. When the dragons are in conflict, the tower, the cosmos, the stable centre of the land cannot endure; there are plagues, misfortune and disasters. Only the proper intervention by a king, magician, shaman (or bishop) can ensure the dragons are in their rightful position at the most powerful place: the centre of the land.

Users of a ceremonial site often believe that not acknowledging celestial events will cause disorder: the Sun will not run its proper course; crops will fail and so on. They believe there is a responsibility on their part to maintain the order of the cosmos. Given its survival in the font imagery and other evidence from Avebury, the ancient British legend of the two dragons suggests the concern of the builders was to try to maintain or correct the balance of their monuments and the Poles, especially as the stars departed from their rightful position in the sky. The builders may have intended the last phases of Avenues, the Sanctuary, the Longstones Cove and especially the building of Silbury Hill to help in holding axial Dragons in place, even as they were being thrown alarmingly off balance by the cycle of precession.

The astronomy shows that the skies at the time of the monument-builders held a dramatic message of precessional shift. In place of a sky, schematically shown in Figure 48c, where the Milky Way and the Northern and Southern Cross upheld a stable and balanced order centred upon Avebury, the sky over the course of the third millennium BCE, was moving towards the situation, shown in Figure 48d, where the Milky Way had fallen from its place around the horizon and the Southern Cross had become lost to sight.

If the legends are applicable they lend weight to the view that the Avebury star-watchers were apprehending precession; but it was hard for them to understand and it was not good news. The legends suggest they would have interpreted a change in the heavens as change upon the Earth. If they built Silbury Hill to mark the loss of the Southern stars, the suggestion is that there was a desire on the part of the builders to resist the immense cycle, to intervene to preserve the existing order. If they were to be successful, like Llud, a founding king, and Merlin, a prototypical magician, then they needed to intervene on a comparably mythic scale.

10

In the Neolithic World

In our species, knowledge of who we are is linked to origins and beginnings, and it is communicated as a mythology. The first obligation to society by young men and women who are being initiated into adult status is acknowledgment of the past, and of its living presence in them as the symbolic embodiment of their ancestors.

Paul Shepard[1]

One of the few remaining stones of the Northern Inner Circle.

Self-consciousness in the New Stone Age

As we draw the different threads of this book together, it is important to keep in mind the obvious: the Neolithic world was very different to our world. Having said that, however, it would be a mistake either to think of Neolithic people as 'primitives,' or to beatify them. Neolithic men and women were physically tough and mentally, socially, politically and spiritually sophisticated. They developed complex relationships and social structures. They pioneered settlement, agriculture, domestication of animals, monument building, trade and exchange. They developed new ceramic, musical, surveying, engineering, astronomical, ritual, and eventually, metallurgical skills. The average Neolithic farmer would have been as keen to hear news, obtain information and improve things to his or her advantage as their counterpart in the Victorian era. But, unlike the Victorian farmers, their piety would have extended deep into the natural world. A relationship with myth and the ancestors, "the symbolic embodiment" of the past described by the human ecologist Paul Shepard above, was central to the Neolithic people of Avebury. Shepard further describes prehistoric people as "autochthonous, that is, native to their place. They lived within a sacred geography that consisted of a complex knowledge of place, terrain, and plants and animals."[2] Moreover, spirits inhabited this world. As this is so utterly different to our world, it makes every aspect of the world of the Neolithic monument-builders extremely difficult to understand.

As people began to emerge from the hunter-gatherer band that had defined human life for hundreds of thousands of years (*Homo sapiens* is at least 400,000 years old) and began to settle, there would have emerged a complex new world of local geopolitical identities and relationships. A bounded place gave rise to new and vital distinctions. The spatial map that each person had in their minds: the fields, the paths, the woods, the rivers, the springs, the hills, the neighbours, the relations and so on, gave rise to a sense of local identity. Each tribal region, each place of ancestral spirit or soul, must have been cause for pride, local dialects, stories, songs and dress, made distinctive in its relationship to other regions. These people were not merged *with* each other or the environment as is often thought; rather they defined themselves through their relationships to each other and the environment.

They farmed, built homes, bred animals, hunted, foraged and traded. The warmer climate and the abundance of wild resources gave them plenty of free time. Sometimes there would have been a relationship to several locations, for summer pasture and winter herd management. Some Windmill Hill people would have lived with their relatives further west (the artefacts are the same), annually returning to their most favoured spot in the high hills when the springs returned. Thus, a large territory and an even larger network of relationships defined their tribal and individual identity. This society was complex and vibrant, and although protocols governed everything, new ideas evidently travelled freely along the paths of transhumance and trade. Archaeologists think it is only a question of time before they find boats from this era of ever-greater size and seaworthiness.[3] These people exchanged goods, news and information at their seasonal gatherings in special places such as Avebury. These meeting places, distinguished by exceptional groves, individual trees and stones, must have stimulated language, consciousness and imagination.

So powerful were the forces of nature, however, and so great their dependency upon and exposure to them, that although many of these Neolithic people would have retained the vigour of youth throughout their lives, most were dead by their thirties. Of the half of women who lived to give birth, an optimistic expectation is that they had three children and were dead by their mid-twenties.[4] The point is this: as a widely separated, pre-literate society relying upon their own resources and with very little cushion from shortages, the Neolithic people's sense of self, language, culture and ways of knowing was embedded in a fully embodied, highly dependent and immediate experience of the natural world that they also encountered as the divine.

In the ancient and tribal world, self-consciousness developed in the context of relations with animals, rivers, trees and forest. The modern mind now thinks of itself as a highly individuated 'I', a sovereign self with individual rights and interests, defined by its separateness from others and the natural world, but in the permeable membrane of the ancient world it would have made little sense. "Context explains all," writes historian Calvin Martin in his eloquent and compelling book, *In the Spirit of the Earth*. Early "hunters drew upon animal and plant origins while beseeching those surrounding other-than-human… for illumination and even dialogue in the fine art of living—living not especially as a human being but as any being that lives."[5]

In the tribal Neolithic world, the self, while quite distinct and rarely more than thirty years of age, was always coming into being, into self-consciousness, within the context of place and relationship—especially through the immediate and sometimes overwhelming relationship with the 'other.' The 'other' may first have been represented by the mother, but was soon extended into the kinship group, then to the frequently dangerous presences of the natural world. The ancient and universal dance and refrain, "I am deer, horse, bear…" and so on, sharpened the distinction between the self and the other, while simultaneously describing the experience of unity within the relationship. The prehistoric mind needed to be focused yet open, both self- and world-aware, intent on survival and on interrelationship. In a sense, there was *only* the relationship, in which the hunter, in the classic example, sought the deer willing to gift itself from out of the abundance of the Great Surround, killed it, and ingested it—so becoming the other—within the never-ending round of appropriate formal rites. The act of butchering, which reveals internal organs similar to those of human beings, always underscores the unity of the hunter and the hunted. Children then as now would have identified entirely with creatures. They would have imputed human intentions and sensibilities to animals, until, with the development of speech and self-consciousness, defining themselves in distinction to them; but still in terms—usually perceived as mythic or spiritual—of the already established kinship.[6] In other words, a rich language and oral and mythic tradition made sense of things.

No doubt the Neolithic people of Britain would have accompanied the seasonally governed times of gathering, occasions of the hunt, trade, alliance-making, marriage, coming of age and gift-exchange with elaborate ceremonies. All things took place, especially the slaying of animals, meat eating and its distribution, in the context of their cosmological function. They would have upheld strong principles of hospitality; meat in particular would have been given out in a manner that reinforced social unity and order. Martin cites accounts of first contacts in which native peoples shared everything with the guest; where they as hosts would have felt shame not to share their enjoyment of the primal abundance. In return, they expected the guest to do the same. As the web of territory-based relationships, alliances and allegiances grew, all would have relied upon keeping on the right side of the neighbours and being accountable to the ubiquitous and strict moral code of implicitly divine law. In this manner, the Neolithic people built strong social networks of relationship, alliance and knowledge, optimising an individual's and a people's chances of success. But all this, although it needs filling out in detail, is imaginable; it was their actual experience of the world that is so hard for us to grasp.

The World Tree

Central to this mode of self-consciousness must have been the relationship of the Mesolithic and the Neolithic peoples with the primal woodland that then covered the land as well as with individual trees within it. Whole forests of broad-leaved and coniferous trees such as the oak achieved the peak of their ecological succession in this era, providing vast and magnificent habitats vibrant with plant and animal life. These places of the trees, especially distinctive groves, would have felt charged with especial spiritual significance, they were protected, 'pure,' and powerful places in which to be. In indigenous tribal societies, each tree, grove or plant is an entity whose properties and powers are capable of influencing the human realm, not just as food, shelter or medicine, but also as a spirit. Dreams, visions, guidance, oracles, health and illness, sexual activity and death belonged to the forest.

The archaeologists Mark Gillings and Joshua Pollard underscore the significance of the woodland to the Neolithic people in their admirable book *Avebury*. They point out that encounters with places inhabited by trees would have increased in significance over time, as people recalled the events that had occurred within them. Clearings in the forest were likely to have been among the first places to become socially important; not only ecologically rich they had a history of how they were formed. There was a story of who made them and who had rights of access to them, the significance of which developed over time; especially if those individuals went on to become important, maybe as progenitors, or if the clearings became settlements or centres for critical activities. As the Neolithic people cleared woodland for grazing, agriculture and for monuments, shamans may have mediated between the spirits of wood, fire and stone, ritually blessing stone axes to avoid excessive offence to the tree spirits. It is intriguing that archaeologists could not find a single stone axe in the West Kennet palisade enclosures, even though the builders must have employed and broken hundreds in its construction. It is likely that woodland framed the Avebury monuments and that the stone avenues originally passed between and under trees. Long barrows may have sat in forest clearings next to distinctive trees. Other woodland places: inhospitable, boggy, thick with impenetrable bramble, gorse and thorn, may have become associated with less than benevolent forces, possibly with 'impure' or 'taboo' ones that should never be disturbed.[7] Spirits who represented destruction, disharmony and death, such as the owl, wolf or wild boar, inhabited them. Over time, the forest landscape became charged with multiple and different meanings and settlements became more separated from nature.

Yet, apart from what constituted auspicious or inauspicious, favourable or unfavourable, the power of nature, of life itself, encountered so forcefully in the wild, in fire and sky, wholly determined human existence at that time. This power was both a blessing and a threat to the people, who must have respected it as divine, and who would have venerated and named it, then told and retold its stories. The divine force they experienced as flowing freely through the Sun, the Moon and stars, through the elements, the land, the rivers, the sea and sky, through plant and animal life as well as their own bodies, has been given many different names. Archaic cultures worldwide have called it *qi, ch'i, jen, prana* or *mana,* native Americans call it Great Spirit, the classical culture called it the *anima mundi*—the soul or spirit of the world. They may have associated this divine force with particular beings: as oak, ash or yew, as the presence of gigantic or animal powers, or as a great and primal mother or father being. Naming these forces gave them recognisable characteristics; routinely recalling them in speech, story and song gave encounters with them shape; while ritual observances—based upon traditions going back to and beyond the Ice Age—

provided the means to make sense of, examine and be in harmony with them.

In some places, the Neolithic people experienced this Earth Spirit as strong, in others weak, in balance or out of balance, as a hostile or favourable manifestation of the *anima mundi*. The ancient Greek and Roman world described the local, indwelling presences as giants, titans, dryads, nymphs, undines, sylphs, *daemons* or *genius loci*, individual 'spirits of place.' Eventually they became divine principles, were given shrines and temples, anthropomorphised and thoroughly personified as pantheons of gods and goddesses with volition and consciousness in their own right. State-sponsored religions provided for their veneration. Some became identified solely with cosmic forces, a Sun God for example; others retained maternal, primal or animistic forms. Yet the primal tree as the Tree of Life or World Tree, retains its simple form and potency in religious tradition worldwide.

The later Celtic peoples allowed the voices of the nature sprits into their verse: "I am a blue salmon," wrote Taliesin, "I am a dog, a deer, a beech." It is evident the Celtic poets enjoyed blurring the distinction between the 'I', the human and the *anima mundi*: "…there is nothing of which I have not been a part."[8] While it was the stones that still conferred sovereignty upon their kings, the sacred groves gave them a context of worship, and the springs provided the Celts with their connection to the source. The poets tell us that the springs contained magical, life-giving and healing powers, were the places of the 'blood' ancestors and the sources of oracular guidance.[9] Far to the south, the ancient Egyptians described how the stone statues of the *nṯr*, the 'divine principles' (many in animal or partial animal form) spoke to the people in the elaborate temples they had built for them. The *nṯr* animated the statues until the day came when they departed and the statues fell silent. The Greeks likewise recorded the time when earth oracles were still active in springs and caves, when nature spirits still inhabited their valleys and mountainsides. Later the oracles became silent as the sacred groves were cut down, primal altars despoiled and sacred springs were silenced. This provides a context in which to assess the melancholy isolation of the modern self: shorn not just of the extended tribal family, but of the rites of initiation and the soul-bond with nature that was our rich Palaeolithic and Mesolithic inheritance.

Sacred Stones: the *Anima Mundi*

In the manner of their Mesolithic ancestors, the Neolithic people inhabited what today we would call a magical landscape. It was magical because of the immediate relationship between the natural and supernatural powers and presences, and the realm of the human. As dreams, visions, use of hallucinogens and childhood experiences still demonstrate to us today the boundary between these worlds was highly permeable. The self could encounter presences in any and every context. The Sun was a divine being, as were the Moon and stars. Lightning was a form of divine power, as was fire. Animals too were powerful beings who held especial spirit power; yet also did stones, water, the wind and trees. A place where, say, the action of water upon stone had made unusual forms, reached by long paths within a forest inhabited by formidable and dangerous creatures, would have been seen as inhabited by an especial spirit. The role of the shaman was to acknowledge and maintain the right relationship with such places, to visit them regularly and make offerings, as well as to make sense of the messages and signs they delivered. A special place such as an unusual tree or cave that local people had long perceived as inhabited by certain, perhaps oracular, forces and consistently made offerings to might occasionally become the centre of special attention.

Gillings and Pollard underscore the probable numinous

significance of the local stone itself to the Neolithic people. They suggest that the remarkable sarsen stones of the Wessex Downs first encountered by Mesolithic and then Neolithic peoples in the woodland and open clearings, and acting as the locus of paths and as landmarks unusual in an area of chalk and otherwise free of exposed stone, would have been acknowledged to have an animate indwelling presence.

Shaped and arranged in the landscape by long geological processes, the scattered and unusual sarsen stones of Avebury may have been perceived as the embodiment of special powers. They may have been associated with the enduring Earth Mother or seen as the work of a timeless and gigantic hand—perhaps as the broken bones of the original earth-shaping ancestors. The stones had inherent gravity, stillness, immutability, solidity and power. Stones in special locations would have had names and stories that invested them with more specific primordial powers; those with the appearance of living, organic forms, may have been associated with the power of particular animals or elements. Some, the most dramatic of all, on hilltops or within the clear rivers, would very well have provided early settings for local veneration of the 'gifting' Earth. There is evidence of sustained ritual activities at rocks for tens of thousands of years in prehistoric Africa, Europe and Australia.[10]

Gillings and Pollard thought that people would have initially visited and used several of the Avebury stones for stone polishing in their original contexts. Thus they may have originally used the huge stone at the back of Avebury Cove as well as an entrance stone at West Kennet long barrow for polishing valuable stones used in social and ceremonial contexts before construction. These and several other stones are scored with groove marks. We know that smaller and portable exceptional stones played a central role in formal social procedures such as gift-exchange. Apart from special stones used for highly polished axes and maceheads, natural cassiterite tin nodules with remarkable features were present on the land surface of Cornwall; in Irish streams, there were beautiful nuggets of gold. Stones exhibiting exceptional planes of symmetry, colour and light probably accompanied special occasions and even conferred authority. Over time, such stones must have become charged with the stories they told, the alliances, the names of the individuals and the lineages they remembered.

Archaeologists have found axe heads that were clearly maces or badges of office; others were just as clearly ornament or offerings. People gathered, exchanged and traded stones over great distance in the Neolithic era and it seems many of these stones in raw or worked form came to or passed through the ways and networks surrounding Avebury. The stones and their sources, particularly the hills and mountains of Brittany, Cumbria, Cornwall and West Wales, conveyed spiritual forces—manifestations of the earth spirit—not considered present elsewhere.

Imagine shamans at or near the quarries for one of the most-prized stones of the Neolithic era, honouring the power of the place and blessing its stones. They may have conducted rites for it never breaking, never doing harm to the bearer, always keeping sharp, always doing deadly harm to its target, and so on. Near one source of especially venerated stone in the Preseli Mountains in West Wales—axes from which have been found at Avebury—an entire Neolithic culture appears to have flourished to this end. Its people built megalithic ritual monuments: dolmens, stone circles, ring cairns, henges, standing stones, and possibly even a cursus, all directly south of and below the visually striking source of their precious bluestones. These stones were considered so special, that dozens of them were transported 250 miles by land and sea, around a perilous coast, to be installed at an early phase of Stonehenge.[11]

The archaeologist Aubrey Burl suggests that stones were enduring symbols of power and status for the Neolithic people, who would have perceived them as holding the qualities of a particular 'spirit of place.' Burl thought that they could have linked axes extracted high on mountainsides with the spirits of thunder and lightning.[12] The more people who visited these sources of stones, the more rituals and ceremonies that went on around them, the more power such stones would have held. Furthermore, Neolithic peoples in Ireland, Scotland and Brittany laboriously carved stones with distinctive symbols: lozenges, chevrons, meanders, zigzags, spirals and cup marks. Archaeologists have found a wonderfully carved mace head at Newgrange and a similar one near Stonehenge. Highly polished flint, jet and shale clearly played a central role in exchange, prestige and mortuary practices. The stones distinguished their bearers, giving them status and authority.

As Neolithic society and resource networks grew and ritual sites developed, it appears that access to the most valuable stones and their sources became increasingly controlled. Not everyone could obtain access to the stones held in the highest esteem. For example, those who could participate in the socially complex axe trade, and represent themselves successfully in the gift-exchange, trade and ceremonial networks, would have found their individual authority and tribal prestige greatly increased. A fine display, in full regalia, with dancers and shamans invoking ancestral and spiritual forces during the presentation of new axes, would have awed any competition, demonstrated spiritual favour and generally increased prestige. The great ritual sites of the Neolithic invariably had a direct relationship to nearby outcrops of stone, hills and mountains that were the sources of the most valuable stone, especially the stones used for functional and ceremonial axe heads.[13] The builders of Avebury had access both to the majestic sarsens of the surrounding hills and to the extremely useful local deposits of flint. At this time, the stones still held power; yet before long humanity would begin to forget that these had once belonged entirely to the Earth.

In the British Neolithic, it may well have been the numinous power of the earth spirit, the resident 'genius' or *daemon* of the forest, the spirit of the mysterious stones lying in their woodland groves, that the men and women of Avebury wanted to house in their henge. Whatever these stones had come to mean to them: enduring, immutable primordial powers, ancestral forces, deities, titanic beings, oracular sources, the life force, the embodiment of divine law, the divine feminine, the *omphalos,* the *axis mundi,* otherworld gateways, or just the marker of the spirit of place within their world, they may have wanted that power held in an enclosure especially built for purpose. Now we might say that the Neolithic people were attempting to control and manipulate their environment through superstitious means. They would have described it quite differently.

Animism & Cosmogony

Representing another order of power from the trees, plants, springs, and stones were the spirits of the creatures. The surrounding broad-leaved forests were home to the eagle, hawk, wolf, fox, boar, lynx, cat, marten, otter, adder, bear, elk, horse, many kinds of deer and the bad-tempered auroch. The marshes, the impenetrable valleys and mountains may have held memories of other creatures either hunted out or driven to extinction in the Mesolithic—giant species. Particular spirits, part animal, part human, dwelt in distinctive places; powerful raptors dwelt on cliffs and treetops; geese and swan filled the wetlands; salmon annually spawned in the rivers and streams. The linking of creatures with cosmogony—narratives of how the world came about in the beginning—no doubt prevailed in stories, songs and the popular imagination. The reading of the flight of birds, the entrails of a sacrificial animal, the appearance of the deer, a big cat or the great bear, everything alive in its totality, provided the content of the earth spirit or world soul. All this, the builders would surely have wanted to be represented in their monuments.

The creatures of the wild and the domestic sphere were central to life and livelihood in the Neolithic era. Their domesticated animals included dogs, sheep, goats, pigs, cattle and oxen; there is even some evidence that horses were in use by this time, with riding probably preceding traction.[14] The ideology of pastoralism, well suited to the warm, damp climate and rich grasslands, now began to prevail over the primal cults of the hunter and his preferred game, such as the deer, elk and bear. The Neolithic people no doubt identified and named individuals, places, clans and tribes as a whole after particular animals and may have regarded particularly powerful stallions, bulls, rams and boars as personifying the potency and terror of the sacred. Possession of herds and prize animals, even of wild ones, such as hunting birds, was probably seen as a mark of status and divine favour. Through controlling the spirit power of the animal, the shaman or spiritual practitioner could travel to the Otherworlds, prognosticate, read auguries, make offerings and seek healing.

Then there was the question of the sky. Not only the Sun, Moon and stars, but also the mysterious comets, meteorites, northern lights, meteorological phenomena: rain, wind and storm, the seasons and the pulses of the tides, all had to be faithfully represented in the henge. As they experienced the heavens, so it was upon the Earth. At the same time, the builders did not simply align their monuments to the heavens, they would also have tried to bring sky beings or power into the henge through homologies or correspondences with things upon the Earth: that is, through animals, stones, trees, plants and so on that were similar to these powers and which evoked them. For example, fire, woods, resins, herbs, extracts, stones and creatures with solar or lunar affinities may have represented those spirits in the ceremonies of the henge. Thus the bear, its pelt and body parts, may have represented the power that allowed the shaman to ascend and descend the cosmic axis of the Poles. Swan feathers may have represented the stars. By evoking heavenly bodies through things that held related numinous, otherworldly and universal power, the people of Avebury retained the integration of the three matrices of life: self (and the kinship group), nature and cosmos.

Yet as Neolithic men and women extended their habitats and developed field systems, trading routes and ritual sites, they also became conscious of and had to systematise for the first time the directions, divisions, numbers, weights, distances, volumes and the whole host of measures, proportions and ratios that today are taken for granted in ordering matter, time and space. Their work in timber, then megalithic alignments to the Sun, Moon and stars have demonstrated to us that the Neolithic people were incorporating abstract qualities into their ritual monuments that went far beyond their immediate daily experience. The slowly increasing size and complexity of their ritual sites now allowed them to explore, incorporate and standardise the more conceptual, mathematical and geometrical dimensions of life on Earth. Here there were no precedents, texts or tables to consult; yet their minds were seemingly as active as any today, and, as population numbers increased, the tasks that required systematisation increased with them.[15] The Sun and Moon provided basic orientations and measures, but it was the movement of the stars that finalised their detailed divisions of time and space. The need of travellers, especially those on ocean-going boats, for accurate times, tides and directions must have directly affected the increase in star lore. The developing navigational skills of the boatmen, as they brought crucial resources and prestigious cultural items into the tribe, must have entered into the refinement of the designs of ritual space. At the same time, the shamans who journeyed to the heights and the depths of the World Tree brought back with them not so much precise knowledge of the heavenly cycles, but rather of the dimensions of consciousness, intelligence and wisdom they represented.

Chapter 7 on the Longstones Cove shows how the monument-builders could have associated complex ratios, even those of Pythagorean theorems, with the exact calendrical marking of the year—in this case provided by Sirius. The great ritual monuments may have defined and become formal markers not only of time but also of number and measure. The distances and orientations incorporated within these templates and known by a few 'keepers,' may thus have provided standard times and measures for the people, as and when they were required. Yet we must also keep in mind that all this would have been subordinate to the celebration of cosmological function.[16]

The Inner Sanctum

Neolithic visitors to Avebury henge entered a context deep with meanings. Some of these meanings were gradually changing, some would have remained the same. Presumably, not every visitor would have had the same experience of these meanings; but there was undoubtedly a highly structured social and ritual framework that determined their encounter with the henge.[17]

While it remains unknown who had access to the inner parts of the henge and who did not, it is clear that the earthworks and the stone settings defined zones of exclusivity. Apotropaic devices to ward off evil or impure spirits would probably have been present on the boundaries, while certain visitors—such as pubescent men and menstruating woman—may have had to follow strict protocols of purification. Moving from its woodland setting, to the clearing or avenues outside the henge, then to the henge and its outer stone circle, and finally into the inner circles, and their central settings, there were many obvious zones of potential inclusion and exclusion. Structures invisible today, of wood, fabric, grass, leather or bone, along with the presence of guards, guardians and other more subtle signs, would have created contrasting zones of varying significance that would have contributed toward the richly varied experience of any visitor to the henge.[18]

Access to the centres where the meanings converged cannot have been for all. These centres would have retained their spiritual potency by virtue of their exclusivity. Visions, the use of psychotropic herbs and mushrooms, ecstatic dancing, healing, tattooing, tests of endurance, oracular consultations, bone, bird, and entrail divination may have been common in some parts of the henge or at sites nearby. Children may have been frightened of visiting parts of or all of the henge, especially at ceremonial times when men and women took on and acted out, no doubt in vivid masks and even lewd regalia, the sometimes-terrifying spiritual forces and archetypes of their age. While perhaps open to all at other times, the right to participate in rituals at the centres, that is, at the deepest levels of knowledge, myth and meaning—of communication with the ancestors, when the heavens became congruent with the stones—must have been preserved only for the elders, shamans, patriarchs, matriarchs and other gifted and prestigious people of the time, just as specialised knowledge and the most sanctified places are held today.

In any attempt to build such a picture, however, we are inevitably faced with too many unanswerable questions: Which entrance did the visitor normally use? Were some entrances to the immense ceremonial enclosure solely for great ancestral stones, others for people? Was the southern entrance, with its long snaking avenue to the River Kennet and the long barrows, a road for the living or for the dead? Was the avenue to the west a path for the spirit of the wheat and barley or the bull and horse? Were some hills and woodlands set apart for the nature spirits, in contrast to others criss-crossed with paths to gain access to water, timber and firewood? Was there perceptible tension between an older hunting ethos that did little to the land and the new pastoral and agricultural value-systems that was effecting a radical transformation of the land through new patterns of ownership and management? How did the builders appease the tree and animal spirits they were disturbing? Above all, what power did these people believe the henge contained? What visions of cosmic order did it originally uphold?

It is a truism to say that the Neolithic people constructed the henge and its stone settings to incorporate the beliefs that prevailed at the time; but this is nonetheless true. These meanings were symbolic and mythic, moral and spiritual, as well as both multiple and homologous. It is likely their beliefs were animistic, ancestral and cosmogonic. Their stones resonated with the surrounding spirit powers they literally quarried from the surrounding world. While the archetypal force associated with the ancestors, which made its presence felt within the blood, must have had its place of power within the henge.

While these monuments would also have provided settings for the shamanic journey to the Otherworld, the road for the recently deceased and the means of communication with creator spirits and the ancestors, more generally they defined the ubiquitous moral presence of natural divine law, and provided the context for its preservation. Here a conservative and implicit order must have held the people accountable. Various gifts and sacrificial offerings including labour would have been required to offset any transgressions and restore the original order.[19] Finally, the monuments had to represent on the ground a profound expression of an ever-growing framework of knowledge—technical, astronomical, calendrical, musical and mantic—obtained from and corresponding to the divine forces of light and fire, as experienced in the Sun, Moon and stars.

Summary

The Windmill Hill people built West Kennet long barrow, on the alignment to Knap Hill, in the second quarter of the fourth millennium BCE. The first appearance of the Crux-Centaurus stars at the beginning of winter, took place over the long barrow at precisely the same time, from 3700-3600 BCE.

Over time, the Windmill Hill people noticed a slight shift in the positions of these stars relative to the fixed points in the landscape. It may have been to observe them better, or simply because these stars were very important to them, that they began to construct a complex megalithic site in the valley below. Avebury satisfied many different kinds of purpose, not just astronomical, but the striking point is this: *the builders oriented the primary megaliths of Avebury to the same stars observed from Windmill Hill.* The first megaliths at Avebury: the Cove and the Obelisk, the Ring Stone, the D feature and the gigantic pairs of stones at the entrances, were oriented to the rising of the Crux-Centaurus stars. These stars rose on the perfectly rounded natural horizon afforded by Waden Hill. The builders may also have favoured the Avebury site because it had appeared to be the origin of these stars, the location of their rising when seen from Windmill Hill.

After 3300 BCE, when the slow descent of the southern portion of the Milky Way meant it became level with and visible around the entire horizon each winter, the Avebury sky-watchers patiently awaited the ascent of the Southern Cross and the return of Cygnus. As pointers to the North and South Poles, these constellations marked the midwinter moment when the Milky Way formed its polar and cardinal synchronisation of the heavens. They would also have anticipated the morning rising of the brightest star then visible in the northern hemisphere, alpha Centauri. Like monuments erected by other prehistoric peoples, they incorporated alignments to this star's jewel-like appearance into many of their subsequent monuments. By 2800 BCE, the white chalk of the immense circular henge, methodically flung up from the sections of the great ditch with its four stone-flanked causeways, mirrored the Milky Way in the winter sky.

The Neolithic people engaged with Sun, Moon and stars on a terrific scale. But, as time went by, there probably came compelling evidence to the henge builders that an early apprehension of the southward descent of the Milky Way was true. They would now have anticipated the eventual loss of some of their symbolically most important stars.

As the sky-watchers on Windmill Hill noted the last star of the Southern Cross, Gacrux, rise lower and lower over West Kennet long barrow around 2500 BCE, and as watchers at Avebury saw the Crux-Centaurus stars set deeper and deeper into the location of Silbury Hill, Avebury became a vast and busy building site. First, the monument-builders made the decision to seal West Kennet long barrow. They packed any remaining unfilled chambers and the passage of the long barrow with earth and stone, leaving the bones inside and sealing the entrance with several huge sarsen stones. At around the same time, they began work on the astonishing Silbury Hill. The emerging mound lay at the centre of a new set of astral alignments, shown in Figure 49. Thirdly, they built the Kennet and Beckhampton Avenues, which terminated at the Sanctuary and the Longstones Cove. Finally, they completed the main Inner Circles of Avebury henge. This exceptional ceremonial complex must now have fulfilled many functions for a large number of people, coming from all over the country to engage in ritual, social and trading contacts in the shadows of the auspicious stones. At the same time, the continued emphasis upon the stone settings that marked the primary axis of the central monument—the astronomical axis honoured by the ancestors on Windmill Hill—showed that the same fundamental stellar concerns remained paramount in the minds of its builders. The diving of Cygnus and the rising of the Crux-Centaurus stars, pointers to the north-south *axis mundi* and Otherworldly portals—like the life-giving local springs, most prominent in midwinter—retained the primary symbolic focus of the henge.

By the latter half of the third millennium, it would have become clear to the sky-watchers that they were again parting company with the stars. Figures 48c and d show the situation. It seems that in much the same way as the Windmill Hill sky-watchers had built West Kennet long barrow and then Avebury in alignment to the Southern Stars, the Avebury sky-watchers, a thousand years later, built Silbury Hill. Seemingly, it confirmed their worst fears about dying stars. The Early Bronze Age builders at Avebury intensified their efforts to harmonise the ancient cosmic narrative between the Earth and the stars, but to no avail. By 2000 BCE, the southern ancestral stars had gone.

11

Monuments of Power: from Moon & Stars to Sun

If you want to connect with cosmic forces to justify your actions... then you pay close attention to the movement of the celestial bodies—their times of appearance and disappearance, their coming together, their occasional awkward turning backward. You monitor the traffic on the road of the sun, moon and planets—the zodiac. You train specialists... There is sound religious and political capital in knowing what is going to happen next through skywatching.

Anthony Aveni[1]

Reconstruction of the central features of Avebury henge seen from the northern bank.

The Rise of Theocracy

The first megalithic, earth and timber monuments in Britain had their roots in a long-lasting hunter-gathering society; indeed, I see the Neolithic monuments as a final expression of the earlier Palaeolithic and Mesolithic era. Sites like Avebury reveal the immense social changes that took place over the course of the Neolithic. Although in many regions it would be incorrect to see the end of the Neolithic and beginning of the Bronze Age as a complete watershed, it is still appropriate to describe this era as the end of an extremely long period of continuity.[2] Without needing to postulate the existence of a full-blown social hierarchy, the Neolithic marks the trend towards new forms of identity, specialisation, social differentiation and centralisation in southern Britain.[3]

As a result of the 'success story' of the Mesolithic, and the gradual establishment of a settled population in Britain, capable of producing a surplus of food and goods and now eager to trade, a vital change had occurred. It is likely these active people had long upheld ancient principles of reciprocity and hospitality—to share what one had with the neighbour and the guest—but now there was also an incentive to produce a surplus, to store it and trade it. Through over-production, a tribe could obtain highly desirable goods: stone, amber, jewellery, hides, quality flint, breeding stock, seed corn, tools and now, the new metals. Gift-giving and reciprocity was now more calculated—a reflection of the ability, the power and the prestige of an individual and the tribe. A new commercial ethos had entered the world. In the ancient exchange between the hunter-gatherer and the land, man had been careful to take no more than was needed. Because of metals, large herds and agricultural surplus and storage, a new value system was to replace the primal relationship with the 'Gift' of the Earth—one over which humans had greater negotiation and control.

As both agricultural knowledge and accuracy of the calendar improved, as farmers and pastoralists worked the land, sometimes too far, to create a surplus, and as new demands were made upon both resources and people to produce the first truly immense works, powerful figures must have emerged in the tribal networks. Some men and women, largely through personal charisma, ability, good health and fortune, would have been able to obtain unprecedented prestige, wealth and power. They may have had many children, creating strong and influential lineages. They may have had large flocks and herds, or outstanding physical, technical, intellectual or specialist skills. The archaeological record, especially of mortuary practices, shows that life was obviously better for some than others. Late Neolithic long barrows do not appear to contain the bones of all who helped to build them, although all ages and genders are represented. Only a selected few were interred here. As the third millennium drew to a close and the Bronze Age emerged, single burials of the rich and powerful, such as of the Wessex Amesbury Archer (c. 2300 BCE) became the norm.[4]

Imagine men and women over the Mesolithic and early Neolithic eras, establishing themselves through their personal ability to participate in rapidly changing social networks involving exchange of resources and information. As these networks grew, as trade and migration increased, such relationships became paramount: it was these that established a person's place in the tribe and what authority and rights they held. The guiding role of a headman or -woman now became essential. Success in the resource networks—largely through skill in the ritual protocols of gift-exchange—meant a tribe could flourish. Gifting a valuable object with an ancestry of supernatural power, for example, established strong relationships and a subsequent basis for trade. Achieving a surplus freed labour for travel and for making objects that supported further participation and status in the inter-tribal social networks. Although only highly prized goods able to resist decay obviously dominate the existing archaeological record, it was the activities—festivals, dances, songs, techniques, skills and especially information—even more than the goods themselves which allowed society to learn, acquire ideas and knowledge, employ new technologies, become stronger, healthier and grow.

There was a strong incentive to trade, to gain the many benefits that trade brought. Sea-faring, leather-backed or even planked boats capable of carrying trussed sheep, goats, pigs and cattle must have travelled far and wide at this time. Although the direct evidence is lacking, heavy axes and livestock must have been transported across the English Channel and around the European coastline, taking in islands as far as the Orkneys and Shetland. Fresh seeds, breeding stock and good axes were invaluable, establishing a tribe, and making the difference in some cases between life and death as settlers opened up new territories. Innovative techniques of flint knapping and axe-making, of farming and carpentry, new varieties of foods, specialty tools, leather, fabrics, furs, ornaments, pigments and minerals, were traded across great distances.

We can see that the individuals who were able to conduct themselves favourably in the complex trading and gift-exchange networks would have gained authority as providers of goods or bearers of knowledge. Their skills may have been navigational, quarrying or agricultural, or an eye for good breeding stock. They may have been a gifted linguist, ritualist, diviner, astronomer, artist, story-teller, musician or dancer. Their talents may well have been a form of currency convertible into direct benefit for their tribe. New information on how to improve the fertility of domesticated animals and the processing of their products, for example, would have been invaluable; while completion of tasks ranging from the successful importation of a prime bull to the erection of a colossal megalith would have become the stuff of news, perhaps of exaggerated stories that would only have benefited the status and reputation of the individuals involved. The development of elaborate personal dress is highly likely; the arrival of new amounts of red and yellow ochre, polished jet and shell, carved tusks, rare feathers, furs and various shamanic objects would have caused great excitement.[5]

In the context of a social system where different bands or clans within the tribe held particular status and rights—for example, certain activities at tribal gatherings and festivals would have belonged to them—some individuals began to stand out. Clans or lineages responsible for specialist activities: divination, augury, music, costume-making, sacrificial offerings, construction, determination of the calendar and so on, would have encouraged and allowed gifted individuals to emerge who had the ability to deliver that knowledge at the main and most prestigious ritual centres—and present it in terms of their own localised tradition.

As populations increased and resource-gathering sites became permanently settled, as storage techniques improved and food surpluses became common, the archaeological evidence shows that certain places became particularly prominent. The trade in finely polished axes and other prestige goods reached a peak at this time, and was accompanied by the rise of ritual sites either in mythically significant places or located at the main junctions of distribution. Where coastal ports, riverside or other places on the main communication routes became significant—forming entrepôts between mining, manufacturing and final re-distribution centres—the local peoples built henges and circles of earth and stone appropriate for handling the complex protocols of exchange. Structures that impressed the visitors would obviously have worked to a host's advantage; but, initially, relationship was everything, the most valuable information was knowledge, the rules of hospitality prevailed, and any meeting, gathering or exchange was always governed by formal ritual observances.

Mount Pleasant near Dorchester, Knowlton, Stonehenge and Marden near Avebury developed great henges, mounds, megaliths and timber circles. In the broader picture, the area between the headwaters of the Rhine and the Danube benefited from a trade that had long used the two rivers to cross the continent. Megalithic culture and its fascination with cosmic cycles also thrived in Denmark, Iberia, the western Mediterranean and Brittany. As boats and navigation improved, migration, especially from central Europe, became widespread. Cornwall and Brittany traded extensively; manufacturing and exporting thousands of axes, while ritual sites beside the axe-quarries of the Preseli Mountains, the Boyne Valley of Ireland, the Cumbrian Fells and the Isles of Orkney grew to unprecedented proportions.

We can imagine that when appropriately blessed by their shamans and elders, when the right offerings had been made, and the signs favourable, travellers would have set off with the appropriate gifts to obtain stone for axes, conduct marriage talks with neighbouring tribes, negotiate alliances, gain the latest news, information and generally bring home the bacon. Through their ability to avoid conflict and operate successfully in the formal networks of ritual and gift-exchange, through favourable marriages, charisma, intelligence and doses of good fortune, some individuals and their lineages at times may have become able to accumulatively obtain and hold onto the sources of good stone, the best areas of grazing, the finest breeding stock and access to the best resource networks. It was they who had the right gifts, the best axes, the most useful information. Thus, they obtained, in today's language 'market advantage;' and no doubt would have sought to maximise this to the benefit of themselves and their people.

As the Neolithic progressed, the archaeological record suggests that certain select groups of men and women began to hold and control access to information, knowledge, and the remarkable and valuable objects that went along with it: such as fine costumes, ancestrally 'charged' stones, jewellery, axe and mace heads, gold and other prestigious items. Possession of knowledge of astronomically significant times, of ritual regalia, talismans and objects to produce at auspicious moments, were all signs of who was endowed with the approval and authority of their tribe, as well as that of the ancestors and the divine. There is evidence that some objects were handled for a very long time before being placed in the ground. Their ownership must have meant prestige and power. It was probably their owners who delivered the news of the turning of the great cosmic cycles upon which depended the wealth and well-being of the people. Gradually, the cosmic laws of Sun and Moon that governed the agricultural year, now held and transmitted through key individuals, replaced the Mesolithic communion with the wild—with the bear, the deer and the spirit of place. Although it was too soon for a complete shift away from tribal-identity and animism to cosmic thunder and lightning gods, the emerging system can best be described as a theocracy, in the sense that there were always a select few who were seen as being especially guided by the divine.

The Late Neolithic Elite

The description above obviously needs filling out and did not apply everywhere. But it suggests how those in command of the resource and exchange networks and of specialised astronomically-derived knowledge, aided by shamans and supported by the tribal elders, could eventually have become powerful enough to form an elite: a group that was in itself capable of influencing, if not wholly determining cultural activities and protocols at the great ritual sites. It is even possible that over the course of time, here and there, distinctive lineages won control of certain ritual sites—the stone and timber circles, the tombs and sacred places—as well as of the finest pastures, watering and trading spots, the best sources of stone, shell and flint, and, later, the trade in gold, copper and tin. This would have allowed such groups to control the networks and settings for exchange, and so maintain their privileged access to the astronomical, calendrical and divinatory knowledge of the great ritual sites that, in turn, supported their authority.

If this view has any credence, it suggests that over the course of the Neolithic and the Early Bronze Age, some tribal leaders at the centres of the richest and most influential exchange networks could have come into a position where they could initiate the construction of new works at the most ancient and hallowed sites. It was their influence and authority that would have facilitated the accumulation of the information and the resources needed to build a new monument. Through the right patronage, gifting, hospitality and the respectful observation of protocols allowing everyone to feel that they—and their ancestors—were included, a group of people with the necessary ritual authority and technical knowledge could have been assembled. Some specialists would have come from within the tribe, others from elsewhere. It seems that most tribes must have had their own ritual sites: unique, distinctive, but also connected to and informed by the wider tribal networks. The evidence suggests a 'Megalithic Diaspora' along the Atlantic seaboard of Northern and Western Europe as stone circles, chambered mounds, dolmens and other monuments were adapted in different social settings. Although local and tribal in character, it seems there was a willingness on the part of Neolithic and early Bronze Age people to collaborate on a few spectacular endeavours.

Thus, while the earliest megalithic monuments suggest communal endeavour, the later building projects of this epoch imply the kind of leadership necessary for planning and organising the labour for exclusive and sustained ideas. Although the evidence is unclear, as the social structure slowly became more uneven it is evident that the human resources required for building something as large as Silbury Hill or transporting and carving the Stonehenge sarsens, reached a point that only a strong central control of such resources could achieve. Whereas the evidence from the much earlier Windmill Hill enclosures suggests groups of self-sufficient people periodically gathered to work and socialise and when supplies ran out they went home, the creation of the West Kennet palisade enclosures, alongside and contemporary with Silbury Hill, suggest something altogether different. As we saw in Chapter 7, livestock held within the palisade enclosures could have (a) served as food for the workers on the mound, (b) given the organisers indication of available resources, (c) provided evidence of prestigious gifting and trading achievements, (d) demonstrated the organisers' obvious personal largesse, and finally, (e) proved their access to great spiritual power.

The tribal leaders who appear to have emerged in central southern Britain and elsewhere in the course of the third millennium would certainly have been perceived as guided and protected by the spiritual and ancestral realms. Their unprecedented wealth was a sign of their wisdom and supernatural favour, as was their ability to gain the support of those responsible for ceremonies at the great monumental sites. The new ceremonialists must have differed from traditional shamans who conversed with the plants and animals of the boundless surround, in that they mediated between the people and the celestial and heavenly powers—especially those introduced by agriculture, fixed settlements and now the great monumental sites. These ceremonialists and tribal leaders—still through personal charisma and skill, as it is far too soon to suggest dynastic succession, even the Iron Age Celts elected their kings—had the opportunity to control activities at the great ritual centres (Stonehenge will be examined in a moment). The most influential, armed with the highly prestigious cosmic knowledge, might have had the chance to embody any concepts about what leadership may have looked like.

Ideas like that of a radiant and divinely inspired leader at the centre of society could easily have accompanied a Bronze Age solar cult. All emanated from a single individual as the representative of the Sun. Such cults appear in some steeply stratified, central European Early Bronze Age contexts complete with gold regalia: breastplates, capes and hats. Two gold breastplates, one square, the other a seven-inch lozenge, were found at Stonehenge Bush Barrow. The 'golden' King Sil is said to have been interred on horseback in Silbury Hill. Perhaps the spread of the idea of leadership—or rather the rarely fulfilled ideal—was influenced by migration from the south, by stories of Egypt and elsewhere, and was accompanied by the trade in horses and gold. It is worth noting, however, that Geoffrey of Monmouth, in his account of the bringing of the stones to Stonehenge, says that it was Merlin who accomplished the task. Although it is impossible to say whether this is an authentic Neolithic tradition or not, the point here is that it was a *magician* and not yet a king who had the authority to transport the stones.

Merlin, Stonehenge & Avebury

Legends from Stonehenge to the south of Avebury stress the association of an exemplary British shaman with this area of England. Geoffrey of Monmouth wrote that Merlin transported the Stonehenge stones by wonderful means. The Stonehenge bluestones most probably came from the Preseli Mountains in West Wales. Geological analysis bears this out. Yet the spectacular Stonehenge sarsens came from the Marlborough Downs near Avebury.

The task of taking up to eighty stones over twenty miles south from the sarsen fields of Avebury along a north-south extension of the ancient Ridgeway to Stonehenge, must have been one of the most conspicuous and renowned feats of the mid-third millennium BCE. The stones were not dressed until they reached Stonehenge, so the forty-ton uprights of the inner trilithons were originally even heavier—the largest perhaps weighing sixty tons. An extremely influential person would have been necessary to survey the route and negotiate with the many local tribes regarding the work involved. Enormous amounts of ceremony and gift giving must have been required before the task could even begin. This person would have known Avebury and its people intimately, not just the people of Stonehenge. The two places at this time must have enjoyed a good relationship—perhaps offering different but complementary services. The task of procuring the sarsen stones ought to have been every bit as difficult as the Preseli bluestones; it involved more people in the area and, once accomplished, would surely have made its way into common lore, assuring the legend of its organiser. If in this manner, a stone-mover, a magician, Geoffrey of Monmouth's 'Merlin,' can be associated with Avebury, aspects of his legend might reflect upon Avebury.

The Merlin legend say that he had the divine gift of the gods, the wisdom of the sages, but human affairs drove him mad. After a battle in which there was great slaughter, he went into the woods, where he became wild. It seems women could entice him back from this state; but Merlin is only content when he settles in the woods with his sister, Ganieda or Gwendydd. The *Vita Merlini* says they observed the stars from a glass castle with seventy doors and seventy windows, foretold the future and uttered prophecies, recorded by numerous scribes. Ganieda was as good at prophecy as he was, but upon Merlin's return to sanity or perhaps his death, his prophetic power was added to hers.[6] The tradition hints at a special place of stars, prophecy, oracle and divination, of records, many personnel and multiple observation points, and a distinctive balance of male and female power.

Gender & Power

Although men could gain social power through their ability to travel to obtain good stone, pasture and breeding stock and thus successfully compete in the resource networks, certain women must also have been well placed to win authority in their areas of knowledge. The Celtic world may not be relevant in many of its details to Neolithic society, but in the Irish *Táin Bó Cúalnge (Cattle Raid of Cooley)*, it is a woman, Maeve, who was queen in her own right, who competed with her husband and subsequently the whole country for right of access to the best breeding bull.[7] Here, no one is surprised a woman could be a queen; the only question is whether others could come up to her standards.

Did some women draw on their time-honoured areas of knowledge to consolidate their authority and power? It appears that women had long presided over the gathering of wild resources, even the processing of the spoils of the hunt, as well as over the hearth. The anthropologist Chris Knight thinks that women, through their menstrual cycles associated with the Moon, determined the most vital social activities, including those of the hunt.[8] Women possibly sent men off to hunt (the process of transforming boys into men) and were very likely involved in the singing and drumming of planning and retelling of hunts, as well as welcoming the spirit of the animal to the hearth. Women would certainly have held plant-lore and remedies, presiding entirely over midwifery, milking, child-care, weaving, basketry, pottery, meat distribution, fire keeping—all matters of the host and the hearth.

Women would also have had specific areas of spiritual knowledge and ritual: healing, dream-interpretation, acting as oracles, the reading of portents, and performing key functions for the dying and the dead. Here and there Aubrey Burl thinks there is a tantalizing clue that women acted in the realm of the dead: corpse dressing and organising bones in ossuaries, long barrows and on the charnel grounds.[9] Women's knowledge would have been transmitted in the course of cooking, storing, butchering and grinding, during leather-, costume-, dye-, rope-, fat-, net- and basket-making. It may have encompassed aspects of house-building, gift-exchange and tool-manufacturing and certainly included much lore and story-telling. Certain women would, no doubt, have been expert singers, lavishly costumed dancers, highly skilled Sun- and Moon-watchers. The archaeological evidence shows a sexual division of activities, but not one that implies women were treated as social inferiors, rather that they had their own powers; in some cases, like that of Queen Maeve, these would have made them equal to the male.[10]

Great Ritual Centres

As society altered in late Neolithic and Early Bronze Age Britain, the theocratic lineages of male and female shamans and elders who presided over all important matters of sexual relations, kinship, marriage, territory, alliance, the spirit world and death, and who could conduct the necessary rituals at the right times and perform the correct social protocols, would have been conducting ceremonies at ever more sophisticated and extensive tribal and inter-tribal ritual sites. As their calendrical, divinatory, astronomical and mythic authority and reputation increased, they would have been called upon to invoke powers of fertility, protection and success in ever more complex networks of diplomacy and politics. It was through their practice of the correct spiritual observances that society remained aligned and accountable to the natural divine and cosmic order, and so avoided serious acts of transgression. It was they who ensured the fertility cycles of rain and sun and who explained when these things did not come. They engineered the megalithic feats and would have operated on behalf of any emerging tribal leaders at great ritual centres like

Avebury, Stonehenge, Knowlton and Mount Pleasant—the scale of whose monuments were beginning to defy the imagination—to maintain the correct procedures.[11] No doubt considerable wealth flowed to them, since every incipient tribal leader would have needed their support. If their predictions were mistaken, however, or their techniques and rituals flawed, this could have led to a serious loss of prestige. An established group unable to adapt to the fluctuations of fortune in the complex resource networks governed by strict ritual protocols would have found itself failing. It would have seemed that the divine powers withheld favour from their ritual centre and had given it to others. All the civilisations that flourished beside the great rivers of Europe and Asia in the Neolithic and Bronze Age grew around the knowledge of the seasons, the tides, the times of flood and gestation.

It appears that at many culturally important centres over the duration of the Neolithic in Wales, Ireland, Britain, Brittany and the Orkneys, the power of place, of the stones, and of ancestral and supernatural powers, steadily moved from being determined by the people as a whole into the directing hands of a tribal elite. These elites were seemingly made up of gifted and mostly male individuals supported by elders and shamans. The movement was propelled by the demand for newer and greater resources, by the production of a surplus that could be stored and traded, by the prestige and success that individuals could win through the exchange networks, by steadily increasing population levels and, by at least 2500 BCE, increased migration. It was also driven by the astonishing growth of major ritual sites such as Avebury, Stonehenge and Mount Pleasant. Those who carried the *'bâton de commandement'* or other insignia to show they were in command of activities at the most prestigious monumental sites would have fed the symbolism of the important individual and centralisation. Although the Neolithic ended, its lasting effects are still with us in the form of a mostly male elite in control of specialist knowledge replacing the ancient, ubiquitous and direct communion between humans and the environment with mediated access to transcendent cosmic forces at centralised ritual sites.

This slow movement towards control of ritual centres by tribal elites was heavily influenced by the deterioration of the climate and by the degradation and the abandonment of over-grazed agricultural land.[12] It was also accompanied by an increase in conflict and competition, leading to defended settlements and the first evidence of warfare. At Carn Brea in Cornwall, for example, a settlement involved in a prosperous axe trade with Brittany, over 700 arrows were fired over its stone walls about the year 3000 BCE. By the time of the carved sarsens at Stonehenge and on, after 2000 BCE into the Middle Bronze Age, highly centralised and defended societies became the norm. This theme subsequently played out with hill fort posturing at hill fort across a bounded landscape tightly controlled by Iron Age chieftains and their 'Druidic' and aristocratic warrior elites. The Mesolithic and shamanic dependence upon the provision of nature, so great that it blurred the boundaries between the human and the world, between the self and the other, and in which even raw stones were charged with immanent presence, became replaced by the autonomous individual acting on behalf of sources of power that ultimately lay beyond the world.

At Avebury, in the late third millennium BCE, the erection of stone circles, coves, palisade enclosures, stone avenues and, above all, the great mound of Silbury itself could be interpreted as the ritual settings for social dramas in which opportunistic tribal chieftains impressed and manipulated the people, appropriated spiritual concepts and reworked symbolic relationships for their own ends. But this would be going too far. In most places, strong kinship and tribal ties formed a network of relationships wholly focused and dependent upon local food production and the ancient communion with the spirits of place. Large areas of Britain had no great ritual sites or any evidence of centralisation. People could marshal boats and sail away with their animals, negotiating their way into new territories, alliances and resource networks. There was a common language over the entire Northern and Western European Atlantic seaboard. In this reading of the evidence, it might be better to say that as long as the late Neolithic ritual sites still worked, as long as they functioned as key centres of knowledge and as important distributors of resources, then no matter how good or poor the local leadership was—or thought it was—they remained the places to be. These were this era's great places of interest, excitement and opportunity. As long as Avebury or anywhere else appeared to retain the sanctification of the divine and supernatural worlds, and were still favoured places of meeting and learning, of feasts and games, and, perhaps above all, of procuring marriage partners, the Neolithic people of the region would have been more than happy to come and labour on the monumental mounds and megalithic settings.

Yet what were the Neolithic people to make of the fact that the ancestral stars on which the old cults at Avebury depended were vanishing? The obvious conclusion was that Avebury had lost the favour of the divine powers. As the Neolithic people struggled with new inequalities, and perhaps a sense of departure from the plenitude of the ancestral hunter-gatherer way of life, they may even have held the Avebury theocracy responsible for the disturbing social and environmental changes of the third millennium BCE. The tumult of the age meant Avebury may have been seen as failing to propitiate the divine powers with its perpetual rounds of ritual observances and monumental endeavours—the latest being Silbury Hill.

If this was the case, it is possible to read the final phase of building at Avebury as crisis management. The astronomy shows that the skies at the time of the monument-builders held a dramatic message of precessional shift. In place of a sky, schematically shown in Figure 48c, where the Milky Way and the Northern and Southern Cross upheld a stable and balanced order centred upon Avebury, the sky over the course of the third millennium BCE, was moving towards the situation, shown in Figure 48d, where the Milky Way had fallen from its place around the horizon and the Southern Cross had become lost to sight. By the end of the millennium the Southern Cross, the pointer to the Southern Celestial Pole, was entirely hidden at the latitude of Britain.

In summary: over the course of the Neolithic certain themes played out in central southern Britain that gave rise to a new form of identity—now conceived in more narrowly human terms, detached from the ancient communion with the land. Along with this arose new institutions of theocratic or divinely guided leadership. This leadership must still have acknowledged the traditional connection with nature; but the main source of its power was the spiritual authority conferred by control of the great ritual sites with all their strict protocols, taboos and attendant networks of information, resources, relationship and knowledge. Released from the direct dependency of the hunter-gatherer upon the land through agricultural surplus, and now engaged with the abstract forces of time, the calendar and the cosmos, powerful individuals could negotiate and manipulate essentially fluid sets of practical and symbolic relationships. Individual leaders clearly thrived—probably more upon collective acknowledgement of their personal ability than any other principle—and in places and at certain times were able to direct the development and the activities of the most significant sites. What is more, the social curve was about to get much steeper.

The Stonehenge Sun

The determination of the Neolithic people of Northern and Western Europe to incorporate the celestial patterns into their monumental sites is evident from the multitude of astronomical alignments that have been found at them. It now seems clear that the astronomical observances of these people went far beyond calibrating the cycles of the Sun and Moon. They reached deep into the realm of the stars. Stellar lore must also have shaped their mythic narrative. Indeed, they went as far as noticing—at least in their own symbolic terms—the slow movement whereby the 'fixed' stars, and especially the Milky Way, gradually rotated against the monumentally marked horizon and the well-known cycles of the Sun and Moon.

Pre-literate, lacking the centralisation and the kind of instruments, numeracy and notation that their Mesopotamian and Egyptian counterparts were developing, we cannot guess how profoundly the Avebury star-watchers may have understood or responded to these astronomical events. Their role was to maintain harmony with the heavens and to receive guidance from the signs they saw there. These sky-watchers read the heavens as they would have read the signs of plants and animals, not to objectively understand the sciences of biology, astronomy and physics, but rather to understand the divine order, the great powers of earth and sky, and make the appropriate ritual observances to them. They did not so much intellectually hold the inevitable mathematics as sense it through their hands-on notation. It was most probably the mysterious proportions and affinities between things that interested them; the patterns and relationships that came from the divine. Yet even if they could predict the movement of the stars, they would have found it much harder to foresee the immense socio-cultural changes that were taking place at this time.

By the time it became clear to the Avebury star-watchers over the latter part of the third millennium BCE that the Milky Way was irrevocably falling to the south and ancestral stars were leaving the sky, it would also have become clear that social interests were changing. New activities along with new monumental forms, especially the single-main internment round barrow, were engaging the attention of the Britons. It may have seemed to an Avebury elite still invested in a traditional order of things, as though, with the turning of the 'Wheel of the Stars,' that one age had abruptly ended and another as suddenly begun. It may have seemed that the impulses sweeping though humanity meant people were not as interested in making spiritual observances to maintain harmony with the heavens—as well as with the Earth for its sometimes grudging abundance—as they were in chasing exciting new resources and technologies and, above all, in developing and maintaining alliances and trading networks that meant immense power for a few.

In the latter part of the mid-third millennium BCE, coinciding with the influx of metals, new ideas and 'Beaker' lifestyles from the Continent, those who controlled the resource networks around Salisbury Plain began construction of a new phase of their already ancient ritual monument at Stonehenge. It was to be unlike anything seen before and it was definitely going to impress the neighbours!

It is obvious that 'Superhenges' like Avebury and Stonehenge made a huge contribution to the momentous changes taking place in Britain at the end of the Neolithic and the beginning of the Bronze Age. As ritual sites became more sophisticated and the labour required at them better organised, greater social status was conferred on those who could provide the necessary leadership to create them. Those who could control the most prestigious ritual sites along with the flow of resources towards and away from them had the chance to become wealthy and powerful. This state of affairs seems to have been especially true of Stonehenge. Those in charge of Stonehenge not only commanded the immediate area, but seemingly also controlled regional access to the newest, rarest and most prestigious goods. These were valuable metals—copper, tin and gold—now entering Britain via trade with Ireland and the Continent. An age of the Sun and metal was soon to replace the dying age of stars and stones.

Already, perhaps hundreds of years earlier, the people of Stonehenge had imported more than eighty stones from the Preseli Mountains in West Wales, arranging them in a variety of circles inside the henge.[13] The transportation of the bluestones had been a triumph. Through a dazzling and highly prestigious display of technology, knowledge and wealth the builders had succeeded in bringing stones of extraordinary power to the henge.

It is worth reflecting further on the symbolic power of the Preseli bluestones. In its natural setting in West Wales, the source of the bluestone is a unified group of jagged and dramatic cairns that originally emerged high above a rugged and heavily wooded landscape. These cairns, at well over a thousand feet, remain spectacular to this day. Carn Meini, Carn Gyfrwy and other carns, as they are known locally, clearly are an especial locus of geological power and would have appeared to the first people of Britain as a place of especial power in the west. The shamans of the Preseli area would have worked to increase the symbolic power of the site, encouraging the powers and animistic presences that inhabited its summit to enter the stones they quarried and shaped for export. The bluestone takes a sharp edge and a high polish and the area flourished as a result of the axe-trade. Four axe manufacturing sites have been found around the location of Glandy Cross, about three miles due south of Carn Meini.[14] The axe, as suggested by Burl, was a symbol of lightning, fire and light for Neolithic people, often linked with high places. A cluster of dolmens, stone circles and other ritual sites, like the 'ring-henge' of Meini Gwyr, demonstrates the ceremonial importance of the Preseli area in late Neolithic and Early Bronze Age networks of exchange. Its spiritual reputation, its remoteness, and the quality of its axes would have been legendary. It operated in close alliance with the people of Stonehenge. The extraordinarily bold move that ordered the importation of a sizeable chunk of the Preseli landscape to Stonehenge even entered oral tradition, being recorded as early as the twelfth century CE by the historian Geoffrey of Monmouth.[15]

The 'new' Stonehenge elite inherited the bluestones and other, far older, features of their chosen site, such as the early Neolithic Cursus—a carefully laid out parallel alignment of earthworks reminiscent of the ecliptic or the Milky Way. They would have been familiar with complex timber structures at nearby henges like Mount Pleasant to the southwest, Marden to the north, the Sanctuary at Avebury, and Woodhenge close by at Durrington Walls. It is likely this group of builders lived and conducted operations from Durrington Walls, where a Neolithic 'town' of rectangular timber houses has been found. They now added to the impact of their monument by deciding to place lintels not of wood but of stone upon a gigantic inner horseshoe of carved sarsen stones, as well as upon a complete outer circle of thirty similarly carved stones. The inner horseshoe originally consisted of five great trilithons with carefully jointed lintels. The lintels on the thirty stones of the outer circle were also jointed to form a stable, continuous and level ring.

The effort of hauling the hard and heavy stone from the Avebury area, then carving it so meticulously was prodigious—nothing like it had ever been attempted before. The builders may even have tried to place lintels upon a circle of bluestones. Enormous amounts of energy and planning went into this phase of Stonehenge. The effort, conceptualisation, design and the carving of the stones were unprecedented. And the spectacular result was just what was intended. As it stood in the last centuries of the third millennium BCE and into the first few centuries of the second, the monument was a reinterpretation of everything that had gone before in Neolithic megalithic culture. It was a stunning promise of a new world. The new Stonehenge can be interpreted as a demonstration of a new form of political power that still drew upon traditional ritual precedents but wanted to break the mould and look to the new. Perhaps most tellingly, little in the way of astronomical sophistication was added to the monument with the sarsen circles. That work had already been done many hundreds of years before. In fact, the new sarsen stones blocked most if not all of the sites early alignments. Stonehenge's single main axis now focused attention upon the solstitial Sun, and only upon certain lunar events that aligned with those of the Sun such as midwinter rising and midsummer setting.

Observers at the centre of the monument could watch the midsummer Sun rise over the entrance to the henge and then up and over the Heelstone and other stones at the terminus of the avenue. To do this, they stood in a U-shaped enclosure similar in size and orientation to the Cove at Avebury. And from the Heelstone and entranceway they could watch the midwinter Sun set through the carved sarsen rings on the same central axis of the monument. Any lunar observances also made through the stone structure were now strictly subservient to those of the Sun. Indeed, it has been suggested that earlier lunar and female cults were now ritually "subsumed" by solar and male agendas.[16]

With its solar emphasis and its design architecture; its ever-increasing zones of exclusivity and its mobilisation of a massive and highly directed workforce, the new Stonehenge clearly provided the means for a small and successful elite to extend authority, prestige and power over an ever larger, wealth-creating resource network. Recent work at Stonehenge suggests burial there was the preserve of a very select few, nearly all male, perhaps an oligarchy.[17] This new kind of tribal leader would still have needed the elders, shamans, ritualists, diviners, augurs, sky-watchers and so on to support and validate their newly emerging solar cosmology; and they may well have drawn such people from sites elsewhere, for Avebury and other nearby ritual sites became neglected, perhaps even abandoned at this time. The old theocracy was over; the time of oligarchy had begun—at least in Wessex. In the round mounds that now dotted the Stonehenge landscape the goods that accompanied these single main burials became increasingly wealthier and more fabulous as the second millennium BCE went on.[18]

Prehistoric British society had changed dramatically over the centuries that Avebury and Silbury, West Kennet long barrow, the Sanctuary and Windmill Hill were built and in use. In the transition from their nomadic hunter-gatherer origins to settled farmers, animal breeders, traders and specialists, the population of the new island of Britain had significantly increased. Now new elites were rising, and not only the tool kits, burials, clothing, prestige items and pottery styles had changed, but above all, concepts of identity and its relationship to knowledge had been radically transformed. As migration, social stratification and centralisation increased, as demand for trade goods grew, the climate deteriorated and as poor farming techniques meant some once fertile land was abandoned, the sometimes violent competition for resources must have been experienced by many as an intense struggle.

Bronze Age Stonehenge, with its central and high status exclusion areas, its grand if technically awkward innovations, displays an entirely different kind of power than the one that had prevailed in the Meso-Neolithic. Natural stone had formerly held greater numinous power and, reverently aligned to the divine order of earth and sky, it had helped regulate the social order. But after the laboriously carved trilithons of Stonehenge it was now clear that a new power was being claimed by the hands and minds of the human. To be specific, power lay in the hands of those few individuals able to control the knowledge and ceremonies held at the most prestigious henge monuments, and fulfil the expectations and demands made upon them by a technically advancing, more sophisticated but increasingly dependent and always potentially violent population. In the new social order, a dwindling number of individuals and lineages actually exercised power, while commanding ever-greater numbers of people, who increasingly depended upon the resource network and its redistribution of goods and information for their economic survival.

It is likely that there was fierce and sometime combative competition among the strongest lineages for control of the information and resource networks. It was becoming necessary to keep one's hand in with a bow, axe or spear. Like the *Ard Rí*, the potential 'High King' of Ireland who would later rule from Tara, Early Bronze Age Stonehenge may have been the expression of the desire to create a central seat for a chieftain or even a 'king' who could unite the many tribes of southern Britain. Often this was less of a reality and more of an ideal, defined only by the legends or the prestige of the objects of those who had once held or had aspired to hold it. Whatever the actual case, these new power structures were central to all that subsequently took place in Britain. They allowed the belief system of a dominant tribe, even a state, defined by powerful chieftains and dependent subjects, to take centre stage, replacing the ancient hunter-gatherer communion with the gifts of nature with the demand for loyalty to the most powerful tribal leader or leaders.

Most significantly, if Avebury was the temple of the Moon and stars, giving mastery of both the lunar calendar and stellar knowledge, then Stonehenge was the temple of the Sun. From the start, Stonehenge had never lost its grip on the primary oscillations of the Sun, regularly clocking them off upon its main alignment. Unlike Avebury—where solar alignments were but one aspect of a complex set of cosmic alignments that lost their effectiveness over millennia—this cycle had never changed. The only thing that changed was the priority of the new Stonehenge builders. In accordance with the symbolism of a single central leader, a 'Sun King,' the construction of the inner stone settings meant only the solstices were visible by the decreasing number of people admitted into the centre or the narrow lines of sight of the henge. The multiple alignments of archaic Stonehenge to both lunar and astral cycles had seemingly been forgotten as Bronze Age society pursued its centralising, and somewhat intangible, ideal of earthly power.[19]

Thus, if Avebury can be seen as the triumph of the Neolithic lunar calendar, tracking both sidereal and synodic months and arduously harmonising them with the path of the Sun, the final phases of Stonehenge can be seen as the triumph of a solar calendar. At Bronze Age Stonehenge, what may have begun as a means of adjusting an ancient lunar calendar became the calendar itself. The Stonehenge builders disengaged the Sun from the cycles of the Moon, established a reliable solar calendar, and developed a symbolic ideology that most probably associated a single ruler, whether male or female, with the Sun.

Stonehenge was going to win in any competition between it and Avebury as its adaptive form meant it could ever more closely approximate the ambitions, ideals and needs of the age. It became exclusive and focused, whereas Avebury had been designed to include *everything*. The strictly solar calendar of Stonehenge could be relied upon to provide accurate information while Avebury's lunar and stellar promiscuity was appearing to drift. Complex, long-standing lunar and stellar cults may originally have offered the same results as the cult of the Sun: fertility, healing, the opportunity for a safe otherworld journey, ancestral veneration, gifts of foretelling and so on, but they would naturally have lost popularity rapidly once their privileged stars were vanishing from the sky. By the beginning of the Bronze Age, Stonehenge, attuned to the simple and absolutely regular solstices, provided a secure foundation on which to build, while Avebury's complexity may have been perceived as trying to hold onto something already lost. In the constantly fluctuating network of individual and tribal allegiances, it was only natural for people in the country to transfer their loyalties.

The archaeology shows that Avebury was neglected not long after the building of Silbury Hill. Stonehenge went from strength to strength for several more centuries, well into the second millennium BCE. By this time, the use of metals in burials, including remarkable gold ornaments that incorporate astronomical and calendrical knowledge, signalled distinctive elite formation.[20] To those responsible for a monument that was now aligned to a lost order it must have seemed as though one age had come to an end and another had begun. Perhaps baffled, confused and lacking the cosmography that could explain what had happened in the heavens and so possibly perceived by the people as no longer attuned to the divine order, the Avebury star-watchers would eventually have left their natural, unhewn stones to sing to each other, to follow the more obvious and well-regulated path of the solar divinity worshipped with carved stone and shining metal. They finally abandoned their subtle lunar cycles, along with the veneration of particular stars, and bowed to the singular Sun.

Notes

1 Neolithic Astronomy

1. 1977, p. 56.
2. During a lifetime of dogged data collection (together with his son, another Alexander), Thom deployed an impressive array of surveying, astronomical and mathematical skills. These enabled him to demonstrate that intentional astronomical orientations at prehistoric sites far exceeded random or chance probabilities. See Heath 2007, passim. Evidence now being collected by archaeoastronomers from all over the world now supports the case originally established by Thom. For example, see Hoskin, 1997, on the stellar alignments of megalithic sites in the Mediterranean. Even the doyens of conservative archaeology, the Egyptologists, now concede that the ancient Egyptians aligned many of their temples to astronomical events, including to the stars. See for example Belmonte and R. Faulkner.
3. Anthony Aveni, Professor of Astronomy and Anthropology at Colgate University NY, has provided excellent introductions to American archaeoastronomy. The work of anthropologists like Tedlock, 1982, is revealing the dynamic relations between indigenous peoples, the calendar and the heavens.
4. North, 1996, xxxvi. John North, who died in 2008, was Professor Emeritus of the history of philosophy and the exact sciences at the University of Groningen. The quotation at the beginning of the chapter is taken from the preface to the second edition of his *Cosmos*, 2008.
5. The lack of a high degree of accuracy is not necessarily a bad thing. It limits the research to broad alignments and avoids the narrow computer accuracy (unrealizable by

Neolithic astronomers) demanded by past models, such as that of Hawkins. See the discussion by Ruggles, 1996.

6. G. Hawkins, 1964, 'Stonehenge: a Neolithic Computer,' *Nature,* 202, pp. 1258-61; F. Hoyle, 1966, 'Stonehenge: an Eclipse Predictor,' *Nature,* 211, pp. 454-6; Heath, 1998, pp. 49-59.
7. Thom, 1967, for example, found the statistical recurrence of stellar alignments at megalithic sites as compelling as those to Sun and Moon, pp. 92-106.
8. Around 3000 BCE in Mesopotamia spring ploughing coincided with the heliacal rising of the Plough and the heliacal setting of the Pleiades. (Rogers, 1998, p.16.) See Ovid's *Fasti* and other Roman texts on agriculture for evidence of the importance of stars in planning the ancient agricultural year.
9. *An Outline Sketch of the Origin and History of Constellations and Star-Names,* Gary D. Thompson 2007-2009, www.members.optusnet.com.au. It is likely that accurate records of the movement of the Sun through the zodiacal houses began in China, Egypt, India and Mesopotamia some time after 2000 BCE.
10. Rogers, 1998; North, 2008, p. 33.
11. As one of many examples, the people of the east coast of Arnhem Land saw the Southern Cross as a stingray being pursued by a shark, the latter representing alpha and beta Centauri.
12. Burl, 1987, ch.1 and 2, discusses mortality rates in the Neolithic, where most men would be dead by 36 and most women by 31.
13. Neolithic pottery and a mix of animal bone is present; the issue may be that so little of the henge has been excavated. Burl, ibid, for example, suggests dwellings and other structures await excavation.
14. Whittle et al, 2007; Bayliss et al, 2007.

2 A Sky-Watcher's Paradise

1. Whittle et al, 1999. Although 'Windmill Hill' was once used to name this megalithic culture the name is now only used to refer to the location.
2. Thomas, 1999, p. 53.
3. Archaeologists generally regard long barrows as territorial markers, whose symbolic features helped to distinguish local ancestral lineages. The orientation of most early Neolithic barrows was to soli-lunar extremes, especially winter solstice sunrise; for example, Stoney Littleton long barrow in Somerset. Sims, 2006, argues that Neolithic interest in the most southern solar (i.e. winter) and lunar events "was to preserve an ancient forager respect for the moon while confiscating it for the novel purposes of a cattleherder lunar-solar cosmology." But North, 1996, makes the case for the long barrows to be primarily oriented to the stars.
4. Waden is pronounced *wa*-den locally, and seems to be a Saxon name signifying either Woden's Hill or *Wēo(h)-dun*, 'hill with a heathen shrine.' The hill was the site of a Romano-British, then Saxon settlement, and so very likely to have had a shrine or temple (J.E.B. Gover, 1936, *The place-names of Wiltshire*, Cambridge University Press).
5. Gillings et al, 2008, p.166, estimates the western stone of the Cove, at around 47 cubic metres and 100 tonnes, as "amongst the largest megaliths in Britain."
6. Pollard & Reynolds, 2002, p. 91.
7. Ibid pp. 91-6. The chalk of the area absorbs rainwater, raising the water table about three months after winter rains begin and activating springs in the otherwise dry valleys around the New Year; hence the local name 'Winterbourne' for places on such streams (Barron, 1976).
8. Gillings & Pollard, 2004, pp. 47-9; Gillings, 2008, pp. 202-04. See Whittle et al, 2007, on the complexity of dating features

of the Avebury landscape.

9. Aubrey Burl, 1999, suggests that the largest stones, those over 40-50 tons, would have needed over 500 people to move them. For example, if one person can exert a pull of 112 pounds, then 500 people would be needed to pull 56,000 pounds, or 25 tons, but with practice, concerted pulling can reach twice that much. While oxen must be included in the picture, and levers and rollers would have made the task easier, the effort of training and looking after the oxen, and also making the rollers, together with ropes capable of these strains, must have been enormous.
10. Some archaeologists, however, such as Mike Pitts, 2000, Mike Parker Pearson, 1998, and Frances Pryor, 2003, introduce symbolic ideas into their discussions: such as stones marking a transition into the "domain of the ancestors" as opposed to wood marking the "domain of the living."
11. Thom, 1967, pp. 89-91. Thom enclosed this area in a 3-4-5 triangle whose corners appear fundamental to the drawing of arcs that define the great Outer Circle, and whose edges, at azimuths of approximately 42°, 132° and 169°, appear to have astronomical significance.
12. Except the Great Pyramid, whose cardinal and stellar alignments circa 2500 BCE acheived phenomenal orders of accuracy.
13. Burl, 1979, p. 173. Two examples of equal-sized Neolithic henges arranged in a row are Priddy in the Mendip Hills and Thornborough in Yorkshire.
14. D.J. Lewis-Williams and D.G. Pearce, 2005, *Inside the Neolithic Mind: Consciousness, Cosmos, and the Realm of the Gods*, Thames & Hudson, London. *The Sacred Mountain of Colombia's Kogi Indians*, 1990, is just one of the extraordinary studies by the anthropologist Gerardo Reichel-Dolmatoff in South America which has helped to illuminate our under-

standing of Stone Age societies.

15. It may be significant that the Ring Stone, placed close to the full Moon marker of the southern circle in this system, lies upon the axis of the two circles. In a pamphlet published for the Astrology Association in 1995, Robin Heath describes a similar lunar counting system, moving around the circle one stone a day, in which the Ring-stone adds the extra hours necessary to make up the phases to 29.5 days (*Megalithic Tour 1994-2009,* available from www.skyandlandscape.com).
16. Lionel Sims gives an account of walking around the 'D' feature to observe the Moon in his 2003 article, 'Entering, and returning from, the underworld: Silbury Hill – where archaeoastronomy meets landscape archaeology:'

    "Walking around the stone row towards the south, and therefore towards Silbury Hill, the increase in the steepness of the angle of view is sufficient for the protruding top of Silbury Hill to gradually dip below the horizon of Waden Hill. By the time we have completed the walk of the row, and ended at the Obelisk, direct viewing... is obscured by the southern entrance stone... Therefore walking counter-clockwise around the 'D' feature towards the Obelisk, the chalk wall of the summit surround slowly sinks and finally disappears at the Obelisk. The Avebury builders have devised through the observer's movement a way to represent a dynamic representation of new moon setting below the horizon".
17. The reason for this difference is that while the Moon is in orbit around the Earth, the Earth is also in orbit around the Sun. The difficulty of ascertaining the exact number of stones in each circle probably reflects the fractions involved.
18. If the Great Outer Circle of approximately 100 stones was an attempt to lay out four lunar cycles (four lots of twenty-five stones with each entrance counting as two or three days),

the Avebury monument-builders would have had the ability to count with very great accuracy indeed. Robin Heath, 1998, has shown that the fifty-six postholes at Stonehenge was the minimum needed to give astonishingly accurate rates of eclipse prediction and he thinks the same was true of the three stone circles at Avebury (pp 54-9). Heath also gives a method of combining lunations and sidereal lunar months using the two inner and the one outer circle at Avebury (pp 194-5).

19. See Heath, ibid, on the calibration of lunar and solar cycles at Stonehenge to measure eclipses. The Hurlers in Cornwall are an example of three aligned stone circles that may originally have possessed 27, 28 and 29 stones.
20. Burl, 1999, pp. 125-137.
21. By engaging with the celestial bodies, I mean interacting with them as traditional hunters might sing to animals before, during and after a hunt. They are, in the words of Claude Levi-Strauss, "good to think" (1963, *Totemism,* Boston: Beacon, p. 89).
22. North, 1996, p. 274; Heath, 1998, pp. 194-5; Sims 2003.
23. Chris Knight, 1991, documents the near universal association of Moon and menstrual cycles. Sexual relations and menstrual blood compromised the 'purity' men needed to engage with the spirit of the animals they were hunting. See also G. Reichel-Dolmatoff, 1968, *Amazonian Cosmos,* University of Chicago.
24. Heath, 1998, op.cit, and Appendix 3.
25. Two codices, the Paris and the Dresden codex, have been interpreted as suggesting Maya knowledge of precession. See Gregory Severin, 1981, 'The Paris Codex: Decoding an Astronomical Ephemeris,' and J. Eric S. Thompson, 1972, 'A Commentary on the Dresden Codex: A Maya Hieroglyphic Book,' *Transactions of the American Philosophical Society,* vol. 71, 5.

3 Windmill Hill & the Mystery of the Moving Stars

1. Collectanae, *Folklore*, 1915, vol. 20, p. 81.
2. See J. Pollard, "good quality flint from sources on the Marlborough Downs" etc., p. 331, and other reports in Whittle et al 1999, for an assessment of the significance of flint for the people of Windmill Hill.
3. Whittle et al, Ibid.
4. While accepting that a single definition of the term is impossible, I take shaman or shamanic to refer to those persons of hunter-gatherer / tribal / often nomadic communities who had specialised spiritual knowledge. They practised ritual, made offerings, read omens, interpreted dreams, communicated with the 'other' etc., on their own behalf or of others, as distinct from 'priests' or those who later served some kind of authority. Shamans 'go between' the worlds, presiding over coming of age initiations and funerary customs in a cosmos perceived as inhabited by spirit forces on multiple levels. See Aldhouse-Green, 2005, p.10 ff.
5. Milk Hill 168°, Tan Hill 178-182°.
6. Source: *Wikipedia*. The double star is visible with binoculars.
7. While it is possible that on many nights in this epoch, *alpha* Centauri and other first magnitude stars could have been visible down to the horizon, an extinction angle of two to three degrees has been assumed, especially for the lesser star *delta* Crucis. Incidentally, the full view of the Southern Cross and Milky Way extended as far north as the 60th parallel of latitude (the Orkney Isles) from the eighth to the seventh millennium BCE.
8. North, 1996, p.83 ff. See previous note regarding the extinction angle. The location of Windmill Hill at the 51st latitude meant that these stars were visible from there for over a third of a precessional cycle—almost 10,000 years.
9. Bayliss at al, 2007, "...we can now date the construction of

the monument to the middle decades of the thirtyseventh century cal. bc (3670–3635 cal. bc at 81% probability)... Overall the infilling of the chambers took around a thousand years."

10. Timber circles with astronomical alignments such as Goseck appear on the continent from as early as the fifth millennium BCE (Gibson, 2005).
11. It seems the astronomy of their Egyptian counterparts was ultimately stellar astronomy. The heliacal rising of the brightest star, Sothis or Sirius, opened the Egyptian New Year, inaugurating a yearly procession of stars defined by 36/37 decans. Upon death, the Old Kingdom pharaohs were held to take their place among the stars. The stars allowed the Egyptians to precisely orient their architecture. See Belmonte, 2001, or Faulkner, 1966.
12. The *heliacal rising* of a star occurs when it first becomes visible on the eastern horizon before sunrise, after a period when it had been hidden below the horizon (or hidden by the brightness of the Sun). Each day after the heliacal rising, the star will appear to rise earlier and thus remain in the sky longer before it is once again hidden by the Sun. Its *acronychal setting* is the last time the star is visible in the sky at sunrise before it sets below the western horizon. A star will reappear in the eastern sky at dawn approximately one year after its previous heliacal rising. The *heliacal setting* of a star is the last occasion the star is visible setting on the horizon after sunset. The *acronychal rising* is the last visible rising of the star on the horizon after sunset.
13. Recently excavated sites such as Nabta Playa hint at the Paleolithic origins of Egyptian astronomical culture. See 'Megaliths and Neolithic astronomy in southern Egypt,' J. McKim Malville, Fred Wendorf, Ali A. Mazar, Romauld Schild, *Nature 392*, 488-491, 2 April 1998.
14. The centre abolishes the "homogeneity and relativity of

profane space" and becomes "the central axis for all future orientation" wrote Eliade in *The Sacred and Profane,* pp. 21-22. It is defined as the point at which there is contact between different planes, Eliade argues, thereby explaining the virtually universal myth of a Cosmic Tree or Pillar joining Heaven, Earth, and the Underworld.

15. Eliade *Shamanism,* 1964, pp. 259-279. See also Ananda Coomaraswamy, 1997, *The Door in the Sky,* Princeton University Press, ch. 2.
16. Eliade, ibid, p. 206.
17. Ibid, p. 269.
18. Aperture measurements for Newgrange calculated from data provided by Viktor Rejis at http://www.iol.ie/~geniet/eng/
19. Mann & Glasson, 2007, pp. 76-84.
20. The builders of Newgrange may also have intended the white quartz stones set around the exterior of this enormous chambered mound to mirror the Milky Way. The paths of the midwinter Sun and Sirius could also have been seen at Stoney Littleton long barrow, west of Avebury, built 3500 – 3300 BCE. The tilt of the passageway to an elevated horizon overcame any problems of stellar extinction and refraction.
21. A posthole near the south entrance of Avebury may be equivalent to the extremely early Mesolithic postholes discovered in what is now the Stonehenge car park. Gillings & Pollard, 2004, pp. 25-6.
22. *Folklore,* 1909, vol. 20, No. 1, pp. 72-83.
23. Arthur and John Hubbard mention the 'wolf platforms' of Martinsell Hill in *Neolithic Dew-ponds and Cattleways,* quoting Richard Verstegan, *Restitution of Decayed Intelligence in Antiquities,* 1673: "The month which we now call January our Saxon ancestors called wolf-monat, to wit, wolf-moneth, because people are wont always in that month to

be in more danger to be devoured of wolves, than in any other season of the year; for that, through the extremity of cold and snow, those ravenous creatures could not find of other beasts sufficient to feast upon."

24. The precessional movement of the stars in relation to the seasonal passage of the Sun is about 50 seconds a year. A second is one sixtieth of one minute, which is one sixtieth of one degree; 360 degrees divide the celestial sphere. The movement of the Sun around the celestial sphere was first accurately recorded using a sexagesimal (x 60) system in Babylon in the early second millennium BCE. David Frawley and others argue that a 360-degree division of a circle could have occurred earlier in India. See Frawley, *Vedic Origins of the Zodiac: The Hymns of Dirghatamas in the Rig Veda*, http://www.vedanet.com. Precessional movement amounts to about one degree in 72 years, so it takes the Sun 360 x 72 years for the winter solstice or the equinox Sun to move around the whole celestial sphere, a total of about 25,920 years.
25. Thom, 1967, pp. 152-58. The 'Hill O Many Stanes' Early Bronze Age megalithic complex also provided a lunar observatory and an accurate indicator of true north.
26. When a star such as Sirius is described as sharing the same path, or rising and setting in the same place associated with the (in this case midwinter) Sun, this does not necessarily mean it is *the* heliacal star, i.e. the last star visible that precedes the rising midwinter Sun. It may be rising much earlier in the night at this time.

4 Avebury: In the Image of the Milky Way

1. Herschel, 1849, *Outlines of Astronomy*, 793.
2. The extinction angle indicates the place where none but the very brightest stars are visible down to a few degrees above the horizon due to the atmosphere of the Earth. See note 11

in Chapter 5.

3. "Over the course of a few hours, an observer would have seen the night sky turning around Crux, the Milky Way forming a complete circle in the sky just above the horizon, and noted the intersection of the ecliptic with the Milky Way at the two points marked by Scorpius and Orion." Mann and Glasson, 2007, p. 90.
4. It may be significant that by this time the orientation of many prehistoric megalithic sites was increasingly toward the south (even lower than the southern rising and setting points of the Moon). Many megalithic sites, for example Mid Clyth in Scotland and Meini Gwyr in Wales, show astonishingly precise north-south alignments.
5. Bayliss, Whittle et al, 2007. The dates are provided by English Heritage, from excavations conducted 2007-2008.
6. John Aubrey, *Wiltshire Collections*, ed. Jackson, 332. Other sources see J. Westwood & J. Simpson, 2005, *The Lore of the Land*, Penguin. For Sulis, see for example Miranda Green, 1986, *The Gods of the Celts*.
7. Mimosa or *beta* Crucis on the left, Gacrux or *gamma* Crucis at the top, and *delta* Crucis on the right. On a level horizon, *Alpha* Crucis may have been visible on some nights on the 51st parallel as late as 2650 BCE. A date of 3000 BCE allows just over one degree for the horizon, the extinction angle and refraction.
8. While it is thought that the summit may have been flattened in the Saxon period to provide a defensive position, evidence as to whether Silbury was originally higher has proved inconclusive.
9. Aveni, 2001, pp. 105-6.
10. Dante, *Purgatorio*, Canto I, 22-25, trans. Dorothy Sayers. Dante probably heard about the southern stars from mariners.
11. Paul Shepard, 1985, *The Sacred Paw*, Viking Penguin. The

Greeks conceived the Great Bear, Ursa Major, as turning the axis of the Poles. Ursa Major as the plough or wain, first recorded in Babylon, came later as farming became the means of subsistence.

12. Ina Wunn, 2000, 'Beginning of Religion,' *Numen*, 47(4). But the evidence for a Neanderthal bear cult must remain provisional. Also Eliade 1964 and Geoffrey Ashe 1992, *The Dawn behind the Dawn*, Henry Holt, passim.
13. *History of Animals*, VI.30.
14. Aldhouse-Green, 2005
15. The myth at this point veers toward later traditions concerning Odin and the Nordic Mead Halls of the Immortals. Shepard, ibid, thinks the myth originally focused upon the Bear Mother; only in the Neolithic did it emphasise the journey of the dying and rising Bear Son.

5 The Crux-Centaurus Stars

1. Dante, *Purgatorio*, Canto 1, 24-5
2. North, 1996, also mentions that the Early Neolithic long barrow Wayland's Smithy in Uffington, Ox., may have been oriented to the same southern stars. The burials at West Kennet barrow were highly organised and articulated affairs. In many cases, the bones were dried or removed elsewhere, indicating complex cultural processes involving the dead. Although archaeologists have found some burials beside the stones of Avebury, what is far more remarkable is the cleanliness of the site, suggesting long-held observation of ritual purity. The users could have added the burials later.
3. Mann and Glasson, 2007, pp. 62ff. Gwynn and Gwythyr are one of many examples of a twin god, often in conflict, determining summer and winter, the Upper- and the Lowerworld.
4. See Aveni, 2001, pp. 103-5 for a discussion on stellar refraction.

5. Even the conservative doyen of British archaeoastronomy Clive Ruggles, thought it plausible that the disappearance of the Crux-Centaurus stars from Son Mas "would have been a crisis, and it was that which caused the sanctuary to be abandoned." *Ancient Astronomy*, ABC-CLIO, 2005, p. 390.
6. Hoskin, 2001, pp. 42-51.
7. Burl, 1987.
8. Only Dames, 1977, seems willing to make the Kennet, Cunnit connection.
9. The 166° azimuth is for the large stones that occupy the northern and greater section of the row. If however the stones of the whole row (where there may have been equally large stones) are included the azimuth is closer to 167° and the dates provided in the text will be correspondingly later.
10. The Ring Stone was a stone with a hole that was traditionally used for vow taking by couples, who frequently knocked a piece from off the stone for fertility and good luck; its fallen remnant is slightly to the east of its original location.
11. At this level of detail, a brief discussion of the *extinction angle* is necessary. In *Megalithic Sites in Britain*, Alexander Thom defined the extinction angle of a star as the "smallest apparent altitude at which, in perfectly clear weather, it can be seen," that is, above the horizon. Thom offered a rough rule that the extinction angle in degrees is equal to the magnitude of the star. Thus *alpha* Crucis, a variable star with a magnitude of +1.4 to +2, can be seen down to 1.4 to 2 degrees of altitude, while Sirius, with a magnitude of -1.46, can be seen right down to the horizon. Alpha Centauri, with a magnitude of -0.27, should also be visible down to the horizon, yet in reality it is not. Thom's rule was therefore only a rough guide, especially since his qualification concerning "perfectly clear weather" seldom applies at

Britain's northern latitudes! In poor conditions of visibility, the extinction angle of a star is much higher, and today, due to atmospheric dust and light pollution, conditions are nearly always poor. A better rule of thumb, but still only applicable to good viewing conditions in the Neolithic, would involve placing the extinction angle of first magnitude stars such as those of Crux and Centaurus at one degree higher; e.g. Alpha Centauri 1°15′, beta Centauri (magnitude +0.6) 1°40′, gamma Crucis (magnitude +1.6) 2°30′, Capella (magnitude +0.08) 1°30′, Deneb (magnitude +1.25) 2° and so on. From these figures, it is immediately obvious how useful a slight elevation of the horizon, albeit only of two degrees, would have been to the Avebury star-watchers. As a result, bright stars would not have appeared out of the atmosphere in an indeterminate manner, but risen crisply upon the horizon or over key markers. Waden Hill to the south, with an elevation of two to three degrees (depending on where the viewer was located within the henge), provided this kind of horizon, as did Windmill Hill to the northwest and the Marlborough Downs to the east, and—at least in some cases—the outer bank of the henge.

12. Gillings and Pollard, 2004, p. 14 and p. 48. The line of stones also may be aligned to the Cove: azimuth centre approximately 167°.
13. No other significant astronomical alignments appear to be indicated by the 'D' feature, although Sims, 2003, makes the case for lunar observation.
14. Apart from the alignments, the quantities of stones in their various settings at Avebury may represent an attempt to approach numerical notation. Jane Sellers points out in *The Death of Gods in Ancient Egypt* that the Babylonians by this time had long established a counting system, based upon the sexagesimal, a base 60 system, derived from measures of barley. The system with its 360 degree division of time and

the sky proved perfect for measuring the heavenly cycles, especially that of precession. Sellers points out that many of the significant "special numbers" not only of Babylon but of the ancient world: 72, 432, 2,160, 25,920, as well as 360, 60, 30 and so on, are the numbers of precession.

15. Milbrath, 1999, Schele et al, 1993, for the Maya. Schele: "... the patterns in the Milky Way and the constellations were directly related to the Maya vision of Creation." Sullivan, 1996, for South America.

6 Silbury Hill

1. *Monumenta Britannica* (Aubrey 1626-1697).
2. Whittle et al, 1999 and 2007.
3. Bayliss et al, 2007.
4. Jim Leary, 'The Silbury Sequence: seeing past tunnel vision,' English Heritage *Research News*, 10, 2008: "We now have at least 15 Neolithic phases ... The mound can be seen to grow through many small events ... the earliest phases of Silbury Hill do not simply consist of one mound but of a number of mounds."
5. North, 1996, pp. 39-59.
6. White, Gavin, 2008, *Babylonian Star-Lore,* London, Solaria Publications, pp. 57-60. White's comments should be treated with caution however. There is a depiction of a bison-headed man in Chauvet Cave, France, possibly dating to 25,000 BCE (Hinckley Allen, 1963, p.150 on Centaurus).
7. For example, Eliade, 1964, p. 467, and J. Nigro Sansonese, 1994, *The Body of Myth: Mythology, Shamanic Trance, and the Sacred Geography of the Body,* Inner Traditions International, p. 60.
8. The lovely Irish legend of *Tochmarc Etáin* is just one example of many Celtic traditions which locate a goddess of sovereignty beside a spring and ancestral mound. Michael Dames, 1976, and Marija Gimbutas are, of course, propo-

nents of the 'Mother Goddess' theory; which can sit happily alongside a fertility theory of the southern stars.

9. Estimated reappearance of middle stars of Crux, c.13500 CE; greatest southern declination c.6000 CE; greatest northern declination c.8000 BCE. Due to the proper motion of each star (and changing magnitudes), they will never be seen in exactly the same relationship again.

7 The Longstones Cove & Other Enclosures

1. *Works & Days*, 383.
2. Gillings et al, 2008, p. 24.
3. Gillings et al, 2008. Pollard & Reynolds, 2002, pp. 96-100. The crossing of the avenue and the Winterbourne (thigh deep in winter) not far from the western entrance to the henge has not yet been found; but its estimated location offers a noteworthy view of Silbury Hill.
4. Gillings et al, 2008, describe the unusual geometry of the Longstones Cove, pp. 126-8.
5. Firstly, any Neolithic/EBA foresights on the alignment to Folly Hill would have been removed in the erection of the Bronze Age barrow cemetery on the hill. Secondly, if any features on the site before 3000 BCE (or in the Longstones Enclosure circa 2800 BCE), e.g., postholes, had midwinter/Sirius alignments, and if accurate azimuths could be obtained for the primary linear three-stone setting and the Longstones Cove, any differences between them (in addition to accurate dating) could conclusively demonstrate Neolithic tracking of the precessional movement of Sirius over Folly Hill.
6. Whittle, 1997. It is interesting that given the number of stone axes that must have been used and broken constructing the palisades, none have been found. It was clearly thought inappropriate to leave them on site.
7. Gillings et al, 2008, p. 203 after Whittle 1997.

8. Pollard & Reynolds, 2002, pp. 113-118.
9. For example: O'Rahilly, Cecile, 1967, *Táin Bó Cúalnge,* from The Book of Leinster, and 1976, *Táin Bó Cúailnge, Recension I,* Dublin Institute for Advanced Studies.
10. Mike Parker Pearson, 1998.
11. Arkadiusz Marciniak, 2005, *Placing Animals in the Neolithic: Social Zooarchaeology of Prehistoric Farming Communities,* University of Arizona, Left Coast Press, provides a succinct account of the manner in which animals were likely to have been perceived over the course of the Neolithic.

8 The Sanctuary at the Crossroads

1. *Commentary on the Dream of Scipio.* Macrobius 395-423 CE.
2. Gibson, 2005, pp 81 ff.
3. Pollard 1992; Pollard & Reynolds, 2002, pp 106-110.
4. Several writers have pointed out how similar the distance is between the diameter of the outer circle of the Sanctuary and the earliest setting of stones at the Longstones Cove, the terminus of Avebury's second avenue, extending to the west.
5. Cunnington, M. E., 1931, 'The Sanctuary on Overton Hill near Avebury,' *Wiltshire Archaeological and Natural History Magazine* 38, 1-11.
6. Mike Pitts, 2000.
7. Gibson, 2005, provides a full discussion of early timber circles in Britain.
8. The alignment of East Kennet around 322° and of East Kennet to Windmill Hill at 327° suggests focus on the setting of stars in Cassiopeia or Leo in the fourth millennium BCE.
9. Gillings et al, 2008.
10. The irregular cross in the arrangement of postholes found at the Sanctuary, with its arms laid out at approximately 305°-125° and 32°-212°, appears to be neither lunar nor solar, but

possibly stellar: aligned to Regulus setting, Sirius rising, Cygnus/Sadr rising and Gacrux setting?

11. An extinction angle of about 1° provides these figures. If Capella is allowed as observed down to the horizon it would have reached an azimuth of 320° by 2550 BCE.
12. A. and A. Thom (1980, 1245) noticed this alignment from the Sanctuary: "a pair of markers with an azimuth of 320° to the middle of Avebury main ring," but said nothing further.
13. Due to the southern elevation, alpha Centauri was lost to view from the Sanctuary after 2750 BCE.
14. Capella 3:30am, alt.1° azm.317°, alpha Crucis below the horizon.
15. Obviously, the crossing-points of the ecliptic and the galactic equator are invisible while the Sun is upon them. But the position of the Sun in the celestial sphere at sunset could easily have been provided by observation of the acronychal rising and setting stars, i.e., the first stars to appear and set on the western horizon after sunset, and, in the case of the rising Sun, by the heliacal or other stars setting on the eastern horizon just before dawn. The question being asked is this: over the period the Sanctuary was in use, could it have provided the means for the sky-watchers to detect a change in the Sun's position as great as 10° and a seasonal shift as much as two weeks?
16. The alignment of a particular day, the Sun and the Galactic Equator seems to hold for approximately 72 years, as precession moves about 1° in that time, and there are, of course, 360° in the whole cycle and close to 360 days in a year. As the solar diameter is about half a degree, the Sun could be said to be over the Galactic Equator for about 36 years, i.e. 1982-2018 CE.
17. This proposal would be supported if alignments to the 'crossroads' similar to those at the Sanctuary were found at Avebury. Sadly, stones that may have been sited on those

alignments from obvious backsights, such as the Obelisk, were removed long ago, whilst trees and buildings obscure the view.

9 Return to Avebury

1. *History of the Kings of Britain*, vii. 4.
2. It is possible that a fourth stone made the Cove a box shape, but this is unlikely.
3. Gillings et al, 2008.
4. Orientations taken from survey by Gillings ibid, p. 154.
5. Altitude of Windmill hill is approximately 2°
6. Deneb became a circumpolar star circa 300 BCE in southern Britain.
7. In some versions of the Earth Diver creation myth, a god sends the bird, or a god makes the journey; sometimes an evil spirit makes the journey. See Mircea Eliade, 1963, *Myth and Reality*, New York, Harper & Row, pp. 21-25; Eliade, 1964, pp. 458-61; Eliade, ed., *Encyclopaedia of Religion* for a selection of Earth Diver creation myths.
8. Aldhouse-Green & Green, 2005, p. 73.
9. Shepard, 1985, p. 66.
10. They also would have noticed, as a result of their permanent markers, that Albireo, the head of the bird, once clear of the horizon at 40°, rose in the same place (but never at the same time) as the most northerly rising Moon.
11. The winter setting and rising of Cygnus over the northern bank of Avebury henge would have provided a method of obtaining true north. For example, by marking the setting and rising points of Deneb or Sadr (approximately 340°/ 330°, and 20°/ 30° from the Cove), then bisecting the angle, the sky-watchers could have obtained a true north-south line. Circa 2800 BCE, the stars of Cassiopeia setting around 333-2° and rising around 27-8°, were perfectly placed to determine true north; these stars were soon to become truly

circumpolar, no longer setting below the northern horizon. Wooden posts or frames supporting plumb lines, with lines of sight eventually made permanent by megaliths, would have provided suitable markers. (Thom, 1967, p. 96.) Bisecting the angle between the setting and the rising of Capella during the spring when the star rose and set in the same night would have given the same effect.

12. Much earlier, in the mid-fifth millennium BCE, Deneb was already making its subterranean northern passage. This star was rising at a time coincident with the vertical 'standing' of the Southern Cross at 160° and also with the rising of alpha Centauri at 140°. The whole of the Southern Cross would have been visible in this era—alpha Crucis a full 3° above the horizon. Given that the 'main alignment' of Avebury, between the Cove and the Obelisk, is 160°, we can speculate that the Avebury alignments may be extremely ancient indeed: possibly part of lore known to the builders' Mesolithic ancestors. The seventh millennium date of the astronomically significant 'car park' posts found at Stonehenge suggests there is a remote possibility that posts or erratic sarsens aligned to stellar events could have been in place at Avebury by the mid-fifth millennium BCE or even earlier.
13. At this time the first magnitude star, Deneb, in a close relationship to Vega on the 340° main alignment and to Capella at 312°, became the prime marker of the northern pole at midnight in midwinter.
14. Viewed from Avebury, Windmill Hill marked the midsummer setting Sun at 310°, or more precisely, due to elevation, the south side of the hill at 308-9°. Beckhampton Hill marked the midwinter setting Sun at 230°, again due to altitude closer to an azimuth of 228-9°. Berwick Basset Down on the Marlborough Downs, marked the midsummer rising Sun at 48-9°, and Overton Hill at the other end of the

Downs, marked the midwinter rising Sun at 129-30°. These azimuths depend upon small differences of elevation and altitude and observation of the top rim or the full diameter of the Sun. The sky-watchers knew it was easier to watch the solstitial Sun go past and then return to a marker than find its extreme northern or southern position.

15. The crucial *Mul.Apin* tablets of Babylon are dated to circa 1000 BCE. Vedic knowledge appears to predate writing.
16. Whittle 1996, p. 360.
17. Ursa Major was the *Septentriones,* the seven oxen of the Romans, whose passage around the Pole turned the wheels of a mill.
18. Both stones and springs held sovereignty for the Celts; they recognised the rightful king by offering up swords and oracular utterances, even brides. Sacred stones were central to British rites of inauguration, a custom that prevails to this day.
19. Fergus Kelly, 1976, *Audacht Morain* ('The Testament of Morann' or 'Advice to a King') Dublin Institute for Advanced Studies. Hancock, W. N., ed. 1865, *Senchus Mór: The Ancient Laws of Ireland,* Dublin and London; reprint New York, William S. Hein, 1983. See also such stories as the *Hidden House of Lugh* and the later traditions of the Grail.
20. G. Reichel-Dolmatoff cites the Milky Way as viewed as semen among many central-American tribes, e.g. 1987, *Iconography of Religions IX, 1,* University of Groningen. Vedic astronomers distinguish the Gemini crossroads as the creator god Brahma—Capella is his heart—and the Sagittarius crossroads as a divine feminine force, Nirriti, who is closely linked with Kali, goddess of destruction and with the power of kundalini. Woden's Path = Milky Way.
21. Nor should we forget the near universal incest taboo. Many societies record an initial sexual transgression in their mythology. This event is often set among the heavens,

establishing and legitimating an incest prohibition that anthropologists generally regard as encouraging exogamy, intra-family stability and the making of alliances (Claude Lévi-Strauss, 1969, *The Elementary Structures of Kinship*, Boston: Beacon Press).

22. In Vedic myth, the two divided parts of the serpent Naga Vasuki came to represent the two lunar nodes and are responsible for eclipses. Although releasing toxin, Vasuki helped the gods obtain the *amrita*, the nectar of immortality. (See the Appendix on the Moon.) For more information on Vedic astrology, see the works of Frawley and Sutton in the Bibliography.
23. *History* vi.17, 19, vii.3; most of this is also in Nennius.
24. Geoffrey Ashe gives an excellent summary of these legends and their sources in *Merlin: the Prophet and his History*, Sutton Publishing, 2006.

10 In the Neolithic World

1. Paul Shepard, 1973, *The Tender Carnivore and the Sacred Game*, New York, Scribner's.
2. "...embedded within a phenology of seasonal cycles." Phenology is the study of periodic biological phenomena. Paul Shepard, *Coming Home to the Pleistocene*, 1998, Shearwater, Island Press, p. 7 ff. Shepard, d. 1996, once described as "the most important American thinker since Thoreau," provides an unrivalled list of prehistoric cultural themes, pp. 170-72. The anthropologist Lucien Lévy-Brühl used the term 'participation mystique' in *How Natives Think*, 1910, to describe the manner in which native peoples did not distinguish between the supernatural and the natural.
3. Seán MacGrail, 2001, *Boats of the World*, OUP, provides an overview.
4. Burl, 1987.
5. Martin 1995, p. 117.

6. Shepard, 1998, p. 45.
7. See the work of Mary Douglas for a discussion of 'pure and impure'.
8. Taliesin, from *The Hostile Confederacy* and *Cad Goddeu.*
9. See, for example, *Tochmarc Etáine,* the 'Courtship of Etain.' Although recorded between the 11th and 14th centuries, the period to which this story belongs is when Eochaid Airem became high king of Ireland circa 134 BCE.
10. The pictographs, paintings, or petroglyphs, carvings, usually describe human-animal interaction.
11. The source of the bluestone is Myndd Preseli, on or near to Carn Menyn. The megalithic sites, such as Meini Gwyr (exactly south of Carn Menyn), are near the village of Glandy Cross. See Figgis, N.P., 2001, *Prehistoric Preseli,* Atelier Productions.
12. Burl, 1987. Of course, several Thunder Gods began life in caves upon mountains, but seemingly not until the Bronze/Iron Age eras
13. A point frequently made by Burl, 1999. See also, Richard Bradley and Mark Edmonds, 1993, *Interpreting the axe trade,* Cambridge University Press.
14. Arkadiusz Marciniak, 2005 and web searches provide lively discussions of the early use of the horse.
15. It is now well-known that the surveyor's art was highly developed at an early time, creating, for example, fields after the Nile flood and the Bronze Age field systems that determine boundaries in Britain to this day. The fields of prehistoric Dartmoor imply systems of surveying, allocation and of labour equal to that introduced by the Romans.
16. Note: template comes from the same root as the word for temple and for time, *tempus.*
17. There is the possibility that some of the skeletons buried in or beside the henges were intruders; one young man beside

Stonehenge had been shot with arrows.

18. These zones can be analysed in terms of the formal and informal, sexual and asexual, sacred and profane, pure and impure, light and dark, elevated and low, natural and supernatural etc. Mann, 1996.
19. The 'Brehon Law' of the Irish Celts maintained a strict list of fines specifying, for example, how many cattle or swine an offender needed to pay to restore a wrong. It was essentially a restorative system of justice rather than a punitive one.

11 Monuments of Power: from Moon & Stars to Sun

1. Anthony Aveni, 2010, *The End of Time: The Maya Mysteries of 2012*, University Press of Colorado, p. 63.
2. Although the Bronze Age in Britain is generally taken to be approximately 2100 to 750 BCE, further divisions describe an Early Bronze Age, 2700-1500 distinguished by a time of ('Beaker') migration, a Middle, 1500-1000 and a Late, 1000-700 BCE. Many think the Neolithic was over by 2500 BCE.
3. Burl, 1987. For a discussion of the evidence for chiefdoms in the late Neolithic and for advanced intellectual skills among the priesthoods of those chiefdoms see Euan Mackie and Clive Ruggles, *Antiquity* 7, 4, (2000) 62-74, *Antiquity* 7b (2002) and related articles. For a magnificent and moving philosophical exegesis upon the Neolithic transition see Martin 1992.
4. Fitzpatrick, A.P., 2003. 'The Amesbury Archer' *Current Archaeology* 184, pp. 146-152.
5. The rare items of clothing that survive from the Neolithic suggest intricate and coloured weaves; for objects, one only has to bring to mind the 300 or so carved stone spheres from Scotland that reveal the Platonic Solids.
6. This is a sample of Geoffrey's prophecies from the *Vita Merlini* in this instance uttered by Merlin's sister Ganieda: "Armorican boar, protected by an ancient oak, takes away

the moon, waving swords behind backs. I see two stars at war with wild beast under the hill of Urien, where the men of Deira and the men of Gwent convened when the great Coel was ruling... A star, having collided with another, falls into the shadows, hiding her own light when the light is restored." Helpful commentaries on the *Vita Merlini* include 'The Esplumoir and Viviane,' Arthur C. L. Brown, *Speculum*, Vol. 20, No. 4 (Oct., 1945), pp. 426-432.

7. O'Rahilly, Cecile, 1967, *Táin Bó Cúalnge*, from *The Book of Leinster*, and 1976, *Táin Bó Cúailnge, Recension I*, Dublin Institute for Advanced Studies.
8. Chris Knight, 1991, *Blood Relations: Menstruation and the Origins of Culture*, Yale University Press.
9. Burl, 1987.
10. In other cases, mentioned by Burl, the skeletal evidence suggests some women were overworked, malnourished and thus infertile.
11. It is possible to see 'proto-Druids' in this picture: that is pre-literate advisors to social leaders chosen for their wisdom, musical and memorial skills.
12. Around 2500 BCE it became wetter and cooler in the British Isles contributing to soil loss and the favouring of pasturage and cattle rather then the growing of grain.
13. Mike Parker Pearson et al, 2009, 'Who was Buried at Stonehenge?' *Antiquity*, 83, 319, pp.23-39, make the case for the bluestones being part of the original monument.
14. Figgis, ibid, 2003. Here is another example of exact north-south orientation.
15. Geoffrey attributed the bringing of the stones to Stonehenge to the magician Merlin. The stones, he wrote, known as 'the Giant's Dance,' had originally been brought by Giants from Africa to Ireland because of their healing properties. The Preselis, traditionally the source of the Stonehenge bluestones, were closely allied to Ireland at the time.

16. See note on Sims and Knight below.
17. Parker Pearson et al, 2009, ibid, suggest Stonehenge was the burial site of the local elite from at least the time of sarsen trilithons, circa 2500 BCE.
18. The gold lozenge, mace and bronze axes and daggers from Normanton Down Bush Barrow just south of Stonehenge date to about 1900 BCE.
19. Sims, 2006, gives a complementary account of this process at Stonehenge. By showing how the sarsen monument came to exclusively focus upon the winter solstice Sun and the minor lunar standstill the "aim of the monument builders was to juxtapose, replicate and reverse certain key horizon properties of the Sun and the Moon, apparently with the intention of investing the Sun with the Moon's former religious significance." Sims builds on the work of Chris Knight, who sees paleo-women's authority and power, especially in sexual relations, subsumed by male agendas.
20. It is possible that on the one hand, the patterns on the gold work of the Bronze Age (note 18) did not understand the underlying astronomy, turning knowledge into cult objects. On the other hand, Bronze Age evidence from Europe, such as the Golden Hats, implies advanced astronomical knowledge.

Appendix I

Precession

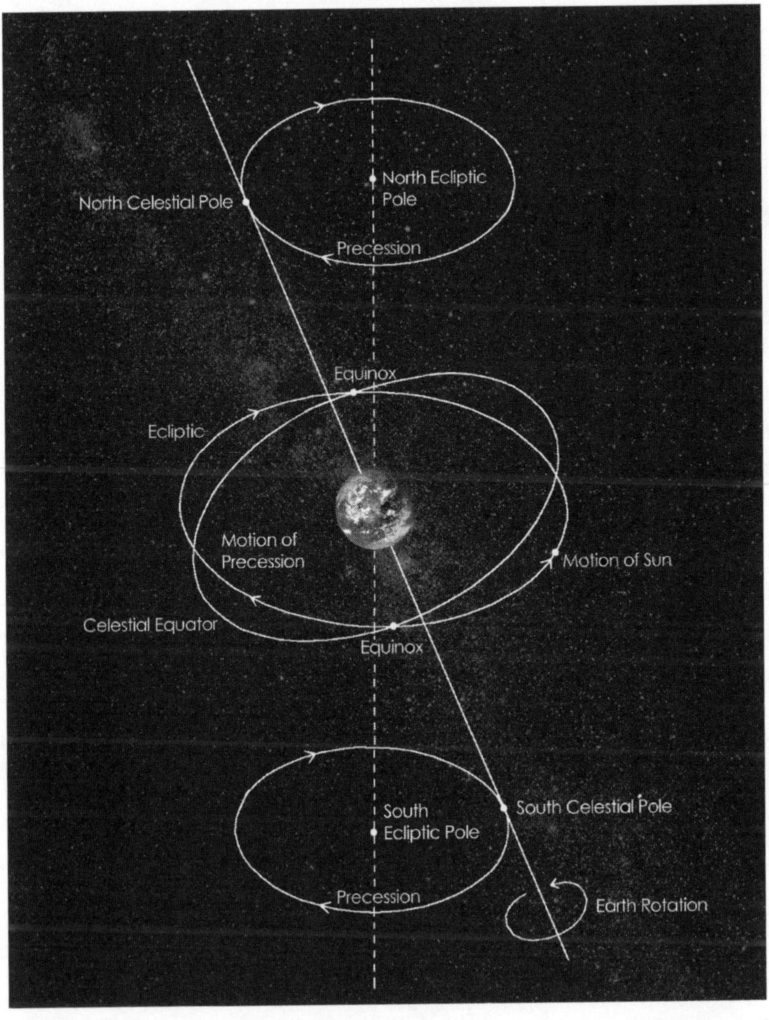

Figure 51. Largely due to the tug of the Moon, the axis of rotation of the Earth turns around the axis of the solar system—the ecliptic formed between the orbit of the Earth and the Sun—over a cycle of

about 26,000 years. As the Earth always maintains the same inclination toward the Sun, one effect of these rotations is that the seasons—most conspicuously marked by the equinoxes and the solstices—slowly move around the celestial sphere, changing their relationship to the backdrop of the fixed stars. Thus an equinox sunrise that takes place in a one-twelfth segment of the celestial sphere, marked by a sign of the Zodiac, will take place in another sign about every 2,200 years.

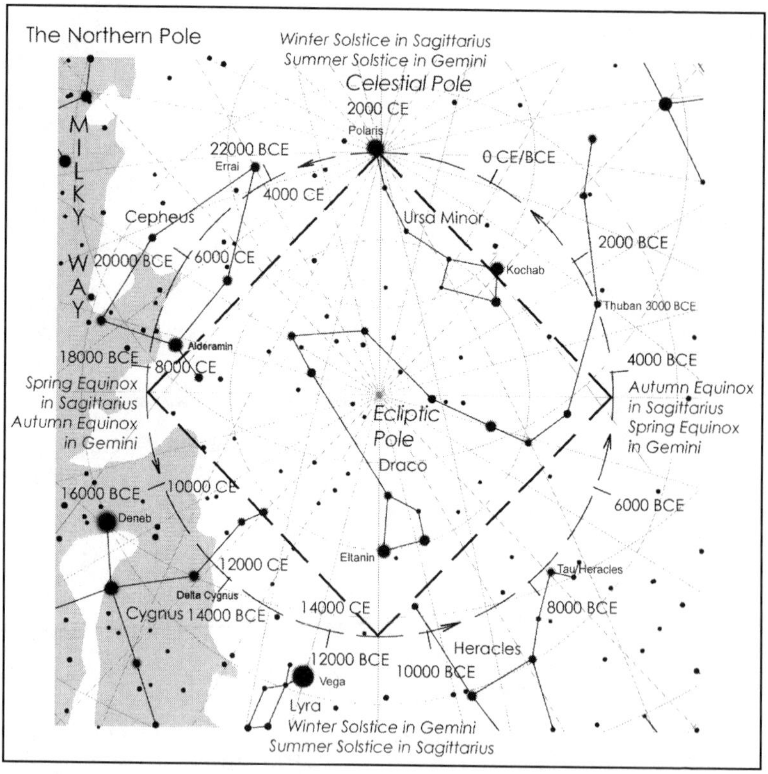

*Figure 52. The celestial poles trace a circle around the sky that can be measured against the stars of the celestial sphere. Every 6,500 years the Northern Celestial Pole, marked by Polaris today, rotates a quarter turn. Thuban (*α draconis*) marked the Pole around 3000 BCE. The Sun, on the path of the ecliptic plane, always crosses the Galactic Equator in the same two places in the sky, but due to precession, the*

time or season of the year this occurs will change. This diagram shows the times when the solstices and the equinoxes are upon the two crossing-points of the ecliptic and the galactic equator in relation to the Northern Celestial Pole. In the current era, for example, the winter solstice Sun is rising in Sagittarius, over the centre of the Milky Way, and the summer solstice Sun is rising in Gemini, over the galactic 'anticentre.' 6,500 years ago, the spring equinox Sun was rising in Gemini and the autumn equinox Sun in Sagittarius, and so on. The diagram suggests a four-fold division of the Great Year based upon the seasonal position of the Sun on the crossroads of the ecliptic and the Milky Way as well as the inclination of the celestial axis to the galaxy. Note the relationship of the constellation Draco to the ecliptic pole.

The Earth rotates daily and orbits the Sun annually. These two circuits define the day and the year. The rotating Earth is inclined to the ecliptic—the plane of its orbit around the Sun—at an angle of approximately 23.5 degrees. The Earth always presents the same inclination to the Sun. Thus, as the Earth orbits the Sun, it receives light and warmth accordingly in the two hemispheres, giving them their annual seasons. As the Earth orbits the Sun, the position of the Sun appears to move annually in relation to the stars that form the backdrop of the celestial sphere, always appearing to rise about one degree slightly before the point it rose the previous morning. After about 30 days and 30° the Sun will move from one sign of the Zodiac to another over the course of the year, moving counter-clockwise through the sky.

The celestial Zodiac or the 'circle of animals' is the broad band of stars through which the Sun, Moon and planets appear to travel. It is customarily divided into 360° and twelve segments (of 30°), while the year itself is divided into twelve months. The stars of the celestial sphere are so distant that we call them the 'fixed' stars, as opposed to the 'wandering' stars or the planets. The fixed stars always appear to move from the same point A to B, never deviating from their course.

The Sun would always appear in the same house of the Zodiac or part of the celestial sphere at the same time of the year were it not for the fact that the axis of the Earth maintains a constant inclination of 23.5 degrees to the ecliptic. This causes the Earth to make a complete rotation around the ecliptic pole approximately every 26,000 years. See Figures 51 and 52. The key to understanding these movements is to keep in mind that while rotating day and night around another axis that is always tilted at the same inclination to the Sun, the Earth is also slowly rotating, like a top or gyroscope, around the axis formed by the ecliptic of the Earth and Sun. The result of this rotation is that the stars appear to very slowly 'precess' or move forward in relation to the Sun's seasonal positions. After a couple of thousand years, the stars and constellations rise about a month later; after 13,000 years, the house of the Zodiac that the Sun formerly rose in midsummer, will now be in midwinter.

The first recorded measurement of precessional movement was by the Greek astronomer Hipparchus in the Second Century BCE. He described the phenomenon as the 'precession of the equinoxes.' At the time, the spring equinox Sun was near the first point of Aries; today it is near the end of Pisces. But obviously, *all* the days of the year precess relative to the celestial sphere, not just the equinoxes. Hipparchus could have chosen another day of the year, such as the winter solstice, as its marker. He chose the equinox since at the equinoxes the ecliptic cuts across the equator of the Earth and thus across an equator projected onto the stellar celestial sphere. From a heliocentric perspective of a spherical Earth, this is very convenient: the rotating 'discs' of the ecliptic and the equator align—everything is level. As the tropical Zodiac used by astrologers since late BCE/early CE has remained anchored to the fiducial point at 1° Aries ever since, there is now considerable confusion between sidereal astrology—the true position of the Sun against the stars, generally practiced in the East—and the tropical astrology that is generally practiced in the West. Neolithic people, in their direct, visual and geocentric world, were likely to have chosen distinctive sidereal markers to observe this phenomenon.

Precession, therefore, is the slow rotation of the celestial axis around the ecliptic axis normally measured in terms of the point of the vernal or spring equinox moving in a clockwise motion backwards through the Zodiac. If the rate of precession is taken as 50 seconds of arc per year, or 1° every 72 years, then 25,920 years are needed for a full cycle to occur—the traditional length of the Platonic or the Great Year—although, in fact, the actual length of the Great year varies between cycles. A 1° shift is now closer to 71.6 years; a full 360-degree rotation takes 25,776 years.

For the past 2,000 years, the Sun has crossed the equator at the spring equinox against the backdrop of the constellation of Pisces and will next be rising in Aquarius. If the Great Year of precession is taken as 25,920 years, then any one seasonal position of the Sun, such as the spring equinox, takes 2,160 years to move through each 30° segment of the Zodiac. The exact date when the vernal equinox Sun will enter Aquarius is disputed; but the date lies somewhere between 2100 and 2500 CE depending on which fiducial point is employed. If the date is based on when the Sun actually rises in the stars of the constellation, then the Sun enters Aquarius much later—closer to 2800 CE.

In the late-fourth and early-third millennium BCE, close observation of just one of their most favoured stars, alpha Centauri, low on the horizon at the time yet bright enough to beat the extinction angle, could conceivably have given the Avebury sky-watchers all they needed to see the effects of precession. While not on the ecliptic, its rising and setting points moved much faster across the horizon than any other star. The close coincidence of Capella and Sirius with the markers of solstitial and lunar extremes would also have allowed them to obtain exceptionally accurate relative precessional information. By tracking the movement of further first-magnitude stars against the Polar axis—leaving aside the then hopeless question of why some stars moved in contrary directions—they would have been in a position to obtain an idea of when the Sun and the seasons would return to the same place. No suggestion is being made that the Neolithic people understood precessional movements in a manner that had grasped galaxies, complex notation, Copernican physics, inclinations or orbits, only that they incorporated what they saw in the sky with the naked eye into their monuments. This process, to them, whether counted in lunar cycles, ancestral lineages or conceived in creation myths of bears or dragons, was the means by which they engaged with the divine forces of their cosmos.

When seen from the Cove or the Obelisk over the entire third millennium BCE, the time when the main stones of Avebury were in place, the fixed stars moved the equivalent of four of the one hundred stones in the Great Outer Circle. Their relationship to the fixed soli-lunar seasonal markers had precessed by about half a sidereal lunar cycle (15 days).

The Avebury star-watchers could also have had the means to track the movement of the North Celestial Pole, since Avebury and other Neolithic sites appear precisely oriented north and south. They could conceivably have achieved this by bisecting the angle between rising and setting stars, especially those in the north and south. In the third millennium BCE, Egyptian astronomers—from whom it is not impossible that some British monument-builders gleaned knowledge—were keenly interested in the Northern Pole and its circumpolar stars. These 'imperishable stars' not only provided the home for the Old Kingdom pharaohs upon their death, but they also provided the means by which their pyramids and temples could be precisely aligned due north. (Kate Spence, 'Ancient Egyptian Chronology and the Astronomical Orientation of Pyramids,' *Nature*, vol. 408

(2000) 320-4, for a description of stellar methods for obtaining the cardinal directions. J.A. Belmonte, 'On the Orientation of Old Kingdom Egyptian Pyramids,' *Archaeoastronomy*, no. 26 (JHA, xxxii 2001) for an assessment of the issue and of the kinds of instruments the Egyptians could have used.) The exceptional astronomical information afforded by Avebury had the potential to provide a small and highly competent group of star-watchers with the means to observe precessional motion, perhaps even with sufficient information for them to understand it was a cycle that would eventually return everything to the same place. Their permanent monuments afforded them the means to arrive at a partial version of this knowledge at an extremely early date.

Appendix 2

The Crossroads of the Ecliptic & the Galaxy

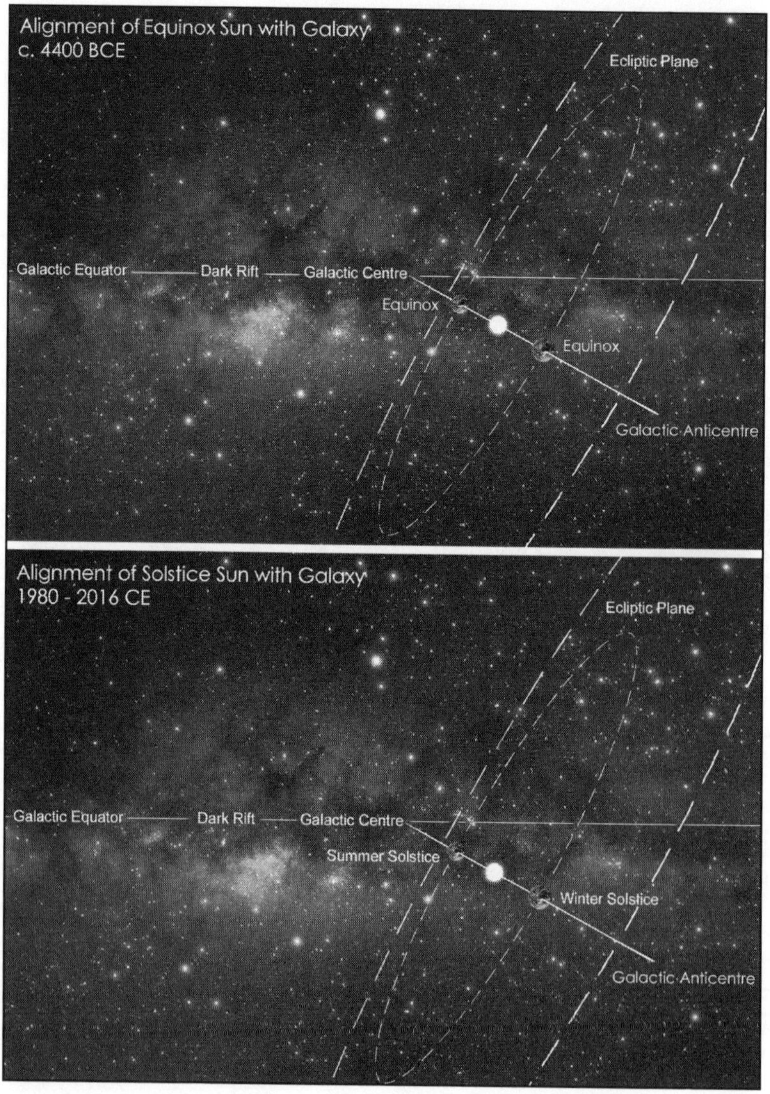

Figure 53. The lower figure shows how the winter solstice Sun is

currently positioned over the crossing-point in Sagittarius, the galactic centre. The summer solstice Sun is over the crossing-point of the ecliptic and the galactic equator in Gemini, the galactic anticentre. In 4500 BCE, as shown in the upper figure, it was the equinoxes that lay on or close to these crossing-points.

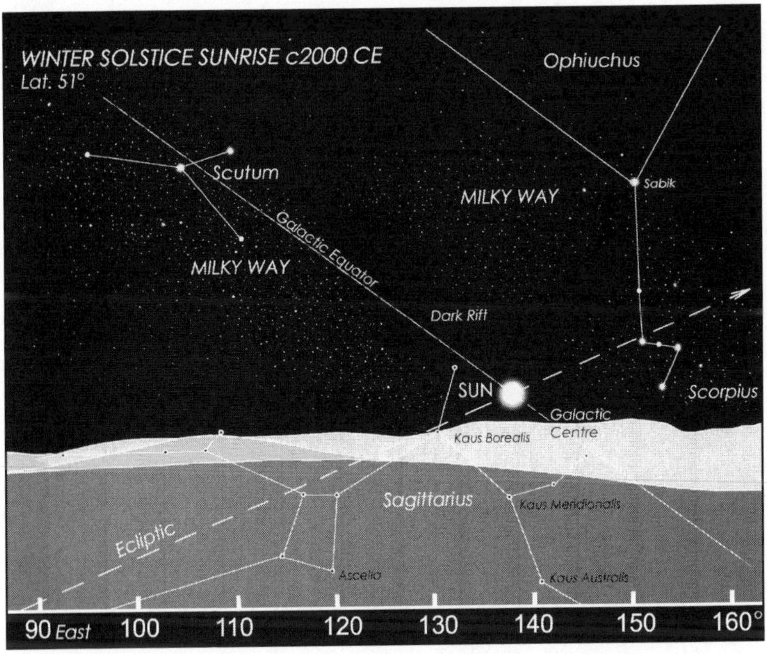

Figure 54. View of the midwinter sunrise at the latitude of Avebury. Dust so obscures the centre of the galaxy that an area known as the 'Dark Rift' hides the light from its stars. The midwinter Sun entered the Dark Rift in Sagittarius about 1920 CE, crossing the centre of the galaxy about 2000 CE. It will pass out of the Dark Rift about 2080 CE, precessing slowly in the direction of Ophiuchus and Scorpius.

In the same way as the inclination of the axis of the rotating Earth is always fixed in relation to the Sun at 23.5° to the ecliptic, so the path of the Sun, the ecliptic, is always fixed in relation to the galaxy or the Milky Way. These are the two constants in our sky. As the Sun, Moon and planets move around and so define the ecliptic, this plane always appears to cross the Galactic Equator (an imaginary line drawn through the centre and plane of the galaxy) at the same two points in Gemini and Sagittarius. Only the time of year when the Sun is upon the two crossing-points will change.

These two crossing-points of the ecliptic and the Galactic Equator are located in Sagittarius, near to Scorpius and in Gemini near to Taurus. The foot of the constellation Ophiuchus, the serpent-bearer, points to the Sagittarius point. The upraised arm or club of Orion as well as the horns of Taurus, point to the Gemini point. The Sagittarius crossing-point lies close to the centre of the galaxy, designated 0° of galactic longitude in 1958, while the Gemini crossing-point lies *away* from the galaxy, the so-called galactic 'anticentre,' designated 180° of galactic longitude. Thus, when the Sun is upon the Sagittarius point, as it is today, the viewer of the midwinter Sun is looking toward the centre of the galaxy at the winter solstice. At midsummer the viewer looks toward the galactic anticentre in Gemini.

The Sun determines our relationship with the galaxy. As the annual seasons of the year governed by the Sun precess slowly around the celestial sphere, in the world of a visual sky-watcher, the two crossing-points with the Milky Way could most conveniently have measured the slowly changing position of the Sun on the ecliptic. These two points became the primary marker of the Great Year in several early cultures including those of Egypt and India.

"Ancient astronomers could detect the long-term precessional motion quite easily by witnessing changes in the time of year when the bright stars underwent heliacal rising," wrote Anthony Aveni in 2001 (p.102). "Through myth and legend the earliest skywatchers transmitted their consciousness of the passage of the vernal equinox along the Zodiac from constellation to constellation." With such a strong memorial tradition the Avebury star-watchers could have accomplished this feat not only by observation of the equinoxes and heliacal rising stars, but also by observation of the two intersections of the ecliptic path and the Galactic Equator located near the galactic core and its anticentre.

In 4500 BC, the viewer of sunrise or sunset at the equinoxes was looking directly along the galactic centre-anticentre axis. At that time, the Sun was rising due east upon the Gemini point at the spring equinox and due east upon the Sagittarius point at the autumn equinox. In 13,000 years, 8500 CE, these positions will have reversed.

There is no law of physics that explains why the ecliptic should cross the Galactic Equator both near the galactic core and exactly opposite it—or at least within a few solar diameters. (The centre of the galaxy is very large; remember the only reason we cannot see its light is because of the all the dust and debris in the way.) The crossing-points of the ecliptic and the plane of the galaxy could have been oriented, like that of other planets in the solar system, in some other direction, and they will be at some distant point in the future because of galactic orbital motion. Precession therefore seems to place the Earth in some kind of ineffable relationship with the Milky Way: almost as though the Earth, through its distinctive ecliptic inclination and the seasonal markers of Sun and Moon, is waving directly at the galaxy.

The Neolithic sky-watchers' visual astronomy only allowed them to see what their markers upon the horizon made possible. It would have become clear from the changing rising and setting times of the stars—especially those in the south—that a slow stellar motion, which included the Milky Way, was linked to the rotating of the Poles. In one age, the Milky Way can turn from vertically overhead and lie flat upon the horizon each night, as it did in the late Neolithic. In another it may change angle very little, as in the 9th millennium before the current era (a pattern that will repeat in the 5th millennium of the current era). These dramatic changes, especially the loss or reappearance of bright stars, must have shown up against the patterns remembered in their oral traditions.

Today, as shown in Figure 53, the Earth is at the point in the Great Year of precession when the winter solstice Sun lies on the crossing-point of the ecliptic and the Galactic Equator in Sagittarius—the direction of the centre of the galaxy. The 0.5° wide disc of the Sun entered this area about 1980 and will depart from it about 2020 CE. At the same time, the summer solstice Sun now lies on the crossing-point of the ecliptic and the galactic equator in Gemini—the direction of the galactic anticentre. 13,000 years ago, in 11000 BCE, there was a complete reversal of these positions; the Sun was on the galactic core at midsummer and on the galactic anticentre at midwinter. At that time, the brilliant star Vega marked the position of the North Celestial Pole, and quite likely entered the mythic record as a result.

6,500 years ago, around 4500 BCE, the North Celestial Pole was close to being at the furthest point *away* from the galactic equator that it will ever reach in the 26,000-year precessional cycle. This coincided with an era when the Sun rose and set on the Sagittarius crossing point close to the autumn equinox, and the Sun rose and set on the Gemini crossing point close to the spring equinox. Both these crossing-points lay on the horizon due east and west, heralded by their heliacal rising stars. No particular star marked the North Pole.

Slightly later, culminating around 2800 BCE for sky-watchers at the latitude of Avebury henge, the Milky Way formed a complete and momentous circle of stars around the horizon as it dipped towards the south. This coincided with the setting of the Sun on the Gemini crossroads upon the horizon in the spring and the rising of the Sun on the Sagittarius crossroads upon the horizon in the autumn. The middle-magnitude star Thuban in Draco marked the North Pole. This was the moment of galactic, ecliptic and polar synchronicity embodied within Avebury. 19,500 years ago in 17500 BCE, these positions were reversed and the Sun rose and set on the Gemini crossing point at the autumn equinox and on the Sagittarius crossing point at the spring equinox, due east and west. It will do so again in about 6,500 years from now in 8500 CE. At these times the axis of the poles and thus of the celestial sphere is tilted near its closest *toward* the galaxy. For viewers at these times in the cycle of precession the Milky Way appears to rotate overhead around the Poles of the sky—an effect especially marked at midnight at the equinoxes.

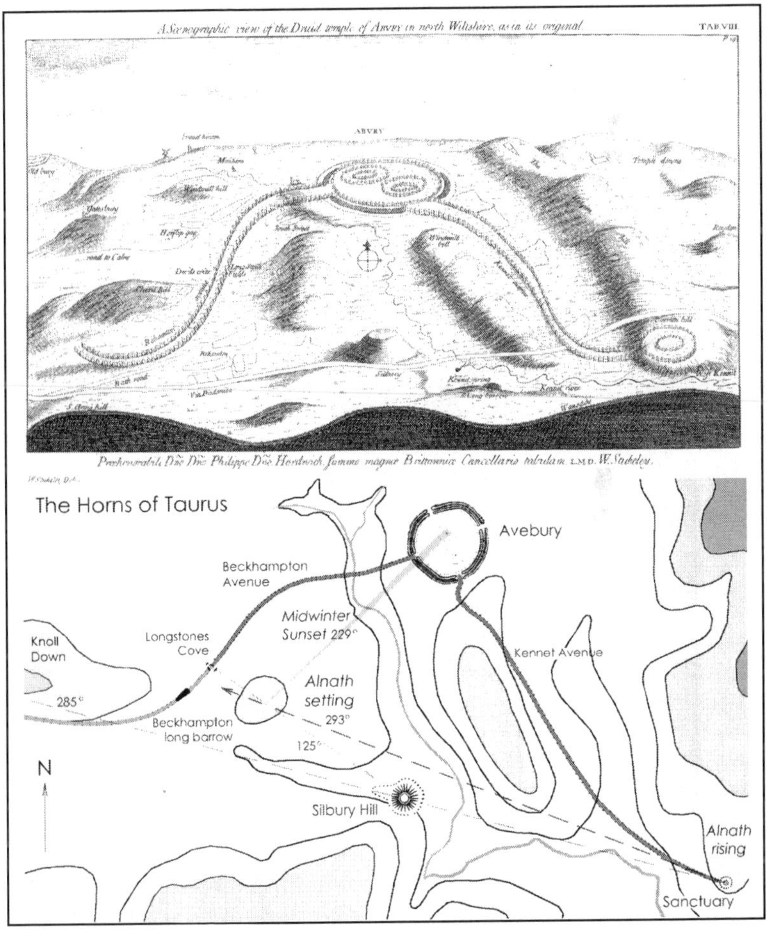

Figure 55. Above: Stukeley's vision of Avebury, c.1740. The two Avenues ran to the Sanctuary and Beckhampton like the head and tail of a serpent. Below: But if, as horns, the Avenues are seen as corre-

sponding to those of Taurus, then Silbury appears as the crossing-point of the ecliptic and the galaxy in Gemini. From the Sanctuary, the terminus of the Kennet Avenue, the point of one horn of Taurus, Alnath (shown in Figure 42), was setting on an alignment to the terminus of the Beckhampton Avenue, the Longstones Cove or Folly Hill, in the late-third millennium BCE. The Gemini crossing-point was setting over Silbury Hill (Figure 40).

As far as the esoteric significance of the crossing-points is concerned they are central in several astronomical traditions. The late Classical author Macrobius (quoted at the beginning of Chapter 8) possibly following a hint in Homer and Porphyry, described the Sagittarius crossroads as the 'portal of the gods' where souls depart, while Gemini was the 'portal of man' where souls come in, that is, incarnate. ("A cavern pleasant, though involved in night,… A lofty gate unfolds on either side; That to the north is pervious to mankind: The sacred south t'immortals is consign'd." Commentary, *On the Cave of the Nymphs in the Thirteenth Book of the Odyssey*, Porphyry, trans. Thomas Taylor 1917, Watkins, London.) While the Greeks overall remain silent or neutral on the matter, Vedic tradition gives considerable details, characterising the Gemini crossroads as the home of the Brahma, the creative male principle, and the source of the mystical substance *soma*, the Ambrosia of the Gods. Vedic lore describes the Sagittarius crossroads as the abode of a death goddess. (See David Frawley, *The Milky Way and the Cosmic Soma*, and other articles at http://www.vedanet.com for a current Vedic perspective on the two crossroads).

These traditions suggest that if Neolithic sky-watchers observed precession they were likely to have conceived it as a dual cycle: with two movements always happening simultaneously, both necessary to the whole. In the same way as the midsummer Sun is actually at the point from which it declines so the midwinter Sun is at its point of return. The same is true for the full, the new Moons and the lunar nodes. In the same way as the Moon can only be eclipsed when it is at its fullest (and furthest from the Sun), so the Sun can only be eclipsed when the Moon is at its darkest (and closest to the Sun). While the equinoxes of the Great Year suggest a balance, a simultaneous movement in two directions, the solstices of the Great Year mark the extremes and the turning points of the cycle; thus, by analogy, the possibility of an 'eclipse'—whatever that may signify in the context of the cycle of precession.

In the highly symbolic, inspirited world of the Neolithic sky-watchers, a lunar eclipse told them of an exact alignment of Moon, Earth and Sun. A solar eclipse told them of an exact alignment of Earth, Moon and Sun. The lunar eclipse of 2010 with the Winter Solstice Sun upon the crossroads of Sagittarius, tells us of an exact alignment of Moon, Earth, Sun, galaxy and Galactic Core. A solar eclipse with the Summer Solstice Sun upon the Galactic Crossroads of Gemini tells us of an exact alignment of Sun, Moon, Earth, galaxy and Galactic Core. The eclipse cycle informs us when these alignments are exact, and at the same time, it adds further, subtler dimensions to their ambiguous and potentially deceptive meanings. (On 14 December 2001, the new Moon at 23° Sagittarius eclipsed the Sun. On 15 June 2011, there will be an eclipse of the full Moon at 24° Sagittarius, and again on 21 December 2011 at 29° Gemini).

The eclipse cycle suggests it might be better to think of the Great Cycle of the ecliptic and the galaxy as another polar dynamic, akin to the cycles of both Sun and Moon. Figure 56 shows it to have the shape over time of a caduceus or a double helix. All is centered upon the cosmic axis, the World Tree. As the two crossing-points revolve, and their cycle interacts with those of the Sun and Moon in a regulated cosmic dance, they reveal a distinctive dynamic found at both the microcosmic cellular level and the macrocosmic galactic level. Our ancestors may have conceived this in terms of dragons; we might see it as the spiralling DNA.

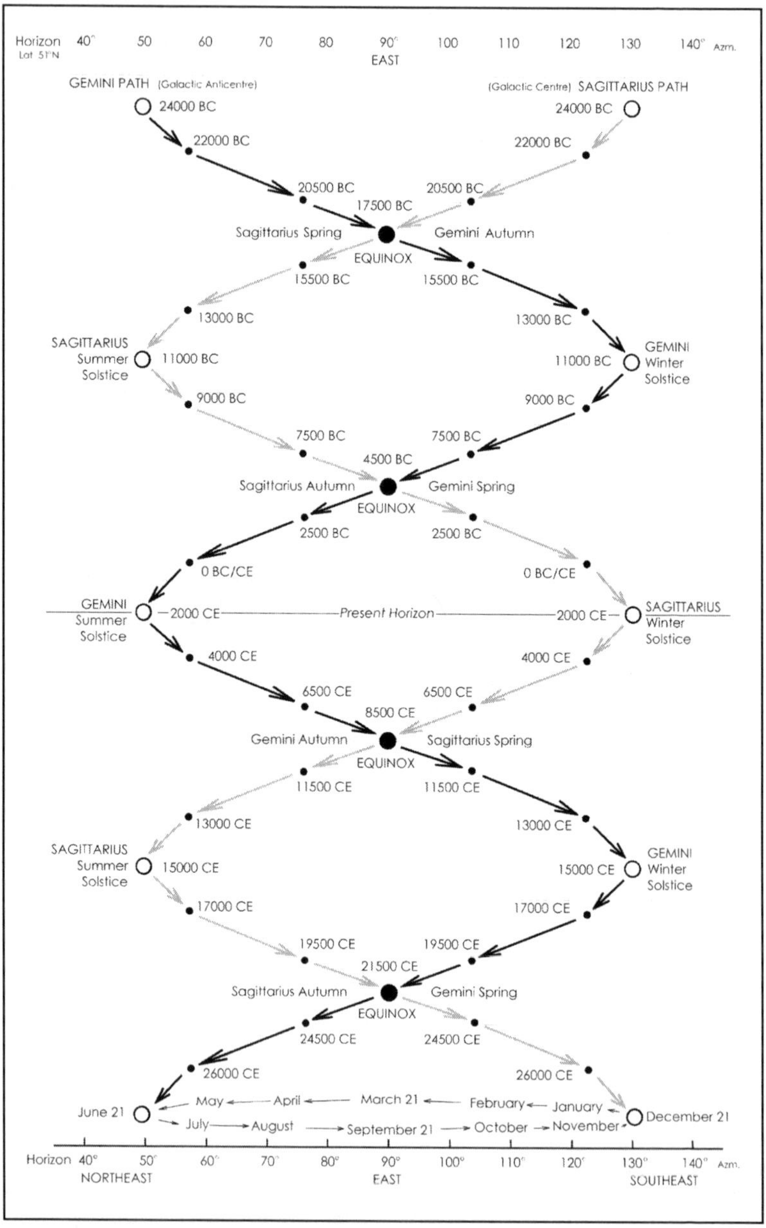

Figure 56. This diagram charts the seasonal change in position over time on the eastern horizon of the rising Sun upon the two crossroads of the Sun's ecliptic path and the Milky Way. The present day, for

example, at the centre, shows the two crossing-points have obtained their extremes: the Gemini point rising at the summer solstice 49/50° and the Sagittarius point rising at the winter solstice 129/30°. From the present day on, the points will appear to change direction, moving through the year, until by 8500 BCE they will be rising due east 90° and setting due west 230° at the equinoxes. The last time they rose with the equinoctial Sun was circa 4500 BCE (when their seasonal positions were reversed). The cycle takes about 26,000 years for all to return to the same place. To read off where the two crossing points are at any time, the vertical axis marks the horizon of any year, the horizontal axis the approximate time of year.

Vedic star lore hints that the seeker will find the *soma* of the gods in Gemini, at the crossroads of the ecliptic and the Milky Way; but it is clear that the path is never straightforward. The Egyptians believed it lay in Sirius—with good reason as we have seen—and oriented their temples towards the star. The Maya believed the divine source lay upon the 'Hearthstones of Creation,' a triangle of stars of Orion, and devised a complex interlocking calendar to tell them when alignments to this and other portals occurred. (For a reasonable assessment of the Maya and 2012, try Aveni 2009, *The End of Time: The Maya Mysteries of 2012*. For Maya cosmology try Milbrath, 1999, Tedlock, 1982 and Schele, 1993.) According to the commentary on the Vedas by the distinguished scholar A.K. Coomaraswamy (1977), the centaur archer of Sagittarius fires his bow at Gemini, while a fierce dragon and other guardians protect its secrets. Only a few will ever obtain the *soma*. Coomaraswamy tells us—in echoes of the Cygnus/Earth Diver myth—that a great firebird flies toward or away from the Gemini crossroads. This firebird rests upon the Pole, protecting it, and in turn is protected by a terrible coiled serpent that often assumes a double form. The Vedas inform us that the lunar nodes, *Rahu* and *Ketu*, are the divided form of this great, eclipse-creating serpent, *Vasuki*, enemy of the Sun and Moon. This dual-serpent wraps around the *axis mundi* of the Poles—gods on one end, demons on the other—forever maintaining or threatening the balance of the world, just like the dragons of Llud and Merlin.

I think it is fairly safe to assume that the Avebury sky-watchers would have used mythic terms like these to describe what they were seeing in the sky. The heavens present us with evidence of a greater, eternal dimension—a superior realm of truth and justice—and so the shamans and monument-builders, wishing to access divine power through their monuments, searched for ways not just to mirror the heavens but also to find, and if possible secure, the sources of life, healing, wisdom and enlightenment that lay there. They symbolically mapped the mysteries of existence in some way onto the sky, the upper world, while mirroring and incorporating the dimensions of heaven into their monuments, and so—like the bear ascending the tree to obtain honey—secure its gifts.

Appendix 3

The Lunar Cycles

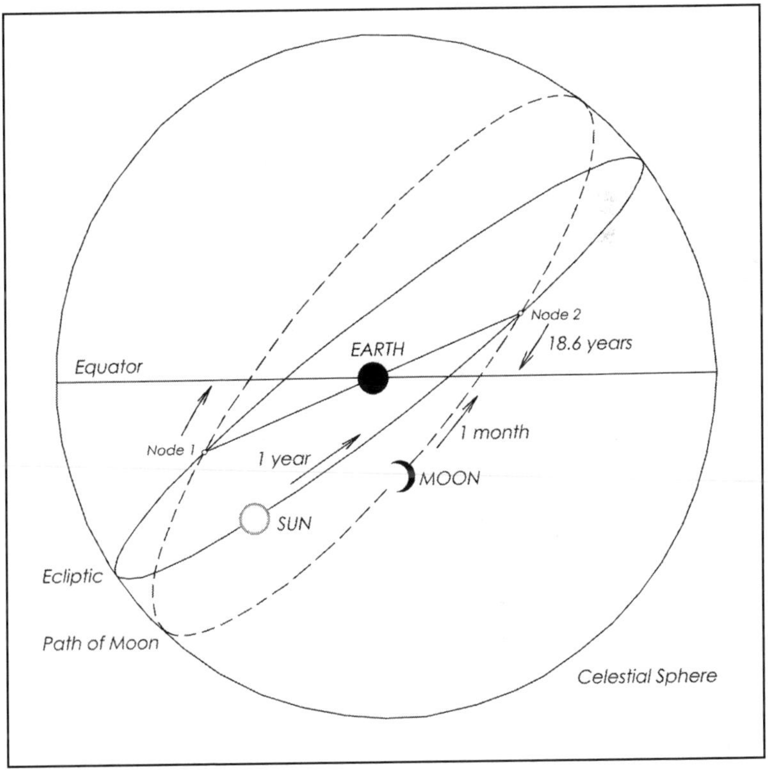

Figure 57. The path of the Moon is inclined to the ecliptic; its line of nodes—the two points where the lunar orbit crosses the ecliptic—slowly moves around the celestial sphere in an 18.61 year cycle, determining eclipses and also when the Moon will be at its highest or lowest in the sky.

The Moon occupies an extremely important, if not the central place, in ancient cosmology and time keeping. The symbols carved on stone at the otherwise obviously solar temples of

Newgrange and Knowth in Ireland look lunar, and they—like the 27/29 stones of the Inner Circles of Avebury—count as decidedly lunar. Lunar counts appear carved on Palaeolithic bone and ivory. The roughly 13° movement of the Moon each day across the broad band of the stars of the ecliptic gave early sky-watchers their first means of dividing the heavens. It takes just over 27 days for the Moon to return to the same place in the stars, dividing time into months, the celestial sphere into 'lunar mansions,' the *nakshatras* of Vedic cosmology and the year into just over thirteen months (360°/13.2 = 27.3).

Although the Moon exerts a powerful stabilising effect upon the Earth, maintaining its axis of inclination, it is intriguing that the Moon is also the major cause of precession. The combination of solar and lunar gravitational forces has made the Earth bulge, causing the slow conical rotation of the Celestial Pole around the Ecliptic Pole.

While the orbit of the Moon follows the apparent movement of the Sun, it is strongly inclined to the ecliptic, crossing above and below it. The Moon rises each night slightly before the place of the previous night, completing over thirteen cycles to every one of the Sun. Long familiarity with the lunar cycles would have brought the sky-watchers the awareness that the lunar nodes, shown in Figure 57—the two points where the orbit of the Moon cross the ecliptic—like precession, move counter to the movement of the Sun. The North Node (when the Moon *ascends* from south to north across the ecliptic), and the South Node (when the Moon *descends* from north to south across the ecliptic), move in a retrograde motion, moving backwards about nineteen days each year, taking 18/19 years to make a complete circuit of the Zodiac.

The Neolithic sky-watchers would not have understood these cycles as we do in terms of orbits, or numbers, but through direct visual experience aided by their sophisticated stone circles. At any time of day or night, they knew where the Moon and Sun—

and their paths—lay against the stars. They knew that when a full or a new Moon was near a node, an eclipse could occur, and in which constellation this would be taking place. They knew that a lunar eclipse could only occur when the Moon was full or that a solar eclipse could only occur when the Moon was new. The many stone circles show they had a vigorous oral tradition and training about these things.

Long experience of the cycle of the Moon could have given sky-watchers at a sophisticated site like Avebury a vital clue in apprehending and describing the cycle of precession. To them, *the Moon might have appeared as a model of precession in microcosm as its line of nodes—the two points where its orbit crosses the ecliptic—slowly moved counter to the Sun in much the same manner as the seasons established by the Sun moved counter to the two ecliptic/galactic crossing-points*. The orbit and nodes of the Moon in its relationship to the Sun may have stimulated early sky-watchers to conceptualise the relationship of the Sun to the Milky Way.

If the Moon provides an analogous understanding of the precessional cycle, could the Neolithic sky-watchers have associated certain points in the lunar cycles with those of the cycle of the Great Year, as was done in early Vedic tradition? (Sanjay Rath, 2008, pp. 117-132.) Although we must also consider the nodes, the 'mansions' and the standstills of the Moon, the correspondences between the full Moon and the summer solstice, the autumn equinox and the waning Moon, the winter solstice and the dark of the Moon, the spring equinox and the waxing Moon, are just too obvious to ignore. But if we were to associate them in this way we would remain where we began, as the precessional cycle still emphasises both crossing-points at the same time. Only if we took an interpretative route that identified, for example, the Sagittarius point and the dark of the Moon with inauspicious forces or the Gemini point and the full Moon with auspicious forces—as is done in the Vedic tradition—could we make an evaluation of the precessional cycle in terms of the phases of the Moon.

The Moon crosses the ecliptic twice each orbit around the Earth, about every thirteen days, creating the possibility of an eclipse. But an eclipse can only occur when the Moon is new or full, that is when the Earth, Moon and Sun are in alignment. When passing between the Earth and Sun, the new Moon on the node can cause a solar eclipse; when the Earth passes between the Sun and Moon, the full Moon on the node can cause a lunar eclipse. The early sky-watchers would have been aware of when these times were approaching. Simple circles of wood or stone upon the ground that tracked the Sun and Moon and thus the crossing-points of their paths, would have allowed them to develop an acute sense of whether the cycles were likely to cause an eclipse or not. Complex sites such as Avebury, would have delivered exceptionally accurate information of this sort.

Now, eclipses follow the retrograde motion of the nodes 180° across the Zodiac, completing one cycle every 18.61 years. It takes about eighteen months for a node to move through each house of the Zodiac. There is therefore, the potential for a lunar or a solar eclipse on the Gemini-Sagittarius axis every nine or so years, although the likelihood of its actual visibility at a particular point on the Earth is much less frequent than this. The combination of their two inner circles of 27/29 stones, gave the Avebury sky-watchers the ability to finely tune their knowledge of when and where the orbit of the Moon crossed the ecliptic. They could track the phases of the Moon in the Southern Inner Circle and the location of the North and South Nodes around the other. They could tell whether the nodes were ascending or descending, and estimate the likelihood of either a solar or a lunar eclipse. And here, at last, in a solar or a lunar eclipse, there is quite a difference between the two directions or nodes.

Early European and Oriental astronomical texts refer to the ascending lunar node, from south to north, as the 'Dragon's

Head' and the descending node, from north to south, as the 'Dragon's Tail.' Vedic tradition refers to them as *Rahu* and *Ketu* and ascribes them significance equal to that of planets. Early sky-watchers knew that if the retrograde path of the lunar nodes took place near the new or full Moon then an eclipse was possible. When conceived as dragons, the nodes devoured the Sun or Moon, and thus were seen as their enemies. While Vedic tradition sometimes sees *Rahu*, the North Node, the Dragon's Head, as auspicious, and *Ketu*, the South Node or the Dragon's Tail as inauspicious, it usually treats them as an axis pregnant with karmic or occult disturbance. (Ibid. passim and Komilla Sutton, 2001, *The Lunar Nodes: Crisis and Redemption*). An eclipse either compounded those possibilities or brought release from them.

Generally, we find that throughout the world, a lunar eclipse is considered less harmful than a solar. Although we cannot be certain what meaning the Avebury sky-watchers attributed to a lunar or a solar eclipse, we again have a serpent-identified double-ended axis, and a good likelihood that the Moon eclipsing the Sun on a descending or ascending node was considered altogether inauspicious. It is precisely this order of symbolism that the Avebury sky-watchers were likely to have associated with the movement of the nodes.

In sum, long and practical experience of the retrograde line of lunar nodes, constantly threatening or promising eclipses, is likely to have provided the Avebury sky-watchers with a key that would have assisted them in conceptualising, understanding and even attributing meaning to the changing seasonal position of the Sun against the equivalent 'nodes' of the galactic Gemini-Scorpius axis. Even if we cannot be sure of the exact details, the lunar cycles gave them a way of thinking about the ebb and flow of life that allowed them to locate themselves among the great presences of the cosmos, and attempt to divine its patterns and purposes.

Bibliography

Aldhouse-Green, Miranda & Stephen, 2005, *The Quest for the Shaman*, London, Thames & Hudson.

Ashe, Geoffrey, 1992, *Dawn behind the Dawn*, New York, Henry Holt.

Aveni, Anthony, 2001, *Skywatchers,* Austin: University of Texas Press.

Barron, R.S., 1976, *The Geology of Wiltshire,* Bradford-on-Avon, Moonraker Press.

Bayliss, Alex, Alasdair Whittle & Michael Wysocki, 2007, 'Talking About My Generation: the Date of the West Kennet Long Barrow,' *Cambridge Archaeological Journal* 17:1 (suppl.), 85–101.

Belmonte, Juan Antonio, 2001, 'On the Orientation of Old Kingdom Egyptian Pyramids,' *Archaeoastronomy*, 26, (JHA, xxxii).

Burl, Aubrey, 1979, *Prehistoric Avebury,* Yale: Yale University Press.

Burl Aubrey, 1987, *The Stonehenge People*, London, J.M. Dent.

Burl, Aubrey, 1999, *Great Stone Circles*, Yale: Yale University Press.

Campion, Nicholas, 2008, *The Dawn of Astrology: A Cultural History of Western Astrology, Vol. 1* (The Ancient and Classical Worlds), London, Continuum.

Dames, Michael, 1976, *The Silbury Treasure,* London: Thames & Hudson.

Dames, Michael, 1977, *The Avebury Cycle*, London: Thames & Hudson.

Eliade, Mircea, 1958, *Patterns in Comparative Religion*, London.

Eliadc, Mercia, 1964, *Shamanism: Archaic Techniques of Ecstasy*, Princeton University Press.

Faulkner, R.O., 1966, 'The King and the Star-Religion in the

Pyramid Texts,' *Journal of Near Eastern Studies*, Vol. 25, No. 3, pp. 153-161.

Frawley, David, 1990, *The Astrology of the Seers: a comprehensive guide to Vedic Astrology*, New Delhi: Motilal Banarsidass.

Geoffrey of Monmouth, *Historia Regum Britanniae*, 'History of the Kings of Britain' written circa 1136 CE.

Gibson, Alex, 2005, *Stonehenge and Timber Circles*, Stroud: Tempus Publishing.

Gillings, Mark, J. Pollard, R. Peterson & D. Wheatley, 2008, *Landscape of the Megaliths: Excavation and Fieldwork on the Avebury Monuments*, 1997-2003, Oxford: Oxbow Books.

Heath, Robin, 1998, *Sun, Moon & Stonehenge*, Cardigan: Bluestone Press.

Heath, Robin, 2007, *Alexander Thom; Cracking the Stone Age Code*, Cardigan: Bluestone Press.

Hutton, Ronald, 1991, *Pagan Religions of the Ancient British Isles*, Oxford: Basil Blackwell.

Hoskin, Michael, 2001, *Tombs, Temples and their Orientations. A New Perspective on Mediterranean Prehistory*. Bognor Regis, Ocarina Books.

Knight, Chris, 1991, *Blood Relations: Menstruation and the Origins of Culture*, Yale University Press

Krupp, E.C. (ed.) 1984, *In Search of Ancient Astronomies*, Harmondsworth: Penguin.

Mann, Nicholas, 1996, *The Dynamics of Space: new approaches in Geomancy*, Mid-Atlantic Geomancy website.

Mann, Nicholas & Philippa Glasson, 2007, *Star Temple of Avalon*, Temple Publications.

Martin, Calvin Luther, 1992, *In the Spirit of the Earth*, John Hopkins University Press.

Milbrath, Susan, 1999, *Star Gods of the Maya*, Austin: University of Texas Press.

Newham, C.A., 1967, *Astronomical Significance of Stonehenge*, Shirenewton: Moon Publications.

North, John, 1996, *Stonehenge: Neolithic Man and the Cosmos*, London: Harper Collins.

North, John, 2008, *Cosmos: an illustrated history of astronomy and cosmology*, University of Chicago.

Parker Pearson, Michael & Ramilisonina, 1998, 'Stonehenge for the Ancestors: The Stones pass on the Message,' *Antiquity* 72.

Parker Pearson, Michael, 2002, 'Placing the Physical and the Incorporeal Dead:

Stonehenge and Changing Concepts of Ancestral Space in Neolithic Britain,' *Archeological Papers of the American Anthropological Association* 11:145-160.

Pitts, Michael, 2000, *Hengeworld*, London: Arrow.

Pitts, Michael, 2001, 'Excavating the Sanctuary: new excavations on Overton Hill, Avebury,' *Wiltshire Archaeological and Natural History Magazine*, 94, 1-23.

Pollard, Joshua, 1992, 'The Sanctuary, Overton Hill, Wiltshire: a re-examination,' *Proceedings of the Prehistoric Society* 58, 213-26.

Pollard, Joshua & Andrew Reynolds, 2002, *Avebury: The biography of the landscape*, Stroud: Tempus Publishing.

Pollard, Joshua & Mark Gillings, 1998, 'Romancing the Stones: towards a virtual and elemental Avebury,' *Archaeological Dialogues* 5.

Pollard, Joshua & M. Gillings, 2004, *Avebury*, London: Duckworth.

Pryor, Francis, 2003, *Britain BC*, London: Harper Perennial.

Research News: Newsletter of the English Heritage Research Department, 10, December 2008, http://www.english-heritage.org.uk/server/show/nav.8336 (issue devoted to Silbury Hill).

Rath, Sanjay, 2008 *Brhat Naksatra*, Sagittarius Publications, New Delhi.

Rogers, J.H., 1998, 'Origins of the ancient constellations: I. The Mesopotamian traditions,' *Journal of the British Astronomical*

Association, vol. 108, no.1, pp.9-28

Ruggles, C.L., 1996, 'Current issues in archaeoastronomy,' *The Observatory*, v. 116, pp. 278-285.

Santillana, G. de, & Dechend, H. von, 1969, *Hamlet's Mill*, Boston: Gambit.

Schele, Linda, Freidel, David & Parker, Joy, 1993, *Maya Cosmos*, New York: Harper Collins.

Shaltout, M., & J.A. Belmonte, 2005, *On the Orientations of Ancient Egyptian Temples I: Upper Egypt and Lower Nubia*, JHA, PP 03.

Shepard, Paul, 1985, *The Sacred Paw*, Viking Penguin.

Shepard, Paul, 1998, *Coming Home to the Pleistocene*, Washington DC, Island Press.

Sims, Lionel, 2006, The Solarisation of the Moon: Manipulated knowledge at Stonehenge, *Cambridge Archaeological Journal*, 16:191207.

Sims, Lionel, 2003, Entering, and returning from the underworld: Silbury Hill – where landscape archaeology meets archaeoastronomy, *Journal of the Royal Anthropological Institute 15:2* See http://homepages.uel.ac.uk/L.D.Sims/

Smith, Isobel, 1965, *Windmill Hill and Avebury: Excavations by Alexander Keiller 1925-1939*, Oxford, Clarendon Press.

Sullivan, William, 1996, *Secrets of the Incas*, New York: Three Rivers Press.

Sutton, Komilla, 1999, *The Essentials of Vedic Astrology*, Bournemouth: Wessex Astrologer.

Tarnas, Richard, 2006, *Cosmos and Psyche: Intimations of a New World View*, New York: Viking.

Tedlock, Barbara, 1982, *Time and the Highland Maya*, Albuquerque, University of New Mexico Press.

Thom, Alexander, 1967, *Megalithic Sites in Britain*, Oxford: Oxford University Press.

Thom, Alexander, 1971, *Megalithic Lunar Observatories*, Oxford: Oxford University Press.

Thom, Alexander, A. Thom & A. Burl, 1980, *Megalithic rings: plans and data for 229 monuments in Britain*, BAR 81, Oxford.

Thomas, Julian, 1999, *Understanding the Neolithic*, London: Routledge.

Whittle, Alastair, 1996, *Europe in the Neolithic: the Creation of New Worlds*, Cambridge: University Press.

Whittle, Alastair, 1997, *Sacred Mound, Holy Rings. Silbury Hill and the West Kennet palisade enclosures: a Later Neolithic complex in North Wiltshire*, Oxford: Oxbow Books.

Whittle, Alastair, J. Pollard, & C. Grigson, 1999, *Harmony of Symbols: the Windmill Hill Causewayed Enclosure, Wiltshire*, Oxford: Oxbow Books.

Whittle, Alastair, Alex Bayliss & Fachtna McAvoy, 2007, 'The World Recreated: redating Silbury Hill in its monumental landscape,' *Antiquity* 81, pt 311, pp. 26-53.

Index

BOOKS

O books

O is a symbol of the world, of oneness and unity. In different cultures it also means the "eye", symbolizing knowledge and insight, and in Old English it means "place of love or home". O books explores the many paths of understanding which different traditions have developed down the ages, particularly those today that express respect for the planet and all of life.

For more information on the full list of over 300 titles please visit our website
www.O-books.net